Great and Unfortunate Things

Great and Unfortunate Things

Jason Arday

with Eve Claxton

SIMON & SCHUSTER

London · New York · Amsterdam/Antwerp · Sydney/Melbourne · Toronto · New Delhi

First published in Great Britain by Simon & Schuster UK Ltd, 2026

1 3 5 7 9 10 8 6 4 2

Simon & Schuster UK Ltd, 7th Floor
199 Bishopsgate, London EC2M 3TY

www.simonandschuster.co.uk
www.simonandschuster.com.au
www.simonandschuster.co.in

Simon & Schuster Australia, Sydney
Simon & Schuster India, New Delhi

The authorised representative in the EEA is Simon & Schuster Netherlands BV, Herculesplein 96, 3584 AA Utrecht, Netherlands. info@simonandschuster.nl

A CIP catalogue record for this book
is available from the British Library

Hardback ISBN: 978-1-3985-4274-7
eBook ISBN: 978-1-3985-4276-1

Typeset in Bembo by M Rules
Printed and Bound in the UK using 100% Renewable Electricity
at CPI Group (UK) Ltd

MIX
Paper | Supporting
responsible forestry
FSC® C013604
FSC
www.fsc.org

To Giff,
with thanks for everything

The axe forgets but the tree remembers.

African Proverb

CONTENTS

Part Three: Sandro and Debs

Part Four: Purpose

Part Five: The Robin

Prologue

It had been two days of interviewing for the professorship, and on the train home from Cambridge, I was exhausted. After getting off at London King's Cross station, I took the Tube as far as my stop, Clapham Common, and walked through Old Town, past the familiar shops and cafés, towards our house, the place where I grew up, where it all began. It was already getting dark, and the lights were glowing warmly in the front window. I turned my key in the lock and went inside. In the living room, my mum, Giff, was in front of the television sipping tea laced with evaporated milk. I've always called her Giff – never Mum – that's just how it's been.

She was sitting in her deep, red, velvety chair affectionately known as The Mothership that, over the years, had come to know the shape of her, even when she wasn't in it. To this day, if you're sitting in that chair, you'd better vacate it as soon as Giff walks into the room; that chair is her sanctuary, her throne, fit for our matriarch, our queen. Like The Mothership, Giff has always been a constant source of comfort for me. I went to hug her and told her I couldn't stay long, that I was just there for an hour or so to pick up some stuff, then I had to leave to get the train to Brighton. I was giving a keynote speech there the next morning.

Giff asked me when I would hear about the job. I told her it might be a few days, maybe more. As it turned out, I didn't have to wait as long as that. About an hour after I got home, my phone rang. It was a Cambridge number, so I answered. The voice on the other end of the line calmly explained that they had made their decision: they were excited to offer me the Professorship in the Sociology of Education.

After the call was over, I came downstairs to find Giff still in her chair. She saw the smile breaking through my poor attempt at a poker face.

'You did it, didn't you, Jason?' she asked.

'No, Giff,' I told her. 'We did. We did it . . .'

We hugged as Giff cried into my shoulder.

Of all the places I could have been when that phone call came in, it was only right that I was home with Giff. Of course she was overjoyed for me, but she had been overjoyed so many times, at every one of my milestones – not just the big ones, but the small ones too.

Given where we had started, there had been a lot of milestones along the way.

When I was three years old, the doctors diagnosed me with autism and global developmental delay, which is a term used when children under the age of five have significant delays in speech, cognitive abilities, motor skills or social skills. My delays were in all of the above.

'There's no one in there,' the doctors told Giff. They said that I was 'deficient', and that I'd never be able to talk, read or write. One doctor insisted I was 'no better than a vegetable' and wouldn't be able to have meaningful relationships. 'He'll never be able to live independently. Never be able to go to school with *normal* children. You might want to place him in long-term care or a home for children with similar difficulties because he's going to need lifelong support.' To them, I was a lost cause.

Giff was devastated, as any parent would be, but she was also a person of faith who had already been through many challenges in her life. Soon after the doctors gave their grim prognosis, something occurred to her: *These experts don't have a crystal ball.* She decided they didn't know what the future held. How could they – or anyone, for that matter – measure a child's potential at such an early stage in his life?

No one wanted to listen to Giff, a humble woman from Ghana without a degree or letters after her name (those accolades would come later). The doctors wanted her to submit to their 'better' and 'superior' judgement, but they failed to see that her lack of formal training actually worked to my advantage because she was able to approach being my parent with an open and fluid mind. Before the word 'neurodiversity' had even been coined, Giff understood the concept: that every human is an individual, unique and whole – and that the world needs all kinds of people. God had made me, and so God, in his infinite wisdom, had given her not a burden but a gift. This was an article of faith for her.

Giff decided to ignore the 'experts'. Instead, she chose to listen to her heart – and the words of the South Asian midwife who had delivered me at the hospital. It had been a difficult pregnancy and labour, and as legend had it, when I finally made my entrance on the 9th of May 1985, the Tears for Fears song 'Everybody Wants to Rule the World' was playing on the radio.

After my arrival, the midwife stayed at the bedside, holding my hand and studying my long fingers. Then she looked at Giff straight in the eye and said: 'Where I come from, babies with long fingers are special. This boy is destined for great things. You hear? You take care of this child.'

'Of course I will,' Giff told her.

When her shift ended, the midwife returned to check on me. 'He's going to do something special,' she repeated. 'I'm telling you: please, please look after him.'

These words made a lasting impression on Giff, and she returned to them again and again when others encouraged her to give up on me. They helped her to envision a future for me that the naysayers couldn't see. 'I don't know what that woman did to you when she delivered you, Jason,' Giff would later say, 'but I always feel like she blessed you with something because you have some truly exceptional gifts, and the things that you've done and experienced are inexplicable. So maybe she was right.'

But there was another prophecy that has resonated throughout my life – one I didn't hear until I was twenty-one years old. It was 2006, and I was on a relief mission in Brazil, working with an organisation installing water pumps in poor communities. We travelled from place to place, spending two or three days in Rio de Janeiro's favelas – shanty towns that cling to the hillsides, stacked with tumbledown houses and shacks.

It was the middle of the day, baking hot, and the sky was a brighter blue than someone who grew up in overcast south London could ever have imagined. We were in one of the favelas, teaching a group of children how to use the new pumps so they could finally drink clean water. I didn't speak Portuguese, but I was paired with a local aid worker who spoke some

English, a woman in her thirties with dark hair and eyes and a gentle, steady way about her. She translated my words, and together we demonstrated how the pump worked.

The children were smiling and attentive, though it was clear they were itching to play football with the makeshift ball made from plastic bottles and cardboard that one of them was carrying around.

At some point, the aid worker studied me as I bent down to help one of the children. Then she said quietly, almost to herself but loudly enough for me to hear: 'You have a very beautiful heart.'

I smiled and swiftly replied, 'That's really kind of you.'

Then she moved towards me and rested her hand on my arm before speaking again. 'I can tell you're destined to do great things. But I also believe you're destined for very sad and difficult things as well.'

It stopped me cold.

'What? Any more than other people?' I asked, half-confused, half-unsettled. This woman had just met me. She didn't know anything about me.

She looked straight into my eyes. 'Yes. I think so.'

We let the conversation drift after that, but her words rattled in my head the rest of the day and late into the night. The next morning, when I saw her again, I pressed her.

'Why would you say that about my life? About great things and sad things and difficult things?'

She smiled almost regretfully. 'Maybe I drank too much the night before.'

'No,' I said. 'You seemed perfectly sober.'

She closed her eyes and then opened them and spoke again:

'It's just a feeling. I could be wrong. But my feeling is that you will face very challenging times, and still, you will achieve greatness. That is God's will. So you must never lose faith.'

After the trip was over, I never saw the woman again, but her words stayed with me and, you might say, her prediction came true. The child whose parents were told he was less than human is now living a life filled with meaning and purpose, yet there has been sadness and difficulty too, experiences that have stretched my faith to breaking point. Somehow, the impossible became the possible, even if the path to get here was winding, fraught with obstacles, never straight.

As part of my job, I'm often asked to give talks all around the country – and the world. Every time I do, people come up to me afterwards, always with the same question: 'How did you do it?' I know what they're asking me. They want me to tell them how I went from the challenges of my early years to being a professor. But it's hard to give them the short version because the truth is, it's a long and complicated story. Was destiny involved? The great and unfortunate things foretold? Or was it because of the system that failed me, and some truly extraordinary people who loved and believed in me, and helped me to overcome those barriers? Or something else altogether? And so, I usually just reply that I didn't do it on my own, and that I was lucky to have a lot of supporters in my corner because it meant that I was never allowed to give up on myself, even when I was desperate to do so. And none of these people were more important than my mother.

The day I got the news about the Cambridge job, I knew that for Giff, it had been thirty-seven years of pure faith, encouragement, dedication, hard work and love. I also knew then what I had always known: that as long as I tried my best – as long as I gave it my all – Giff would be happy. Her love is unconditional and all-encompassing in that way. Cambridge was a quite remarkable and unimaginable cherry, but for Giff it was not the cake.

The cake was all in the moments that came before.

Part One

Giff

Chapter 1

A Different Timescale

It's a strange thing to spend almost twelve years of your life without language, and then to have to describe that time using only words, as I'm doing here. Most of my memories of my early childhood are of generalised images, sounds, sensations, feelings, rather than specific events, perhaps because language helps us to form memories, and I didn't have access to that until I was older. But there are at least two core images of my childhood self that stand out to me.

The first is of being in our kitchen, either tethered by a cloth to Giff's back or perched on her hip. Both gave me a great vantage point, and I would cling on while she worked, her hands always in motion as she finely chopped tomatoes, onions, peppers and scotch bonnets, fingers crumbling Maggi seasoning cubes into the dish of the day. She'd lean over the stove, and I'd tip with her, feeling the steam rising and then cooling on my skin as she took the cook's privilege of tasting the edge of the wooden spoon, assessing for flavour and of course the spiciness – the hotter the better. Ever resourceful, she could make one pan of soup or stew last for four or five days, adding to it, heating and reheating. Her favourite to cook was the Ghanaian staple light soup, with its fiery tomato-infused broth, as it had a longer shelf life and was also the least labour-intensive to assemble while holding a toddler on your hip or having them harnessed to your back. I'd watch in fascination as the soup came to a boil on the stove. From that same perch, I saw bread rise, cakes ripple and biscuits thicken. When she took the bread out of the oven, Giff always tapped the bottom of the loaves with her finger so she could feel the density and hear the hollowness. Then I'd watch her cut the first slice, the knife serrating through and the steam emerging from the bready insides. On the days when there wasn't enough food in the cupboard and we had cereal for dinner, Giff added evaporated milk and sugar to sweeten the experience, making it taste more like pudding. Even ketchup and corned beef sandwiches were delicious when Giff made them. The smell of her cooking saturated the house, giving the air a thickness that clung to my clothes, so that every time I went out, it was like carrying a bit of home with me.

My other core memory is of sitting in room three of our local health centre: an altogether different experience; this was a small, blank-walled, antiseptic space with a couple of beanbags to sit on, a single window, and a table with some blocks and other shapes laid out on it. I spent hours and hours of my childhood in room three. After I was diagnosed with autism and developmental delays, the local council granted me multiple hours of speech therapy, three days a week, every week, for the best part of ten years.

All children are born non-verbal, but most children start using words around their first birthday. That wasn't the case with me. When I started speech therapy around the age of four, I had yet to talk, had only just learned to walk and still needed someone to spoon-feed me. I didn't play with toys much because I didn't seem to understand their purpose, and when I did show interest in them, I would often break them. While most children learn to colour with crayons by four, I didn't have the fine motor skills for that, nor did I have the cognitive processing to understand when someone showed me how to do it.

In addition to my various delays, I had sensory sensitivities too, especially when it came to loud noises. As a result, I often struggled to leave the house, and Giff had to find all kinds of ways of distracting and soothing me so we could get to my speech therapy sessions on time. Outside the house, I was acutely aware of everything – every sight, every sound, every vibration. Even the air particles felt different to me after we left the cocoon of home. Inside, the air was thick like a blanket, full of the scent of Giff's cooking and her love, but outside, the air felt much thinner, which made me want to immediately turn back. The problem was, as much as I wanted to retreat, I also didn't want to leave Giff's side, so I kept going, my shoulder brushing against her hip as we went, eyes fixed on my feet to ground me, up the narrow set of steps that led to the main road. The trees and bushes on either side of the steps were overgrown, so Giff had to push them aside, and I'd close my eyes, bracing myself, not just for branches springing back at me, but for the dreaded rumbling roar of the main road: cars speeding, buses chugging along, the whistle of a bike going by, the stray runner from the morning doing his loops. At the top of the steps, she'd make sure to offer me her left hand, my favourite because it had a keloid scar that had formed after she gashed herself opening a can of tuna once. I loved that smooth, protruding scar. Sometimes I'd rub my thumb against it, other times my lip. If I happened to be on Giff's right side, I'd run around to grab her left hand so I could feel the keloid, distracting myself from the growl of the traffic as we went.

Eventually, we'd arrive at the clinic, a low-level yellow-brick building with a cold, hard glass front door. If I refused to go inside, Giff had her methods of persuading me. One of these was to give me a five-pence piece from her purse. As soon as she handed the coin to me, I became transfixed by the light reflecting off its gleaming surfaces, the queen's head on one side and the crowned thistle on the other. Giff had cleverly figured out that a five-pence piece was perfectly designed to capture my imagination and could therefore be used to successfully occupy my attention as she ushered me through the door.

Inside, the clinic was as unappealing as it was clinical. No pictures on the walls, just chipped off-white paint, and underfoot, scuffed floor tiles giving off the unpleasant whiff of industrial bleach – typical of an underfunded public-sector building in south London in the late 1980s.

We sat in the waiting area while I examined my prized silver. When it was time for the session to begin, my therapist, Katrina, came striding through the swinging glass door on the other side of the room. A round-faced young woman with hair in a ponytail, Katrina had glasses sitting on her nose and a weary smile on her face.

After she came to collect us from the lobby, we'd make the short walk to room three on the ground floor. Inside, I'd plunk down on one of the beanbags, and Giff would whisk away the five-pence piece, gesturing that she would give it back to me when I'd successfully finished the session. Giff had already learned that there were many ways to communicate with me without using words. All she had to do was squeeze my hand as she retrieved the coin and widen her huge brown eyes, and I knew exactly what she meant.

Once Giff and the coin had gone, I was left with Katrina and the wooden blocks and shapes set out on a table in front of me. Katrina's mouth started to make noises. What was she trying to tell me? I had no idea. I could register sounds, but I couldn't shape them into meaning. Occasionally, I'd attempt a response, a barely audible 'ah' or an 'oh' – a syllable at most, but nothing that added up to a real word. As Katrina might have said, 'There is no clear path through the *cognitive and developmental blockage*.'

In every session, she would go through the same exercises, the identical sequence of words and parts of words, pointing at pictures, trying to get me to say something. But with nothing visually exciting to grab my attention, I'd lose interest almost immediately, becoming internally stimulated instead. That's when the colours in my mind – the ones I've been able to see for as long as I can remember – would begin to activate. By blinking my eyes, I was able to send bright orange, blue and green smoke clouds swirling around room three. I'd watch them explode against the all-white walls, completely occupied and entertained by the fireworks of my imagination. Sadly, Katrina couldn't see the smoke clouds, just my staring, vacant expression.

Despite my therapist's best efforts, nothing could distract me from this entertainment except maybe the true object of my desire: the shiny coin waiting for me, along with Giff, back down the hall. And so, as the session progressed, Katrina's tone started to shift, her voice no longer sweet and imploring but clipped and direct instead. Even if I didn't understand her words, I could recognise the signals that something about her was changing. She'd rub her face, and her glasses, which started the session resting on the bridge of her nose, would move north until they were sitting on top of her head.

When I first started going to speech therapy, Katrina was freshly trained, new to the field, and certain she could make a difference in my life. But after many months of unsuccessful sessions, her youthful optimism and enthusiasm started to wear off. One day, as I was waiting in the lobby with Giff, Katrina burst through the glass door, arms swinging, looking more resolved than ever to *make progress*. She marched me back through the doors and down the hallway towards our usual room. Giff followed, and after I settled into the beanbag, she bustled off again, taking my five-pence piece with her. That day, we went through the usual exercises, Katrina frowning throughout, the double lines between her eyebrows creasing deeply. Tension filled the room, and I began to feel the heat rising on the back of my neck. My safe haven, Giff, was in the waiting room. Out of sight.

Katrina's calm-on-the-surface demeanour finally began to crack, revealing the simmering irritation beneath. A look that told me she was not best pleased with me flashed across her face, then she bent down and paused for a moment before putting her hands firmly on my narrow shoulders. Then she started shaking me. For the first few seconds, I thought it was a game; I actually laughed at the motion of the shaking as it rocked my head back and forth on my neck. But my laughter made Katrina shake me even more vigorously, and my smile quickly vanished as her grip tightened and I felt the pinch of her finger pads digging into the skin on my arms. A desperate and exhausted figure, my flush-cheeked therapist finally let me go, her glasses now dislodged from their position by the sheer force she'd exerted while shaking me.

In truth, whenever I was alone with an adult who wasn't a family member, I was fair game for that person to take advantage of me because I had no way to verbally report their wrongdoings. It was just that Katrina was the first person to actually do this.

While I didn't have words at the time to describe what had taken place in room three, I somehow understood that what Katrina had done was wrong. As I came back through the swinging glass door into the waiting room, I sprinted away from my therapist, nearly bundling Giff over as I crashed into her well-cushioned hip. She made a little 'oof' sound on impact. I put out my hand in anticipation of the five-pence piece, and Giff handed me my reward. Then I turned back to look at my therapist, her cheeks still bright red. Perhaps she felt confident she could count on my silence. But she would one day be proven wrong. The words would eventually break through, just on a different timescale from Katrina's.

Chapter 2

Intrinsic Worth

Growing up, Giff was my safe haven, but also my superhero, my biggest champion, and a woman whose reserves of patience and intelligence are the reason that despite my many challenges, I'm able to sit here and tell you my story.

I have very few photos of myself as a child, but my favourite is of me aged two, sitting on Giff's hip as usual, in the garden outside our house. Giff is in her mid-twenties in the photo, wearing a white dress with white beads around her neck and looking very much as she does today – her beautiful, round baby face smooth and unwrinkled, her naturally dark-rimmed eyes looking straight at the camera, her expression open and welcoming. Even though my hand is in front of my face, you can tell that I'm smiling.

'People used to call you Sunshine,' Giff recalls, 'because you were always smiling. They remembered you for that – that and the dark lines around your eyes.' Like Giff, I've always had dark-rimmed eyes. When she was a girl, her teachers chastised her for wearing eyeliner – often physically punishing her for flouting strict school rules about make-up, even though her eyes were that way naturally. From the time I was born, people asked Giff,

'Did you put eyeliner on your child's eyes?' To which she'd respond, 'Of course not, no! Why would I do that?'

Giff has always been short but strong, someone whose arms were made stronger by pounding banku and fufu with the wooden spoon known by Ghanaians as the Banku Ta. Those arms lifted me onto her lap so she could read to me, and even when I couldn't understand the words, I loved the sound of Giff's voice, the rhythm of the lines as she recited them in her soft Ghanaian accent (which she believes to this day sounds quite British, much to my amusement). Those same arms picked me up and deposited me onto the worn carpet in front of our second-hand TV before leaving me there to go and wash our clothes in the bath by hand with Dreft soap flakes. After her many tasks were done, I'd hear her pad back into the living room and drop into her chair in front of the television with a weary sigh.

When I was very young, my dad, Joseph, worked as the head chef of a cafeteria at a supermarket, and later in the same role at a manufacturing company. Sometimes, he'd bring home prime cuts of meat from his work, exclaiming, 'Only the best for my family!' Every day, he'd get up at the crack of dawn to iron his uniform, including his tall white chef's hat referred to as the 'toque blanche', before leaving at seven and rarely returning home until eight at night. Dad was always meticulously clean-shaven and well-groomed, and as I got older, it was my job to polish his steel-capped work shoes until they gleamed. He took a lot of pride in his work and his appearance. I can still picture him coming in the door after fourteen hours at work, bone-tired, only to wake up the following morning and do it all over again. After James Brown, he was certainly the hardest-working man in show business – or at least the catering industry.

Everyone thought Giff was a single parent because my dad was always at work. 'A job worth doing is worth doing well' was his mantra. My work ethic definitely comes from him.

Because my dad worked such long hours – and Giff didn't have anyone else to take care of me – I went everywhere with her, from supermarkets to picket lines and protests and church on Sundays, not to mention classrooms and therapists' offices. That was fine by me. I never wanted to leave her side; even at home, I followed her from room to room.

My parents are both Ghanaian, but they met and married in London. When Giff learned she was pregnant for the first time, she prayed to God for a daughter, and when she eventually ended up with three boys, she reasoned, 'If I cannot have girls, I am going to bring you boys up *like* girls.' In West African culture, the women are expected to wait on the men, but Giff put an end to that tradition – at least in our house. 'If anybody's doing any waiting on, you boys will be waiting on the women,' she'd say. 'I do not want any of you to think a woman's purpose is to serve you in any way, shape or form!' As soon as we were old enough, all three of us boys learned how to cook, clean and keep house.

Around the time I was born, my parents moved into our yellow-brick council house, with its white windows and doors, red roof tiles and patch of garden at the front. The interior was modest to say the least, with two bedrooms and a bathroom upstairs and a living room, kitchen and toilet downstairs. The walls of the house were flimsily constructed, its low ceilings covered in a prickly, swirling stucco; the staircase was narrow with shallow steps, as if everything had been made to the smallest and cheapest specifications possible. I shared a bedroom with my two brothers, the three of us sleeping in two bunk beds. When I look back at it now, I cannot comprehend how we all fit into that minuscule space.

We were the first family to live in that house, starting in 1985. It was one of the last council houses to be built in Margaret Thatcher's Britain, right before the Tory government began its systematic defunding of social housing. During this time, many council houses were sold off to those who could afford to buy them, leaving everyone else with a dwindling number of government-subsidised properties that rapidly began to deteriorate. Even though our house was new when we moved in, it was poorly ventilated and collected damp, which led to mould growing in the windows and ceilings. Today, Giff suffers from severe asthma, which I'm certain is due to all the musty black patches she diligently wiped away at over the years, even though they always grew back again.

Our house was cramped, and not just because five people were living in three rooms. We also had *a lot* of stuff. Typically, Africans like to hold on to their possessions. When something comes into the house, it stays in the house. Giff collected all kinds of things, and so did my dad – papers, trinkets, wooden figures, miniature cars, fabrics, books, boxes filled with who knows what. By the time we were teenagers, the house was packed floor to ceiling, with barely a space to put your feet. I remember the time a West Indian guy came to install a cable upgrade; he took one look at our place and exclaimed, 'This whole house gonna burn up! This house is a fire hazard!'

Despite the crowded conditions, the excess of stuff and the fact that when you live in social housing, you're always looked down on – deemed to be on the lowest rung of society's ladder – I still consider myself very lucky to have grown up in that house, the stable point in our universe. Other children may have wanted new things, such as bikes and computer games, but I just wanted everything to stay the same. I was rich, but money was not my currency. I had something invaluable: my parents' love.

Back then, Clapham and south London were home to a lot of families like ours, not just Africans, but West Indians, Colombians, Portuguese, everyone straddling the same struggles: overcrowded living conditions, unstable employment, elusive upward mobility. There was a lot of criminal activity and gang violence in our area as well, and we all lived with the constant fear of becoming collateral damage in someone else's fight. From the bedroom I shared with my brothers, I would tweak the curtains and see the tree outside the window, and beyond the branches, the small area below that was home to parking spots and rubbish bins. Concealed from the street, this was a place where unsavoury characters came to hand over who knows what, where wads of money changed hands and fights broke out. Looking out of that window was like watching a film; there was always some kind of drama going on.

It was very common in those days for people to get rushed or mugged. When Giff was pregnant with me, she was held up at knifepoint. The guy emptied her purse and then asked her, 'Haven't you got anything else?' To that, Giff replied: 'I'm eight and a half months pregnant and I've got a one-year-old with me. You've taken everything I have, and now you're asking me if I've got more?' It's difficult to intimidate Giff. What she lacks in stature, she makes up for in mettle.

~

After I was born, people came to visit to see the new baby, as is common in most African families and cultures. Then the date was set for my naming ceremony a few weeks later. During that ceremony, called an Outdooring, you bring the child outdoors and give them a name, then introduce them to their relatives and call on their ancestors to help celebrate them, and welcome them into the world. Traditionally, Ghanaians give their children the name of an older relative. My dad insisted on Atta Kwei for my middle names, after his brother, my uncle Henry. But Giff chose my first name. When she was pregnant with me, she'd been reading a lot of Greek mythology, and the story of Jason and the Argonauts was her favourite. She couldn't have known then that my life would involve so many trials, obstacles and tests of courage, just like that of my mythological namesake with his quest for the Golden Fleece.

At my naming ceremony, Giff received a lot of blessings and praises because she'd given birth to a second boy. Of course, she didn't agree with this preferencing of male children over female children. She believed she was just as good as, if not better than, any of the men around her – in fact, her entire life is a testament to this – but that was the culture she came from, so she accepted the blessings with good grace.

Once the excitement of my naming ceremony was over, everybody went on with their lives, and Giff was left with the responsibility of caring for me and my one-year-old brother, affectionately known as JJ (short for Joseph John). For the first few weeks of my life, a nurse came to our home regularly to check on us, and after that, Giff went to appointments at our local clinic. She was beginning to have concerns about JJ, who was still not speaking. Meanwhile, I didn't babble like most babies, and I didn't respond when people said my name. At first, when questions arose in Giff's mind, she kept them to herself. She wondered if she was maybe overreacting.

But as time went on, she became increasingly worried. When she went to the clinic, they would tell her that JJ should be clapping his hands or pointing by now, but he wasn't doing either. She began to ask the doctors and nurses questions, which did not endear her to them, and they started getting irritated. The feeling was mutual. Giff told them, 'Don't keep telling me about what you think my child *should* be doing. If he's not able to do these things, then how do we remedy that? What do we do?' The people at the clinic didn't seem to have anything else to offer her.

Before long, she went to our doctor, a Ghanaian man. At least with him, she felt safe to speak freely and could do so in her mother tongue, our regional language, Ga. He listened closely to her concerns. 'If I'm right,' she said, 'and there's something wrong, what else can be done, apart from going to the health clinic? Please tell me if you think I'm overly concerned because I can see other children are developing at a different pace.'

Our doctor referred JJ for psychological testing first. JJ was three and a half years old when he was diagnosed with autism. Because Giff was seeing many of the same delays and patterns in me, she took me for testing a year later, when I was three. Back then, my diagnosis was referred to as autistic disorder or classic autism – or sometimes as Kanner's autism after Dr Leo Kanner, who studied autistic children in the 1940s, noting their difficulties with social interactions and communication and their 'restricted' interests and patterns of behaviour. In years to come – before autistic spectrum disorder (ASD) became the most common description – the doctors told Giff that my complex needs were also reflective of Asperger's syndrome, a term coined in 1979 by the British psychiatrist Dr Lorna Wing and named after the Austrian paediatrician Dr Hans Asperger. I was also diagnosed with developmental delays (now referred to as global developmental delay).

Giff had never come across any of these terms or people before. At first, she had no context for what the doctors were telling her. To confuse things further, JJ's autism presented very differently from mine. His case was considered somewhat more hopeful because he was beginning to acquire some language and was able to verbalise words from a young age, even if he couldn't put sentences together until he was nearly seven. My language delays were much more severe: I simply didn't speak. Meanwhile, the doctors did not mince their words. They said I was 'dumb' (in the medical sense), 'slow', and there was no point in educating me because I couldn't understand anything. According to them, my future was bleak.

'That's the way Jason's going to be, and that's the way he's going to be forever,' they told Giff.

They didn't just diagnose me – they wrote me off altogether.

~

When Giff talks about this time in her life, she describes going through a kind of bereavement, with the initial shock followed by feelings of disbelief and anger, followed by overwhelming sadness. After my diagnosis, she cried every day for a number of months. She asked herself over and over again, *Why me?*

In every interaction with the doctors and nurses, Giff felt they were giving her fewer and fewer reasons for hope. At that time, it was still the Dark Ages in terms of people's understanding of autism. The first time the word even appeared in the *Diagnostic and Statistical Manual of Mental Disorders*, known as the *DSM*, was in 1980, just five years before my birth. Had I been born a decade earlier, I would have been diagnosed with childhood schizophrenia. What was known about autism back then was based on the observations of a handful of doctors studying a very small number of children. These theorists had taken their observations and codified them in the *DSM*, and as a result, their misconceptions and misinterpretations became gospel, even though their descriptions were based on their interpretation of external symptoms, rather than any kind of understanding of the actual autistic experience. Then and now, the *DSM* is steeped in the language of deficiency. It talks about 'deficits' of social communication. It describes 'repetitive and restricted behaviours'. It discusses symptoms causing 'impairments'. It looks at autism from the perspective of an outsider observing behaviours and labelling them as 'abnormal'. This was what doctors relied on to make diagnoses – and they still do.

Giff knew what the doctors and nurses were thinking: *This Black woman must have done something wrong to have two children with the same diagnosis. What other reason could there be?* They told Giff I was slow to speak because she talked to me in Ga, and this must have caused or at the very least contributed to my 'developmental confusion'. They were always asking what she was feeding us, wanting to know if she was reading books aloud to us, suggesting that she wasn't exposing us to the 'right environment'. The concept of 'refrigerator mothers' – an outdated theory that autism was somehow caused by a mother's emotional coldness to her child – should have been fully debunked by the time I was diagnosed, but the assumption that mothers were to blame was still alive and well in the health clinics of 1980s and 1990s south London. Giff felt that no one was listening, that everyone was telling her what she was doing wrong, but not what could be done to help. She lived with the constant threat that these 'experts' would decide her parenting was 'inadequate' and take her children away, which happened to so many other mothers of colour back then.

While Giff was pregnant, she'd had all kinds of dreams about what her baby would be in the future. Like any mother, she'd had aspirations for me, and now she felt as if all those hopes had been taken away from her. Yet in the depths of her despair, she was able to draw on her roots. In Ghanaian culture, there is a mythological creature called the Sankofa whose head faces backward to look at its tail. Symbolically, the Sankofa is a reminder to turn to the past in order to move forward into the future. After many months of being beset by sleepless nights and tears, Giff followed the lead of the Sankofa bird and looked to her past. Her parents had divorced when she was very young, and she was raised by various family members all over Ghana, which had forced her to become adaptable. At this auntie's house, there was one set of rules, and at that auntie's house, another. Her ever-changing circumstances had made her resilient, independent and strong. She'd had to become an expert in figuring out how to blend into her environment to survive. As a result of these past experiences, she realised that she was confident and had reserves that she could draw from in her current time of need.

She also had her great faith in God. One day, she woke up and said to herself, *These are testing times for me, but God doesn't give us a burden that is too great to carry. If he thinks I can carry this load of two children with similar diagnoses, one year's difference between them, then maybe I'm stronger than I think I am.*

Giff decided to stop listening to the so-called experts. 'I don't accept that' became one of her most-used phrases. She believed from the bottom of her soul that both her sons had intrinsic worth, and that whatever happened, we were precious and should be treated with the utmost love, care and kindness. The doctors told her that there was 'no one in there', but this idea of believing in something you couldn't see was familiar to her from her faith. Just because God wasn't always visible, that didn't mean he wasn't there. She decided the same could be true for me.

Chapter 3

Sequence and Sameness

Around the time of my diagnosis, Giff discovered she was pregnant again. She was determined that this time, she would be blessed with a girl. Our dad insisted that his daughter should be called Josephine in his honour. But it was not to be. Instead, when I was four years old, my brother Simon was born. You might have thought I'd be jealous of this new baby who had taken my position as the youngest in the family. Instead, I was fascinated by him. I thought he was the coolest thing. I loved to look at him when he was in his buggy or strapped to Giff's chest. Small and smiley, he had such a beautiful face.

To my parents' understandable relief, Simon started speaking around his first birthday, the typical age for that milestone. As it turned out, he was a bit of a prodigy, able to read and write fluently from the age of four. Meanwhile, anything to do with language was still lost on me. When I was about five, the doctors ran tests on my hearing, as I still wasn't speaking, and I was found to be profoundly deaf in my left ear. I started wearing a hearing aid, which was supposed to help and support with language acquisition, but it didn't seem to make much of a difference in my case.

Without words, I was prone to feelings of frustration that I couldn't fully control or redirect. Many times, the emotions would rise up in me and, with no other outlet for communication, I'd begin to feel a kind of intense heat building at the back of my neck, a signal that a situation was quickly going from bad to worse. Then my hands would begin sweating and my eyes would dart feverishly around the room. In an attempt to calm myself, I'd start rocking and humming, and when that wasn't enough, I'd find my way to a corner and begin banging my head against the wall, first softly, then harder and harder until all I could hear was the smack, smack, smacking sound, blocking out everything else. The rocking, the humming, the head-banging – all of these were forms of stimming (short for self-stimulatory behaviour), an attempt to self-soothe, to try to regulate myself.

Many times, Giff had to give up whatever errand we were supposed to be running because I was distraught and couldn't leave the house – and she couldn't leave me. Through trial and error, she came to understand that if she tried to pull me away from the wall or restrain me in any way, this only made things worse. Instead, she would put cushions all around me to mitigate any harm and wait for the meltdown to run its course.

At age four, I started school. Giff learned through experience that the only way to avoid a meltdown in the mornings was to have a routine that we followed religiously before we left the house. I'd have to watch the same cartoons on television. Then I'd eat the same bowl of cereal – Weetabix – with milk that was the same temperature as the day before. I'd have to wear the same clothes, put on in the same order. Sequence and sameness were vitally important to me. There could be no surprises, not even a scintilla of a change, or this would trip me up and I'd go into a meltdown, with little to no hope of recovery. But as long as everything went to plan, we could leave. Socks on, shoes on, coats on, and off we went. The sameness – the routine of it all – was soothing and helped to ease my way.

Separation from Giff was terrifying, however. Just the sight of the school gates was enough to set every nerve in my body on edge. I'd cling to her, my fingers like vices. Then we'd wait together in the playground until the teacher came out of the looming red-brick building with a huge, heavy, wooden-handled bell that she started waving up and down unrhythmically, the clanging of the bell making me clench my teeth in my head. The other kids began lining up in lockstep, and then suddenly Giff was kissing me on the head, and her hand was slipping out of mine; there were kids all around me, and she was gone.

I was in a place where no one understood me, I didn't understand anyone, and I couldn't communicate my distress, at least not using words. At home, Giff always knew what I needed – sometimes before I knew it myself. If I was thirsty, she had a glass of water for me. If I was hungry, she was there with a snack. If I couldn't calm myself, she knew how to let my meltdown run its course while still keeping me safe. I needed her in my eyeline at all times because she was the one who could speak up and advocate for me. But at school, I was on my own.

Inside the classroom, I was supposed to listen and follow instructions. Right away, the teacher would start shouting at me because I wasn't doing what everybody else was doing. Confused and scared, I'd begin to feel the intense heat at the back of my neck again. Before I knew it, everything started speeding up, like the world was on fast-forward, and I'd begin rocking and humming, then I'd get myself to the corner of the room so I could smack my head against the wall, obliterating everything else.

Giff told my teachers never to touch me when I was melting down. She explained to them that they needed to put cushions around me to protect me. To their credit, they would try this, but they were too scared to let the meltdown run its course and so they would often restrain me, pinning my arms to my sides, which only made things worse. That's when they'd have to call Giff. Ten minutes later, she'd come running into the classroom, calling out my name. Then she'd bend down to my level, turn my body to face hers, and cup her hands around my eyes, pressing the outer edges of her palms to the sides of my face so that all I could see were her big brown eyes staring into mine. Everything else – the entire world – got blacked out, like a total eclipse of the sun. 'Look at me, look at me, Jason,' Giff repeated. Slowly, I'd stop the rocking, the humming and the banging, consoled by Giff – my port, my lighthouse, my dry land, all rolled into one.

These constant calls from the school left Giff tethered to the house. On one very rare occasion, she decided to go to our local shopping centre, the Arndale, to get something. The teachers called and called, but there was no one at home. This was before everyone walked around with a phone in their pocket. By the time they finally got hold of Giff, I'd banged my head so hard I'd split it open and had blood running down my face.

After this incident, the teachers told Giff that they could no longer have me in a classroom with other children, that I was a danger to my fellow students. This wasn't exactly true; I wasn't a danger to anyone but myself. Even so, I got put in a classroom on my own with a single teacher, segregated from the rest of the school. I didn't have words, but I had eyes. I knew I was different.

~

As a child, I spent a lot of time alone with adults staring down at me.

On the doctors' recommendations, Giff began taking me to a hospital clinic that she was told could help us. For me, these sessions were much worse than speech therapy with Katrina, even factoring in the time when she shook me. Here I found myself in a brightly lit room with nothing to play with, just adults with clipboards, watching me and writing things down.

Inside that room, these adults showed me pictures of shapes and told me to connect them to other shapes. I had to point to a triangle and connect it to other triangles. The shapes meant nothing to me, so I immediately disengaged. With nothing to focus on, I started running around. The people with clipboards wrote this down. Then they picked me up and put me on a chair. Every time I got off the chair, they picked me up and put me back on it again. I had to make eye contact with them for what felt like hours, I'm assuming because they felt that sitting still and maintaining eye contact were skills I needed in life. I was a little kid, but the people with clipboards seemed to expect me to act like an adult.

They knew – because Giff had told them – that I couldn't tolerate complex loud noises: an engine running, an exhaust backfiring, cars speeding up when the traffic lights change, motorbikes grunting, sirens wailing. I couldn't isolate the sounds or distil what they meant, so these kinds of noises simply overwhelmed me. When we were out of the house, Giff often had to cover my ears with her hands, or sometimes I'd cover them myself, trying to block it all out. Even at home, the sound of two metal pans clattering in a sink or a fork scraping on a plate could send me into a frenzy.

At the hospital, the people with clipboards wheeled in a TV and video player on one stand and a radio and cassette player on another. Then they pressed play and turned up the volume extremely high. Multiple irregular sounds filled the room: car noises, piercing animal calls, doors slamming. Did they think if they subjected me to this cacophony for long enough, I'd be able to manage the 'real' world? The problem was too many loud, harsh sounds were torture for me. I started throwing myself around, banging my head on the floor and the walls. The clipboard people continued to play the noises, even as I started to melt down – all the while watching and taking their notes. They told Giff that they would help me, but I believe they were trying to 'fix' me, taking the pieces of me apart so they could put me back together like some kind of robot who would follow their commands.

I wish they could have understood that the behaviours they saw as 'deficits' were simply the reactions of a small child trying to cope with being overstimulated. All human beings take in information through the senses – sight, sound, smell, taste and touch – and pass that information through the nervous system to the brain and back again. But those of us with autistic brains receive way more sensory information than people with neurotypical brains, which can cause us to be more easily overwhelmed, which in turn can lead us to shut down or focus on a single thing in order to remain calm. And there's nothing we can do about this. It's just how we're made.

To this day, if I'm in a room and there's a lot of complex background noise, I can quickly struggle with such a large amount of sensory input. Over the years, I've learned to hide any outward displays of discomfort so nobody can tell. But if I want to continue chatting with the person in front of me in a noisy room, I have to isolate the sound of their voice, collecting the words that are coming out of their mouth and putting them together in my mind. Then I have to think about my response, digging into a memory bank of words and phrases that I've collected over the course of my life to be able to come up with an appropriate reply. I pride myself on holding space for people, speaking well, and being personable, but the reality is that it takes a massive amount of mental energy for me to have a conversation with someone in a room where there are lots of other people speaking. But that's just me.

Even within the autistic experience, there's a lot of diversity – every autistic person is different. One person might be dazzled by bright lights overhead. Another might be touch-sensitive and shy away from a hand on the arm. Someone else might crave that physical connection and enjoy it. Individuals vary. Giff saw this in the differences between JJ and me. For example, JJ loved the sensory satisfaction of pressing LEGO bricks together and building intricate constructions that kept him happily engaged for hours. I didn't like playing with LEGO. It did nothing for me. I was extremely sensitive to noise; but this didn't bother JJ as much as it did me. Giff understood that we were individuals, and she begged our teachers and therapists not to compare us or necessarily use similar approaches. 'They are not the same,' she said, 'and you need to treat them differently.'

What the people with clipboards wrote down during those

long and torturous hours I spent with them remains a mystery to me, but I know what *I* took away from the sessions: I learned to block things out, to numb myself to pain, to shut down. To this day, there's part of me that's still anesthetised. The numbness gets in the way of my relationships – often I can't be fully present, can't connect. I just switch off. The damage has lasted decades. But the people with clipboards weren't around to see that. I honestly think that if someone had said jumping off a cliff would 'cure' me of my autism, they might actually have considered making me do it.

Chapter 4

Trial and Error

As time went on, Giff began to recognise that the professionals had an extremely limited vision for me, so she started to develop her own strategies through a simple system of trial and error. She noticed that when she washed our clothes in the bath, I loved to trail my hands through the water. So she started letting me massage the soapy wet clothes, whooshing them around, splashing, and having the water ripple back at me. It calmed me down immediately. Other times she'd get me to sweep the floor: the sound of the brush against the carpet, the swishing noise, the rhythm of the motion, the way you have to use your body to make the brush move worked for me. All I was doing was pushing the dust around the room – I wasn't actually cleaning anything – but that wasn't the point. The motions helped me to regulate.

Without knowing anything about 'sensory-friendly environments', Giff created them. When she won a giant purple stuffed elephant in a raffle, she gave it to me and this four-foot-tall furry animal came with us from room to room. Giff used Elephant to help me practise interacting with people. 'Here's how you shake hands,' she told me, holding out Elephant's trunk and teaching me to squeeze it with just the right amount of pressure. Giff believed that a firm handshake was a sign of good character, so we practised squeezing that trunk over and over again. She also cuddled Elephant to show me how to give a hug and then said to me, 'Your turn. Now *you* hug the elephant.' And when Giff saw that I was on the verge of a meltdown, she'd put Elephant in the corner so that I'd bang my head against the big fluffy animal instead of the wall.

Her interventions weren't just innovative – they were driven by necessity. Giff had to survive living in a very small house with three boys, two of them with complex learning needs, where at any given time of the day, at least one of us was melting down or making some kind of mess. It wasn't always pretty. At a very young age, I was fascinated by the texture of things that were soft and squishy. At some point, I must have discovered that my faeces had this sought-after quality, because I started smearing my crap on the walls. I just wanted to feel the squishiness of it between my fingers while watching the patterns it made as I spread it all around. This was the kind of sensory feedback I craved, but it was Giff who had to clean everything up, scrubbing the walls with bleach and putting me in the bath to disinfect me. Eventually, she figured out that she could give me a tube of toothpaste to squeeze instead. The gloopy paste squishing into my hands was just as satisfying for smearing – and a lot more sanitary as well.

Often, I struggled to fall asleep at night, so Giff would take me for walks around the streets of Clapham, trying to instil a sense of calm in me. I loved the quietness of the city at night, the dwindling of the traffic noise, the darkened sky overhead and the comforting yellow glow of the street lamps, the sound of my body swishing against Giff's side as we walked. It was like someone had turned down the volume on the world.

During the day, I usually had a lot of energy to expend. Wrestling was a favourite activity for us brothers, and we spent a lot of time writhing around on the living room floor, our arms and legs flailing, breaking lamps, side tables, anything in our path. We especially enjoyed jumping up and down on the sofa like it was a trampoline, then power-bombing off the arms and crash-landing onto the carpet. This was the best kind of feedback for me – that feeling of my body thudding down on the floor with a proper thwack gave me so much satisfaction. Realising that she couldn't fight it, Giff placed cushions strategically around the room and prayed we wouldn't get hurt. Meanwhile, my dad sanded off the sharp edges on tables or other surfaces, all in a desperate attempt to childproof the front room.

At some point, I remember our parents buying a beige-coloured sofa and two matching armchairs on a 'buy now, pay later' plan. The new set came with detachable cushions, which were useful for putting around the room as protection. The three of us brothers quickly discovered that if we jumped off the arms of the sofa, we could flip over and crash-land on our backs in the middle of the seating with a magnificent thud. We performed this trick over and over until, about two months after the sofa arrived, one of us jumped off the arm and landed in the middle to the sound of a loud crack. Whatever underlying structure was holding the sofa together had completely broken. Thankfully, Giff wasn't in the room at the time and our dad was at work, so, knowing we were about to get into massive trouble, we covered up the sofa's sunken middle with a couple of the cushions. The next time Giff sat down on the couch, it basically folded up on either side of her.

She was furious, but somehow we escaped her wrath because she was convinced that the sofa was defective. JJ and Simon did not try to persuade her otherwise, and I didn't have the words, even if I had wanted to tell her – which I definitely did not. Sadly, the couch was already out of warranty, so our parents couldn't return it and were stuck paying off that broken sofa for many months to come. To this day, they have yet to find out which of their sons was responsible for the somersault that killed the couch.

Another place we could go to expend energy was Clapham Common. Otherwise known as the Common, this triangle-shaped stretch of mud and grass was one of our favourite haunts. Growing up, we didn't go on holidays or for weekends away, so a trip to the Common was our biggest treat. Giff had a talent for turning a simple outing into an adventure, getting us ice lollies from Iceland supermarket and then releasing us to run around in the wild. On the Common, I was like a bird out of its cage. I could kick a ball around with my brothers or go to the playground to play on the swings or hang on the monkey bars. Suspended above the ground on a cargo net or leaping in the air, I experienced the feeling of free fall that every child should experience. On sunny days, when the muddy ground had hardened, I could lie on my back with my eyes closed and watch the sun shining through the red patterns of my inner eyelids. Without any tasks to complete, or people with clipboards staring down at me, or teachers trying to get me to read, or therapists telling me what to do, I was happy. Just mindless. On the Common, the weight I carried around with me every day was gone. Those were perfect moments; they just never seemed to last long enough.

~

'If you do things differently from us, he will never learn anything,' the therapists, doctors, social workers and teachers kept telling Giff when she got tired of following their instructions because she could see they weren't working.

'I *am* doing it differently,' she told them, 'because when I do it my way, it has an effect.'

Giff decided to learn Makaton, a method of communication that relies on a combination of spoken words, hand gestures and visual aids like pictures and symbols. She went to classes and gained her level one and two qualifications, and because Makaton is very visual, this system worked well for me.

Her approach was to break down each concept and repeat it over and over, slowly and patiently, using a lot of pointing and pictures, until it began to sink in. She also spoke to me at length about whatever it was she was trying to impart to me, always with the assumption that I was competent and could understand her, even if there was no indication yet that this was the case. Giff was determined to give me a simple command and have me follow it – something that I still couldn't do at almost seven, and that the 'experts' had told her was impossible (because, again, there was 'no one in there'). For example, she wanted to teach me to take a bite of an apple on command. To do that, Giff, a very good artist, would first draw a picture of somebody biting an apple. Then she would enunciate the word 'apple'. Next, she would show me the actual fruit and demonstrate how to take a bite. Finally, she would place the apple down in front of me, saying, 'You take a bite.'

We did this for several weeks, but I still couldn't follow the instruction. According to Giff, I started getting fed up and frustrated and would throw the apple on the floor. But she was determined to keep going. She thought to herself, *He's only a child, so even if he throws the apple away, I'll just pick it up again.*

Giff can still remember the moment when she told me to bite the apple and I did it. She was elated. Praises were given. It had taken us many months of practice, but this was a huge milestone. From that point on, Giff realised that no matter how long it took to teach me a task, we would carry on.

Once I'd finally mastered how to take a bite, she began to teach me that there are different ways of eating the apple. 'You can either eat it whole, or you can slice it into two and eat it, which is called a half,' she explained. 'Or you can divide it into four, which is quarters. If you want it sliced, you can move your hand like this in a sawing motion, and I'll cut it for you.' By breaking it down and doing it in stages, she knew we'd get there eventually.

The next time we went to see a doctor or a social worker, Giff brought along an apple, told me to eat it, and when I took a bite, she said, 'Look, he's *listening*.'

Chapter 5

Out of Reach

I was very lucky to grow up with a mother who instinctively rejected the kinds of narrow definitions that others imposed on me. She was a strong Black African woman who knew that forcing anyone to conform to a single standard of 'normal' was wrong, and that there were many ways to exist in this world. She told herself, *With every ounce of strength I have and every breath I have in me and as long as I'm alive, whatever Jason can be, he will be. If the most he can do is to pack shelves in a supermarket, fine. He will do it and do it exceptionally well. If that's his path, then I'll make sure he walks it to the best of his ability so that when I'm no longer here, he'll be able to look after himself and keep a roof over his head.* Somehow Giff was able to tune out the advice of the 'experts' for long enough to listen to my silence and discover within it what I really needed.

But there was another thing propelling me forward at this stage in my life – something as fundamental as her devotion – and that was my innate drive to do something *when I set my mind to it.*

In those days, my parents had a set of four champagne glasses that they'd been given as a wedding present. They kept these glasses in pride of place in a cabinet in the front room. I knew the glasses were special because unlike the other glasses in our house, these ones sat there on display in that cabinet, twinkling away, catching the light from the front window.

Back then, my way of understanding an object was first to look at it and then to touch it – often pressing it against my cheek to get a better feel for it. But if I *really* wanted to find out what something was made of, there was only one way to do that: I'd have to drop the object on the floor or bang it against the nearest hard surface to see if it would shatter into pieces. This gave me enormous pleasure.

Without being able to understand or use words, I was always looking for this kind of feedback from the things around me. I loved to slam cupboard doors so I could hear the thwacking sound they made. (To this day, if I'm on my own in the house, I'll go into the kitchen and slam some cupboard doors, just for the sheer joy of it.) Another great urge was to snatch something out of someone else's hands. If one of my brothers was playing with a toy and I could grab it from him when he was least expecting it, that *really* satisfied my desire. The phrase goes 'Look with your eyes, not with your hands', but looking could never be enough for me. I needed to touch, grab and smash it.

Giff had a lot of ornaments – little figurines that friends or family had brought back from holidays, ceramic fridge magnets, that type of thing – and if one of those got into my long pilfering fingers, it was the biggest thrill for me to take that trinket and destroy it. As a result, she'd put everything away in cupboards under lock and key or high up on shelves. 'When his hands aren't busy, he breaks things,' she always said. She made sure to give me tasks around the house, like sweeping the floor or helping her wash our clothes in the bath – anything to distract me from my wrecking missions. Keeping my hands occupied was a full-time job.

Throughout my early childhood, the four champagne glasses sat in the cabinet, far out of my grasp. I became obsessed with them. From the age of six, I gazed up at the glasses on a daily basis, dreaming of taking one down and pressing it against my cheek, then holding the skinny stem in my fingers and snapping it clean in two. Giff would often find me looking up at the cabinet with greedy determination, and she'd widen her eyes, letting me know that she knew exactly what I was thinking. As I grew a bit taller, Giff took the glasses and placed them on a higher shelf in the cabinet, much to my dismay. Every time I had a growth spurt, she put the glasses on a higher and higher shelf. There was only so far she could stretch, but she managed to keep moving her precious wedding set to safety. This went on for something like two and a half years.

Then one day, when I was about eight years old, Giff must have gone out. My dad was upstairs. My brothers were otherwise occupied. This was my opportunity. I assessed that I was tall enough to get to the glasses if I climbed up on something. I pulled out a chair from under the table and placed it in front of the cabinet, then I got up on the chair and moved the sliding doors to one side so I could get my fingertips to the highest shelf if I stood on tiptoes. I slowly nudged the bottom of one of the glasses forward until it was at the edge of the shelf, then I took it out and held it in my hands, marvelling at it, watching the smooth, transparent surface gleam in the light. Holding it against my chest, pressing its cool surface to my face, kissing it, I was entranced. I had longed for this moment, and now it was finally here.

As I climbed down from the chair, I was still carefully carrying my prize. I knew I could get into really serious trouble for this, so I had to make it worth it. I held the stem in my two fingers and thumbs and got ready to do the deed. I waited, just to savour the moment, then I took a little inhalation of breath and applied pressure with my fingertips. The stem was so slender it snapped instantly. A beautiful whisper of a snap. If I think of the top-five times I've experienced pure joy in my life, that moment is right up there. I'll never forget it. Snapping the stem gave me everything I needed and wanted; I was ecstatic.

After I broke the stem, I stood there for a while, holding the pieces, admiring my work. Then I realised I didn't know what to do with the broken parts, so I just climbed up onto the chair again and put them back on the shelf in the cabinet. I was so young and naively bold, I didn't even think to hide them. When Giff came home and saw one of her wedding glasses snapped in two, she knew exactly who the culprit was – that broken glass had my name written all over it. As predicted, I got into massive trouble. Giff's eyes pierced through me as she calmly and quietly told me off, emphasising every word. Her threats of a smack fell on deaf ears as I was sent to my room. That glass was older than I was! It had huge sentimental value. Giff spent the rest of the evening attempting to repair the broken stem, sighing in exasperation as she tried and failed to superglue it back together.

But to me, it had all been worth it. I had been thinking about climbing that mountaintop for over two years. I wanted something, I maintained focus, and the fact that I had waited so long only increased my sense of pride when I finally accomplished my goal. While Giff was furious with me about the broken glass, it also taught her that if something was out of my reach, I would keep climbing and striving until I got to it. In time, Giff and others would find more productive ways to harness that potential.

Chapter 6

Connection and Communication

One of Giff's biggest teaching tools in those days was the television. Back then, we had a Hitachi, a deep black box with fake wooden panels on the sides; it sat in the corner of the living room, beaming out sound and light at all times of the day and night. When I was about eight or nine, we got cable television, which meant we suddenly had a lot more channels, to everyone's great delight. Television was our family's number-one form of entertainment in those days. Like a lot of people struggling to make ends meet, we relied on the TV for escapism, that sense of being transported to other places. And for me, the visual medium of TV was ideal because unlike a book or the radio, it didn't require me to understand everything that was being said to follow along.

Of course there were times when Giff used the TV as a distraction. She would sit my brothers and me in front of our favourite cartoons to give herself enough time to make dinner, clean up or wash the clothes. But whenever she could, she sat down and watched the programmes with us. Giff narrated everything that was happening on the screen, using the characters and the stories to introduce me to various concepts. There was a children's programme back then called *Nellie the Elephant*, based on the song about an elephant who packs her trunk and says goodbye to the circus. Giff remembers using Nellie to explain the concept of independence to me. 'Nellie wanted to be independent – she wanted to do something different – and so she went off on her own path,' Giff pointed out. 'One day, you will grow up. And even though I will still be here, the time will come when you will want to be more independent. Right now, you're always holding on to my skirt, but eventually you'll want to leave the skirt. That's called being independent.'

Another programme we watched was *Rosie and Jim*, about two rag dolls who lived with the owner of a houseboat on a canal. 'Not everyone lives in houses,' Giff would tell me. 'Rosie and Jim live on a boat on the water, and because of that, they've been trained to be careful not to fall in.' Here she would mime falling into the water and splashing around for me. 'Rosie and Jim have learned that it's dangerous to fall in. That's what everyone has to do, Jason. We have to learn how to be safe.' The next time we were out on the street, Giff would say, 'Remember Rosie and Jim? They live on the water. We have our house, and we live on a road. You have to stay safe by not running into the road, just like they have to stay safe by not falling into the water.'

Whenever possible – and that was most of the time – there was a lesson to be learned. It was never just TV for TV's sake.

Beyond teaching us about concepts like independence and safety, Giff used television programmes to expose us to any series that included positive Black role models. As we got a bit older, that meant we watched a lot of American shows like *Moesha*, *The Fresh Prince of Bel-Air* and *Sister, Sister*, since in those days, there were no British equivalents of these kinds of programmes about aspirational Black families except for Trix Worrell's brilliant *Desmond's*. Giff wanted us to see what that looked like; she wanted to spark some kind of ambition in us.

TV was our portal. It exposed us to all kinds of places and experiences that we could never have afforded to go to in real life. Growing up, we watched almost every kind of sporting event: football, rugby, basketball, tennis, athletics, you name it. We watched a magazine programme called *Trans World Sport* on Channel 4 that featured interesting and informative sports stories from all around the globe. Giff made sure that sport – another good vehicle for conveying life lessons such as the importance of teamwork and being a good loser – was always 'on the curriculum' at our house. 'Some people think that winning is the only thing that matters,' she would say, 'but it matters more to learn how to lose with grace, because you're probably going to spend more time losing than winning in life.' For me, watching sports was particularly exciting because I didn't need language to understand what was going on.

And then there were Giff's soaps: *Neighbours* and *Home and Away*, the two Australian programmes that were on television every single weekday of my childhood, with omnibus repeats on weekends. We always watched together, never missing an episode, and often catching the repeats as well. As a neurodivergent child, living in a world that often seemed chaotic, confusing and overwhelming, I loved that those soaps came on every day at the exact same time and in the same order. I was rigidly attached to the routine of watching these programmes. Just knowing that when I got home from school, I would be able to tune in with Giff made my hands sweaty with anticipation. From the second the theme songs started up, I was locked in, hyper-fixated. A spaceship could have landed in the living room, and I wouldn't have noticed. All I wanted was to find out what happened to the characters next. Until a few years ago, when *Neighbours* was taken off the air, I'd watch it religiously. And to this day, I still watch *Home and Away*, using it as a way to tune out, as pure escapism. It's my equivalent of meditation.

Thanks to these soaps, and TV in general, my understanding of the human experience expanded. I learned about emotions – fear, sadness, joy – and about relationships. In watching television shows, I could see other people's struggles, and I found ways to connect their problems to those of real people in my life – and to my own as well. And like the characters on television, I started to have my own dreams, all with Giff at my side, explaining, narrating, making clear.

~

Not long after I started primary school, Giff met a woman who worked there called Brenda. Brenda told us about her church, Hanley Hall, which was a short walk from our house. We started going there every Sunday for the service and Sunday school. What I remember most about Hanley is the songs: 'Morning Has Broken' by Cat Stevens, 'The Family of Man' by the Spinners, and a religious version of the 'Do-Re-Mi' song from *The Sound of Music* that started 'S for sin, a dreadful thing . . .' These weren't traditional hymns, and they were accompanied by people playing musical instruments, often the kids from Sunday school. I sat in a pew with Giff and my brothers, letting the vibrations from the voices of the congregation and the instruments buzz all around me. But unlike the sounds and vibrations of the traffic, these ones actually soothed me.

As soon as I heard the first note, I'd start bopping up and down in my seat, humming and rocking back and forth, tapping my hands on the pew in front of me. At school or outside the house, everyone always wanted me to stop my stimming, but at Hanley, I could let the stims flow in time to the music. This was a huge relief and source of pleasure for me. Sometimes Brenda or her sister, Sofia, who had both worked with children with special and complex needs, would have to take me out so I could calm down a bit. They weren't punishing me – they were changing the scenery so I could have a break, and they always brought me back in after a few minutes. In their eyes, I was as much a part of that congregation as anyone else.

Hanley Hall welcomed people of all backgrounds who wanted to learn about God and to worship; it didn't matter that I couldn't speak. There was a ritual and a repetition to Hanley that I loved. We went every Sunday at the same time, and while the passages from the Bible changed, we always did the same things and sang the same songs. I didn't spend a lot of time around other children apart from my siblings growing up because I was either in therapy or segregated from my classmates. But at Hanley Hall, I was allowed to be with other kids. There were no clipboards, no one assessing how inept I was; that in itself was affirming. And just when it looked like things couldn't get any better, we'd have a snack after the songs. I'd wait to get my treat from the box of biscuits, and while I never knew which kind I'd get from the assortment, I knew I'd get one, and this predictability provided another layer of comfort.

As Giff observed me at Hanley, she was beginning to recognise the importance of music and movement in giving me a way to express myself and let out my emotions without words or having a meltdown. We listened to a lot of music at our house. My dad had a large and wide-ranging record collection: James Brown, Jimmy Cliff, Jimi Hendrix, Santana, Miles Davis and so many others, as well as African musicians like Orlando Julius, Ladysmith Black Mambazo, Manu Dibango and of course Mama Africa, the queen of African music, Miriam Makeba. Paul Simon's *Graceland*, which featured so many of my dad's favourite African musicians, played on repeat throughout my childhood. On the rare occasions when he happened to have a day off from work, I remember watching my dad as he put records on his prized Sharp turntable in the living room – carefully removing the disc from its sleeve, holding it between his two palms at the edges, and lining it up over the spindle in the middle of the record player. Then he'd drop the needle, and there'd be the familiar short crackle before the song started up. The music of Jimmy Cliff in particular spoke to my dad's struggles, sorrows and frustrations as an African Black man trying to find his way in a foreign land. I remember the pained look on his face and the slump of his shoulders as he'd play 'Many Rivers to Cross'.

Giff could see that as soon as my dad put on any record, no matter how sombre, my whole demeanour changed. I'd start moving my body in rhythm, rocking, humming, clapping my hands or tapping on the nearest object, nodding my head. Giff had a tambourine and a mini drum that she gave to JJ and me, and we followed her lead as she clapped along to church music, African music, rock and roll, pop, R & B and old-school music, you name it. Her tastes were even more wide-ranging than my dad's. Before I could speak, music became a massive point of connection and communication for my parents, my siblings and me. Through music, I entered a conversation that I could fully comprehend and participate in through the beat.

At that time, Enya was one of the biggest stars around – and Giff loved her music. We listened to songs like 'Orinoco Flow', 'Book of Days' and 'Caribbean Blue' with Giff often comparing the flowing, rushing sound of the music to water.

'This is a song about the ocean,' she told us as we listened to 'Orinoco Flow'. 'You've never been to the ocean, but when you stand at the water's edge, you can hear the sound of the waves as the tide rushes in and the seagulls cry overhead. If you look out at the water, people are doing different activities. They're swimming in the sea, they're sailing. You can't just jump into the water. People need to learn how to swim. They learn how to do things like sailing. One day we'll visit the ocean together.'

Giff would play a song over and over, until slowly I began to connect a melody or a change of key or a lyric or a hook or a riff with feelings and experiences. Often, she'd use the lyrics to help me understand concepts. One of her favourite songs back then was 'Head over Heels' by Tears for Fears.

'Listen closely, Jason,' she'd tell me. 'This is a song about love and what it feels like to love someone. That's what head over heels means.'

Just as my dad went to the songs of Jimmy Cliff and others for consolation, Giff turned to music for support. Often, she played her church hymns, singing and clapping along, giving praises to God. But there was one secular song she would play more than all the others: Simon and Garfunkel's 'The Sound of Silence'.

'Jason, if you listen to the words, you will understand they are about the feeling of isolation,' Giff told me. 'It's a song about darkness being a familiar companion, someone who visits you more than once in your life. It's about what it means to be alone, when you can't connect with others. It's a sad song, but it's touched a lot of people because everyone feels sadness at some point. It's something we cannot avoid.'

Giff carried around her own sadness, even if she didn't always show it. She was the mother of three young Black boys, two of them with disabilities, and despite her complete devotion to us, she was regularly judged and demeaned, her wisdom called into question. I can see now that 'The Sound of Silence' spoke to these painful places, and even if I didn't fully understand the words, I could sense the emotions behind them.

The therapists at the hospital had tried to turn me into a robot, but music was my WD-40, lubricating my hinges and joints so that I would have access to feelings, to what it means to be human, to move, slide and bend in time to the rhythm, letting the meaning of melody resonate in my heart.

Then there were the times when Giff stopped narrating the songs, when the two of us would just dance to the music together in the front room. Some of my fondest memories of childhood are of dancing with Giff, her spinning me around, both of us feeling unencumbered, free just to be.

Chapter 7

Observant

For the first few years of my education, starting when I was four years old, I went to the closest special needs primary school to our house. And one day a week, I went to the local mainstream primary school, Heathbrook. Giff tirelessly campaigned to have JJ and me moved to Heathbrook full-time because she strongly believed that we needed to be in mainstream classrooms in order to flourish and fully develop. Nowadays, mixed-needs classrooms are the norm for most children, but in the 1990s, Giff was ahead of her time. The 'experts' felt there was no point in moving me because I couldn't speak and was 'never going to improve'. Giff felt that if no one was expecting me to improve, I would stop trying, and it would turn into a self-fulfilling prophecy and so she fought to have me moved along with JJ. Speaking up in this way was risky, not only because she was a lone woman in a sea of male experts – not to mention the only Black person in the room – but also because Black women who challenged authority figures in this way often ended up having their kids taken away from them.

Eventually, Giff succeeded in having us moved to mainstream school, first with JJ and then with me. At the age of seven, I started at Heathbrook full time. This meant I finally began wearing a uniform. Until then, I'd always worn my own clothes to Heathbrook on the one day a week I went, which immediately singled me out from all the other kids who wore uniforms. Now I was finally going to be like everyone else, much to my delight. Giff procured the uniform from a second-hand sale at the school. The top was made of a thick, deep navy blue wool, with an embroidered crest on one side of the chest, and the collared shirt was crisp cotton. I loved that uniform instantly. From a sensory point of view, it was perfect – the shirt was like the softest armour, and the fuzzy knit sleeves could be pulled down to rub against the tops of my palms. Then there were the light grey polyester trousers, with a single pleat in the front and a zip fly. Sharp.

The night before my first day of wearing a uniform to school, I was delirious with excitement. That evening, Giff opened up the creaky ironing board, stood it to attention, plugged in the iron, and filled the steam compartment with water. While she waited for the iron to get hot, she turned the uniform items inside out. Our iron was temperamental. It had been known to stick, marking the fabric, so everything got turned inside out to avoid any damage to visible areas. Giff drove the iron over the clothing with great purpose and precision, saying, 'Jason, we are going to do this every day. When you value clothes, they last longer.' She believed that dressing and presenting nicely were important, that you should always put your best foot forward – and as a former seamstress, she also appreciated the importance of looking after your clothes. I stared up at her, smiled and nodded. It was my way of saying thank you, absent the words. Giff leaned over, kissing the top of my head. Then she neatly folded the ironed clothes and placed them on the arm of the chair for me to wear the next day.

The morning arrived. Giff moisturised my face with a mixture of Palmer's Cocoa Butter and Johnson's Baby Oil, the light reflecting off my cheeks and forehead as I looked in the mirror. Then she retrieved my name-tagged uniform from the arm of the chair downstairs and dressed me in front of the mirror, telling me how handsome and grown-up I looked. I examined myself, the crisp edge of the pleat on my trousers, the starchy cut of the collar, my shiny new Clarks shoes, the neat belt wound around my middle, the embroidery on my chest looking like a medal already received for valour. I felt a sense of pride and well-being and stood slightly taller.

Then I rushed out of the door, eager to walk the ten minutes to school – something I'd never felt before. As we entered the playground, it was clear to see that I looked the same as everyone else. We were all in uniform. I was no longer an outsider. The bell rang, and the well-drilled pupils ran to get into their class lines. I hung back, savouring the feeling of Giff's hand in mine for just a second longer. 'Make sure you're good,' she told me, 'and you have a good day. I love you.' She kissed me on the cheek, fondly using her thumb to rub off the red lipstick left behind.

Then, head held high, I walked into the classroom alongside my classmates. The teacher addressed us with a 'Good morning, children', and everyone except me responded, in a perfectly rehearsed chorus, 'Good morning, Miss James. Good morning, everybody.'

Right after that, I saw another teacher appear at the door. While the other children were enthusiastically sharing tales of their weekends in show-and-tell, this teacher quietly removed me from the classroom and whisked me away to a small room with one solitary window. Besides the teacher, I was the only person in the room. It was a world away from the busy class of a few minutes ago.

The teacher didn't explain why this was happening to me or what I'd done to deserve such treatment. In some ways, he didn't need to. Ever since I'd started at primary school, the teachers had been removing me from the classroom, claiming that it was too stimulating for me, that I needed to be on my own in case I upset the other children with my meltdowns, which had only continued. Despite Giff's best efforts, I had been segregated again.

I learned a harsh lesson that day: while my uniform represented belonging, I was still 'different'. The only time I saw other children was when we went outside for a break. After that, I was ushered back into the room, alone except for the teacher, once again. Suddenly I didn't like my new school uniform anymore. I just wanted to go home. I wanted to be with Giff.

~

Meanwhile, Giff kept fighting, insisting that my teachers innovate their approach to my education, even if her suggestions fell on deaf ears. For instance, when I was being taught to write the alphabet, I made little to no progress for some time. 'It's not enough to show Jason the alphabet on a blackboard if he has problems holding a pen,' Giff pointed out. My fingers would often get sweaty, and I had problems with my grip. When no one else had any ideas of how to help me, Giff did her own research and tracked down a former work colleague who had been an engineer. He helped her to procure a special pen that would make writing easier for me. 'There is no such thing as a one-size-fits-all approach,' she told my teachers, repeatedly reminding them to treat JJ and me as individuals.

School was a place where JJ did well, excelling at maths and anything to do with computers and technology. Meanwhile, my younger brother, Simon, had been identified as 'gifted' by his teachers and had overtaken me completely. This didn't trouble me. It just made me appreciate him even more.

For my part, any progress I made was excruciatingly slow. The therapists gave Giff exercises to do with me at home that involved following a list of instructions, but these didn't interest me, and before long, she gave up on them. But one thing she didn't give up on was her desire for me to learn to play and interact with others, even if the school kept insisting on segregating me. When she noticed how much I enjoyed kicking a ball around with my brothers, she approached the coaches who ran an under-elevens football league and persuaded them to take JJ and me on, even though I still couldn't speak. 'If you look at the expression on his face,' she told the coaches, 'that will let you know his response.'

This was part of Giff's plan to make sure that I was exposed to other children, that I could understand the value of teamwork and collaborating with others to achieve a collective goal. After that, JJ and I played football every Saturday. As exhausted as Giff was after waking up early every morning to get the three of us to school, she'd rouse herself on Saturday too, dropping us at the park and then waiting for the match to end.

When I was playing, it didn't matter that I couldn't speak. It didn't matter that I felt singled out at school. I was part of a team there. I could do what the other children did – sometimes even better. My physical coordination rapidly improved, and I became a good player, someone people wanted on their team. Thanks to football, I started making my first friends. Even though I couldn't answer them when they spoke to me, we were all celebrating the same victories and commiserating the same losses. To this day, I still play football with some of the people I met at that time. These are lifelong friendships that the 'experts' told Giff I would never be able to form.

~

When people hear that I used to be non-verbal, they always assume it was a terrible experience. They feel sorry for me – pity me, even. 'Oh, it must have been so difficult not to be able to speak.' But to be honest, it was the opposite. Being silent allowed me to spend my earliest years quietly observing and learning to understand human beings and their interactions with one another. Most people, assuming that I couldn't hear or understand what they were saying, ignored me, and this gave me a lot of time to listen, a skill that has served me very well as an adult. Even before I could fully understand language, I was deducing, synthesising and absorbing information. I don't think it's a coincidence that I ended up working as a sociologist – someone who studies societies, and the many ways that people interact.

During the first almost twelve years of my life, I had to be hypervigilant, alert to people and what their facial expressions, gestures, body language, postures and tones of voice meant, in order to interpret that and navigate around it. I picked up on all kinds of social cues as a result. As a child, I learned that a half-smile, a raised eyebrow or the crease of a frown often said a lot more than the words someone used. I learned to discern the difference between someone slumping or putting their shoulders back, and what that said about their mood. I was alert to tone of voice, and how it changed when people were frustrated or upset. I saw how adults sometimes approached each other with a handshake and other times a hug or a kiss on the cheek. I observed the amount of space people left between them when they stood chatting. Often, I couldn't stop staring – so much so that Giff had to teach me it's rude to stare. Sometimes she'd give me a quick pinch on the leg or arm to remind me, and other times she'd have to apologise on my behalf. 'I'm so sorry my son keeps staring,' she'd say. 'He's still learning not to do that.'

I was fascinated by people, incredibly interested in them. All these years later, I'll notice if someone has changed one tiny thing about their appearance – about the way they've tied their hair back or how they twiddle a necklace between their fingertips. I'm especially attentive to the flickering of emotions as they flash across people's faces. Many times, I can sense how someone feels without even asking. Gestures are powerful signals too. One of my abiding early memories is of watching two men standing on a street corner. The first man was crying and the second man hugged him, holding his head tightly, just letting the guy cry on his shoulder. It shattered the images of masculinity I'd been exposed to while watching cartoons and television dramas. And it changed how I thought. To this day, I hug people when I sense that's what they need. The cliché is that autistic people don't like to hug, but again, it all depends on the person. To me, a hug feels like an exchange of energy, a spiritual thing.

Giff once told me, 'Even though you couldn't speak, one thing I did notice was that you made people feel good. People always remembered two things about you: "That boy, that middle one, Jason, he always shook people's hands and he always hugged people," they'd say.'

If making people feel good was a skill, it's one I had mastered at a young age. And I was about to develop another skill – one that would forever change my life.

~

Giff has never forgotten the moment, but for some reason, I can't locate the memory in my bank of mental images, so I have to rely on her telling of this story.

I was at speech therapy with Katrina, who, after the shaking incident, had levelled off to what could be considered a baseline of snappiness and shortness. For nearly eight years, multiple times a week, Giff and I had dutifully gone to speech therapy. Over that time period, I'd made so little progress that the local council was on the verge of pulling the plug on my funded support. If this had happened, I would have lost access to speech therapy altogether. That's not something I would necessarily have been sad about – and I'm pretty sure Katrina would have been relieved as well.

But miraculously, just a few days shy of my twelfth birthday, I spoke. It was at the start of one of my sessions, and Katrina had just said, 'Hello, Jason.' At that moment, I was fiddling with my hearing aid, which was bothering me, and then I took it out of my ear and said hello back to her. Thankfully, Giff was there, so she could witness the moment.

Giff screamed, 'Say that again!' And so, I did. Not only had I spoken, but I had said the word correctly in context. Until this point, I had said bits of words and made various noises blurted out of context, but I'd never offered a reply at the right time, with the right word. Neither Giff nor Katrina could believe it.

'Can you say anything else?' Giff wanted to know. On that day, I couldn't, but over time, other words came to me.

The naysayers had told Giff that this would never happen, that if I wasn't speaking by age four or five, I would likely never go on to develop language skills. 'I do not accept that,' she told them. Some years later, in 2013, a study by scientists at the Center for Autism and Related Disorders in Baltimore showed that the vast majority of autistic children with severe language delays at age four actually do go on to be able to speak. Giff was proven right yet again.

In my earliest days of speaking, I mostly just repeated what other people said. This is known as echolalia, and it can be quite common in neurodivergent children. Repeating what other people said was a way for me to acquire more language, finally forming very simple sentences, and getting to know the sound of my own voice. Giff's delight at my new-found speaking skills soon turned to exasperation after I parroted absolutely everything she said for days on end. This was so annoying that she joked that maybe it hadn't been such a good idea to teach me to speak after all.

Even so, the timing was fortuitous: I had said my first words just months before starting secondary school. People were delighted that I could finally speak, but this development came with a cost: I could no longer silently observe everyone as I had in the past. When you're wordless, you're allowed to live in your own world and absorb your surroundings. There's a freedom to that.

The expectations were different now.

Part Two

Practice

Chapter 8

Outside the Classroom

Back in the mid-1990s, Southfields Secondary School was a grimy red- and yellow-brick Victorian building, five storeys high, with tall white-framed windows, not the shiny, new premises it is today. Initially, I went just a few days a week, while also still attending Heathbrook primary, until I was fully integrated and went to Southfields every day. I had to take a bus to get there, and at first Giff went with me so I could learn the route. After that, I was allowed to go with my brother Joseph, who had been at Southfields for a couple of years already and now went by his full name, instead of by JJ. Joseph didn't like having to take me on the bus with him because he was extremely punctual and loved school, especially his favourite subjects, maths and computers. In the morning, he'd leave the house before me, Reebok backpack on his shoulders, racing off in the distance, while I barely had my shoes on. I was chronically tardy, hated school, and still couldn't read and write at the age of twelve. I often made Joseph late because he had to wait for me as I dawdled to the bus stop. My parents often joked that my older brother was going to open the school gates in the morning.

When I got off the bus at the other end, the feeling of dread at the sight of the Southfields building would overwhelm me. My stomach would be in knots as I walked towards the school gates, every step a fight against the instinct to turn around and run home. Going in through the gaping mouth of the school entrance meant being swallowed by the chaos of the hallways and the constant echoing hubbub of students, school bells, shouting teachers and squeaking floors. I had to brace myself every single time.

You would have thought I'd at least be excited about wearing my new uniform: black trousers and a white polo shirt under a royal blue top. But I knew better, having learned from primary school that wearing the same outfit as everyone else didn't mean that I was going to be treated the same way as them. Sure enough, on my first day at secondary school, I was sent off to the special educational needs (SEN) classroom, with about eight or nine other students. The Education Act of 1993 had done away with the term 'educationally subnormal' that had been used to describe people like me, replacing it with the term SEN, but the smell of stigma still hung heavy in the air. Joseph was considered a SEN student on paper but was gradually taken out of the SEN track because he showed so much aptitude.

Back then, Southfields was known as the best place in southwest London for students with special needs. The SEN programme was run by Miss Rita McCann, a middle-aged woman with jet-black, tailbone-length hair, big eyes and very long eyelashes. Inside the classroom, we each had our own computer terminal, hooked up to a learning platform called SuccessMaker. Miss McCann was there to assist us with the programme, which was focused on developing our literacy and numeracy skills. I still didn't have any real linguistic fluency, nor could I understand anything to do with numbers due to my dyscalculia, which I was diagnosed with while at Southfields. Miss McCann was dutiful and attentive, and I did try, but I didn't make much progress.

The great thing about Miss McCann was that she believed in the potential of all children, including me. She told Giff she had full confidence that one day I would be able to read and write, that the cognitive gears would finally click into place and that everything would begin to flow from there. This meant a lot to Giff, as no one had ever told her that before. For a short time, I was able to benefit from a kind and diligent educator who was passionate about children with different learning needs. Miss McCann understood that when I repeated what she had just told me, I wasn't being rude, it was because of my echolalia, which was helping me to acquire language. But my time with Miss McCann was short-lived. Two years after I arrived at Southfields, the local council took away the funding for the programme, and that was the end of that. SuccessMaker went, and so did Miss Rita McCann. Around the same time, the council also cut funding for my speech therapy sessions, so after ten long years, that was the end of those too. I never saw my therapist, Katrina, again.

After Miss McCann left, I was put in a regular classroom with a rotating series of SEN support assistants. The main thing I remember about these assistants is that their breath always seemed to smell intensely of tobacco and caffeine. They would sit next to me in every class, tapping with a pen on a word in the textbook, trying to get me to understand it. And when I couldn't, they used the same pen to bang on my knuckles, all while breathing down my neck. I often wonder if the reason

I've never wanted to smoke cigarettes or drink coffee is because it takes me back to having my knuckles rapped.

'You're not trying hard enough,' they'd snap. 'Why don't you understand things?'

~

Despite Giff's continued efforts to teach me to read – she would sit with me for hours, reading books aloud, pointing at the pictures, trying to help me see the connections between words on the page, sounds and concepts – nothing was helping. Giff was doing her best, but my brain could not make the link. I was stuck.

At Southfields, students were split up into four sets, or streams. Top set was where all the really clever kids were placed, and I was always put in bottom set, which meant I was generally with other kids who were struggling with basic academic skills. Bottom set was somewhere between a nursery and a madhouse: kids talking over the teacher, laughing, passing notes, getting into fights, always causing some kind of ruckus. I don't blame the school for this situation – Southfields had just lost its special needs department due to budget cuts. Most of our teachers weren't given the training or the resources to manage classes of more than thirty kids with a variety of support needs.

Meanwhile, I had no idea what was written on the blackboard and couldn't make head nor tail of the textbook in front of me. I've always struggled to understand people's voices when there's a lot of background noise, and as my classroom was the noisiest in the entire school, it was very difficult for me to discern the teachers' words, let alone the lessons they were trying to impart. If I'd been able to dial down the volume of the classroom, the way I could on a stereo, I might have stood a chance. But that wasn't possible, so I simply had to endure the cacophony. The therapists with their clipboards had trained me well, but that didn't mean it wasn't misery. I remember thinking, *This is never going to end*, as I desperately waited for the 'pips', a loud sound signalling the lesson was finally over.

The teachers at Southfields knew that I was a SEN student and couldn't read, but that didn't mean I avoided being called on in class. English was the worst subject for me in this respect. When I was about fourteen, we started studying classics such as *Animal Farm*, *Of Mice and Men* and *Romeo and Juliet* – texts that might as well have been written in Greek for all I knew. The teacher, Miss Rowan, a younger woman with wire-framed glasses, would often ask students to read aloud in class.

When I first arrived in Miss Rowan's classroom, I would still occasionally repeat the teacher's words under my breath in an attempt to process their meaning. Inevitably, Miss Rowan heard me muttering something one day and her eyes fixed on me.

'Sorry, Jason is talking over there,' she told the class. 'Jason, could you read this passage, please?'

My heart sank to the pit of my stomach.

Miss Rowan must have known my limitations, but she had called on me anyway, presumably to send a message to the rest of the class: '*If you don't settle down, you'll be asked to read next.*'

I just sat there, frozen, because I had no way of understanding the letters on the page. My support assistant prodded me with her pen; obviously, that didn't help. After a few agonising seconds of silence, the rest of the students erupted in laughter, jeering at me, calling me dumb. I bowed my head, completely ashamed. There's that phrase about wishing the ground would open up and swallow me whole. I would have given anything for that to actually happen; I just wanted to disappear. After that Miss Rowan glared around the room, and everyone else in the class settled down in case they got called on too.

In my years at Southfields, perhaps the biggest lesson I learned was to sit as still as a rock, not saying anything in class to avoid being exposed. I'd tuck my chin into my chest and sink down in my seat, praying the teacher wouldn't notice me. This also meant suppressing not just my echolalia but also my stims – my need to tap, hum or rock to regulate myself. If I made even the slightest movement or sound, I was at risk for being called upon. The problem was, making myself as small as possible while suppressing my stims took so much mental energy that there was no way I could pay attention to the lesson, even if I'd been able to discern what the teacher was saying in the first place.

If you can believe it, in addition to failing miserably with reading and writing in English, I was also supposed to be learning Spanish. Our Spanish teacher, Miss Dominic, was one of those people who, as far as I could see, really struggled to keep control of a bottom set class with over thirty students in it. Before long, I became convinced that I was Miss Dominic's scapegoat. All I had to do was glance at someone sitting next to me or out of the window, and that seemed to be enough to get me banished from the classroom: 'Jason, get out of my class!'

Other kids were far more disruptive than I was, but it felt like I was the one who usually got punished. On reflection, I think it was because Miss Dominic knew I was polite and mild-mannered, and I would do anything she told me to, including leaving the class on command. Other kids would have stood up to her, but I'd just walk out to the hallway and wait outside until the class was over. At least it was quiet out there. After the bell went, I'd go back into the room to collect my bag and coat, and there was Miss Dominic, looking like she had been pushed to her breaking point yet again by my classmates. Even though she had cast me out, I was the one who ended up consoling her, asking, 'Are you okay, Miss?' On several occasions, she even apologised to me.

Miss Dominic wasn't the only one sending me out to stand in the hallways alone. The other teachers did it too. That is one of my major memories of Southfields: being outside the classroom, segregated again, waiting for it all to be over. At the end of the day, I'd run to the bus, where I would finally gain some relief. Giff had saved up her money and bought me a chrome-coloured imitation Walkman from Alba with headphones and trailing wires. I loved that 'Walkman' with a passion. As soon as I was on the bus, I'd put on my headphones, press play and just block out the world. The relief I experienced as soon as I could hear that music was life-affirming. I'd get lost in whatever track was playing, finally able to let out my humming and tapping as I listened. Even though Giff made me promise that I wouldn't wear my headphones in the street, in case I got distracted when I was walking around, that moment of release on the bus ride home became something I looked forward to all day long.

~

Like the teachers at Southfields, my fellow students didn't always give me the easiest time. They ridiculed me for not being able to read and write, and they laughed at the way I spoke. All those years of speech therapy meant that I had learned to emulate Katrina's intonation and tone of voice, which made me sound vaguely well-spoken, as though I'd had a lifetime of elocution lessons. Even as an adult, people find my regional-neutral accent hard to place. A friend once joked that I sound a quarter street and three-quarters private school boy. Not only did I have a weird accent, but I was also into guitar music, which was not typical for a young Black kid growing up in south London in the 1990s. My favourite bands and musicians were Oasis, the Stone Roses, the Verve, Paul Simon, the Cranberries, the Beautiful South, Tasmin Archer, Skunk Anansie, Nirvana, Pearl Jam and Paul Weller, to name a few. I knew people thought my taste in music was strange, but it didn't bother me. I had this sort of unshakable sense of self, bestowed on me by Giff. And so, the low-level bullying of some of the students became part of the Southfields landscape, like the dull-coloured yellowing paint on all the walls, cracking and flaking, so that you didn't really notice it anymore.

I did make two really good friends at Southfields: Chris and another kid called Jason. Chris was in top set and Jason was in second, but despite our academic differences, they were very kind to me. When my brother couldn't walk me to the bus because he was busy with other activities, Jason and Chris went with me instead, pointing out the number 77 that I needed to take so I wouldn't end up on the wrong bus (I still couldn't make out the numbers). Sometimes, I'd go round to their houses after school, and we'd watch wrestling and Ali G on television, or we'd head to the park and kick a football around. Jason was half-Mauritian and Chris was strawberry blond with freckles. We became a trio, me with the Afro I was trying to grow to emulate one of my heroes, Jimi Hendrix.

Even without having much practice at friendship, I already

knew how to walk up to people with a winning grin because I'd seen Giff do the same. I knew how to make someone feel better by putting a hand on their shoulder after they missed an easy goal because I'd seen my friends at football do that. I started to really enjoy the back and forth of conversation and the joking around of having mates – how it felt to tell someone a story, making them smile or laugh back at you. I found out that all my years of observing others had served me well. I still wasn't able to read or write, but I was naturally good at being around people – a skill that would serve me well in years to come.

Chapter 9

The Power of Repetition

One day, I remember having this epiphany: *When I go to school, I don't learn anything.* I told Giff how I felt. She said, 'Are you giving it your best, Jason? Are you paying attention?' And I had to admit that I wasn't because it just didn't seem worth it. That same year, we were allowed to get a lunch pass and leave the building to get food, so I started a regular habit of bunking off in the afternoon. I'd leave school, pick up a box of chicken and chips, and then get on the bus and flee the scene, heading straight to Rileys snooker hall.

Snooker was my newest passion. After the success of football, Giff was always on the lookout for other sports I could try. Tennis, cricket, swimming – she introduced me to anything on offer in the area. One day, she was watching golf on television and noticed that there was a lot of repetition involved, with the players swinging their clubs over and over again. She'd already learned through observation that repetitive motions, such as sweeping the floor, were soothing for me. We couldn't afford golf lessons, but a few weeks later, a snooker match happened to come on TV. Giff watched as the players carefully lined up the shots on the table before potting the balls in the pockets.

She deduced that snooker was similar to golf in that it was about executing the same movements over and over – and getting a ball in a small hole (except in the case of snooker, with a green baize instead of a putting green). *Right*, thought Giff. *I think that's something that Jason would like.*

There was a snooker hall not far from our house called Rileys. When Giff asked me if I would be interested in going, I nodded yes. Before long, Rileys had become a sort of second home to me. The woman on the door was named Amy. I'd ring the bell, and she'd buzz me inside as under-eighteens were allowed in as long as they left by 8 p.m. Rileys was gloomy and quiet – an adult space frequented mostly by men sipping on pints and pulling on cigarettes. Beneath low-hanging lamps, the green baize of the tables glowed and trails of smoke hung in the air. Giff would pay by the hour for the table, and then she'd leave me there, providing the staff with strict instructions to keep an eye on me and explaining that she'd come back to collect me later. She knew that if anything untoward happened, I was savvy enough to run home and get her, since Rileys was so close to our house.

The club didn't just have snooker: there were slot machines, dartboards, lots of pool tables too – American pool, British pool. Snooker was downstairs and pool was upstairs. I gravitated to snooker because that's what Giff had shown me on television.

There was this one player, a tall and sinewy older guy with dark hair named Michael, who showed me the technical ropes and became my unofficial coach. It was Michael who taught me how to walk into the line of the shot, then make the right stance: one leg ramrod straight, with the other bent, while folding your body over the table.

'Whatever you do, do not move your head, Jason,' Michael told me, explaining the golden rule of snooker. 'If you move your head, you throw the cue off line.'

Soon enough, I learned not just the stance but how to feather the ball, moving the cue back and forth rhythmically three and a half times, while flicking my eyes between the cue ball and the object ball, pausing as I drew the cue back, then striking straight through the ball and the line of the shot. If I did it this way, always in the same way, the cue ball would be on a string and the object ball would always land straight into the back of the pocket, Michael explained in a very simplistic way.

The more technically proficient I became, the more consistently I achieved this. Michael taught me where to strike on the white ball to get it to do what I wanted. He showed me how to stun, screw and run-through, plain ball or with side, and the names of these shots became a part of my vernacular. He also taught me how to do potting drills (exercises you practise to help improve your pre-shot routine and ability to pot the balls in the pocket, which is how you score points) and how to construct big breaks (break-building), which is the secret to winning the game (the value of the points scored in a single visit to the table is called a break, and your turn continues as long as you keep potting one ball after another without missing). I had a natural aptitude and was hungry to learn.

There were lots of older guys in the club, not all of them as honourable as Michael. I remember a lovable rogue named Fred. Ropey and potbellied, he had a really bad gambling problem and invited me to play against him for money. I agreed but I wasn't good enough to beat him yet, so this was a bit unethical – he was basically taking pocket money from a schoolboy.

When Michael saw this, he jumped in, saying, 'You should be ashamed of yourself, Fred! You shouldn't be doing that!' But it was also a good learning experience for me, because thanks to Fred, I learned how to play for money, which began to work to my advantage as I got better at the game.

As Giff had predicted, I loved snooker. It's a very repetitive and diligent sport. Your hands, your eyes and your whole body have to work in unison to create that 'feel' on the shot. I grew to love the sound of the thwack when the balls hit each other, and the thunk when the object ball hit the back of the pocket. There's a rhythm to the game that I would get lost in, just as I got lost in music. All the other sounds of the snooker club, the kind of complex noises that usually bothered me – the ping and clatter of the slot machines, the clanking of people in the kitchen, the chatter of the men at the bar – just faded away.

'Monotropism' is a word that people often use to describe how the autistic brain can home in on a single task or special interest, becoming completely focused for very long periods. I certainly hadn't heard of the word, which had only just been coined by the autism researcher Dr Dinah Murray when I started frequenting Rileys, but there's no doubt that my monotropism became a major asset in the snooker hall – and throughout my life. I started going to Rileys every afternoon, sometimes playing for up to six hours a day. Thanks to the intensity of my focus and all the hours I put in, I improved so quickly and showed such aptitude that the club let me play for free. This was their way of sponsoring me; the only thing I had to do in return was to clean the tables for them. People often left ashtrays on the side of the table, and inevitably, they'd get knocked over, spilling ash onto the baize. Sometimes a lit cigarette would even burn a hole in the fabric. This used to drive me mad because I liked the cloth looking pristine, so I was happy to clean up in return for 'free lights', as it was known (because when your money ran out, the lamp above the table was switched off and you couldn't see well enough to keep playing).

After leaving school, usually at lunchtime, I'd go straight to Rileys. I always left my cue behind the bar at the club so it would be waiting for me when I arrived. To my knowledge, no one at Rileys ever questioned why a young boy in a school uniform was playing snooker all afternoon: that place was full of insalubrious characters who weren't going to report a truant. Meanwhile, as far as I know, my teachers at Southfields didn't complain when I wasn't at school in the afternoons. At least they had one less student to worry about in the mayhem that was bottom set.

~

One morning, I was in Miss Dominic's Spanish class, and I remembered I had a Maryland chocolate and hazelnut cookie stashed in my inside jacket pocket. I've always had a sweet tooth, so I took out the cookie and put it into my mouth whole in an attempt to hide it from my teacher. Of course, Miss Dominic noticed this and decided to choose that moment to ask me a question. I couldn't answer because I had a mouthful of cookie. 'Get out of my class now, you stupid boy!' she insisted. I guess I asked for that one, seeing as I shouldn't have been eating in class.

It was the last lesson before noon and I already had my lunch pass, so I grabbed my coat, left the school, hopped on the bus, and went straight to the snooker hall. Rileys had a special room upstairs with a match table, which had finer baize and narrower pockets, making it much more challenging to play. At a certain point, I was allowed to practise on that table too. On one side of the room, there was a big glass window, which meant that people could watch me as I worked on my line-ups and various other drills. A line-up is when you put fifteen red balls all in a line in the middle of the table; first you pot a red and then you pot a colour, then you alternate between reds and colours, attempting to construct a break with the aim of clearing the table. I was fast, meticulous, flawless. It got to the point where I was in such perfect control of the cue ball during a line-up that I would barely miss a shot.

At that time, I had so little control over my life. I couldn't make myself read or write. I couldn't make myself learn numbers. I couldn't make myself intelligent. But I'll tell you what I could do: I could definitely dish up on the green baize. At school, no one ever acknowledged me for being good at anything other than sports, but when I was in the snooker hall, everyone knew me as 'the Black kid who can play'.

The same day that Miss Dominic threw me out of her classroom, I made my first century break in a line-up. This is when you amass one hundred points by successfully potting at least thirteen reds followed by the high-value colours in a single visit. As I potted one shot after another, people at the club began gathering at the window to watch me, and soon I had dozens of spectators. After I potted the last shot, everyone erupted in applause. I had my arms in the air, holding my cue, incredulous that I'd done it. I remember thinking to myself, *Well, this is a bit different to how I felt five hours ago, getting thrown out of Miss Dominic's class.*

To celebrate, Rileys gave me a free burger and chips with a

couple of sachets of mayonnaise and a big Fanta. I was so chuffed with myself, I felt like a king.

~

At home, I squirrelled away all the money I was winning at the club under my bed. I didn't tell Giff, my dad or even my brothers, because then they would realise how much school I was missing. But from time to time, I'd put a few notes under my brothers' pillows or in their drawers so they could spend them on whatever they wanted. Because I struggled reading numbers, I didn't know how much the notes were worth, so I gave my brothers the biggest ones, hoping these were the most valuable. I always wanted to share everything and anything I had with them, and they were pretty stoked by these gifts from their brother, the overly generous tooth fairy.

Giff, who was all-seeing and all-knowing, eventually cottoned on to the fact that I was rolling in cash. I think she was concerned that I had started dealing drugs because one day she confronted me. 'I'm going to ask you a question, Jason,' she began, 'and I want you to tell me the truth, even if you think I'm going to be angry, upset or disappointed with you. I'll always be on your side, but if you lie to me, then I'll be much more annoyed with you than if you tell me the truth.'

'Okay, Giff,' I replied.

'Where do you get this money from?' she asked, showing me a healthy wad of notes that she'd found stashed under my bed.

'From playing snooker,' I replied.

Giff was sceptical. Even though snooker had been her idea, she had no clue how good I'd become or how much time I was spending at the club practising and playing for money.

'I want you to take me down to the snooker hall and show me how well you play,' she said, clearly not convinced.

So off we went.

'Play like you normally would,' Giff instructed.

I scattered the balls, collating a cool 77 break, manoeuvring the white ball well and potting with precision. I was feathering and delivering the cue perfectly straight. Given that I'd not been playing for that long, this was really impressive. A year later, I would record my first century in an actual match, a total clearance of 122 points in a single visit. Still my highest break to date.

'My God, you've got a real talent, Jason!' Giff exclaimed proudly. 'You can play like they play on TV!'

After that, she stopped questioning me on how I made my money.

Before long, I started playing in the junior leagues, competing in snooker tournaments all over London, wearing my waistcoat with a Rileys logo on it. The entry fee was always twenty pounds, and if I got to the latter stages, I was guaranteed a prize of at least eighty pounds. A couple of times, I won the competition and made about three hundred pounds. It got to a point where I became so good that I could afford to have my own snooker cue made by John Parris Cues, the best cue maker in the world. I told them my story, and they gave me a towel with the Parris name on it to wipe the cue and my hands. I've kept it to this day.

My brain was so clear when I was playing snooker: I knew that all I had to do was concentrate on this one pot, and then the next one, and the next one. The only way to screw up was to miss balls. It was like I'd found all the answers on this twelve-by-six-foot table. Everything made sense to me there. As I got better, I started thinking two shots ahead, three shots ahead. If you're really gifted, you can think four or five shots ahead. I was never that good, but I knew that if I just kept potting, I'd have a decent chance of winning. The objective was clear, and there was nothing else in my life that was as simple as that. I *wished* all of life could be like that, where I could just do the same thing over and over and succeed.

Giff started using snooker as a metaphor, referencing everything back to the game. She still does occasionally. 'Practice makes permanent, Jason,' she told me. 'The more you repeat a task, the better you will get.' This understanding of the power of repetition eventually helped me when I learned to read and write, in my career, in almost everything I've done since. Another lesson: 'If you miss a shot, don't focus on the failed shot, focus on the next opportunity.' This has been applicable to so many other facets of my life.

Who would have thought that one of the best therapies of my childhood would be found not at a hospital or clinic but in a dingy, smoky snooker club in southwest London? Once again, Giff and I were going beyond the limited prescriptions of my teachers and therapists and finding our own ways to help me thrive.

Chapter 10

Walk This Way

It wasn't easy to be the mother of three Black boys in London in the 1980s and 1990s. Back then, the far-right British National Party (BNP) was holding regular marches and rallies across the capital. And that wasn't the only threat. Police brutality and harassment, particularly against Black youth, was widespread. The year I was born, 1985, the Black community in Brixton – not far from where we lived in south London – rose up in protest after a mother was shot in her own home when the police came there looking for her son, in the second of the Brixton uprisings.

Both Giff and my dad did their best to prepare my brothers and me for the reality of being Black in Britain. They made sure we knew that people were going to judge us on the basis of our skin colour, at school, in the streets, wherever we went. As a kid, you don't ask to become skilled at negotiating prejudice; you don't want to become a master of the art. But you don't have a choice. If you don't figure out how to manoeuvre around it, my parents explained, you were going to get beaten down – sometimes figuratively, other times literally.

In an effort to protect my brothers and me, Giff began

schooling us in what to do if we were ever stopped by the police. Beginning from the time I was about twelve, we'd role-play in the living room, with Giff as the policeman, interrogating us, ordering us around. I actually enjoyed these sessions and would smile and giggle at Giff pretending to be a copper. But she remained deadpan. 'Jason, this is no laughing matter. The police do not need any encouragement to lay hands on you, or even worse, kill you.'

She trained us in the correct body language. 'Stand up straight, but keep your body open and soft. Lower your shoulders, keep them relaxed,' she instructed. 'Try to maintain eye contact and put your hands in a position where they can be seen. The police are trained to react to any sudden movements.' Giff's instructions were simple, consistent, and clear – which meant I could easily follow them.

But Giff wasn't just educating us about how to protect ourselves, she was teaching us how to stand up for others too.

'Action is always needed,' Giff told us. 'You must either use your presence or your voice to speak truth to power. Society is unjust, and you have a moral obligation to do whatever you can to disrupt that in small and big ways. Always use your presence to mobilise the greater good. One person's suffering is all of our sufferings – you must give everything you've got to help your fellow brother and sister.'

At least once a week, Giff took me with her to Lady Margaret Hall Settlement community centre, on Wandsworth Road, where her local activist group met. She was one of the senior leaders, and she went to Lady Margaret to advocate on behalf of immigrants and others who needed support, including people who were looking for housing or jobs. She also used to take me to a sewing club there, where she helped new arrivals and others learn to sew.

Starting when I was very small, I also went with her to anti-apartheid rallies, anti-BNP marches and Free Nelson Mandela protests. Then, in 1993, when I was about to turn eight years old, Stephen Lawrence, the eighteen-year-old son of Jamaican parents, was brutally stabbed to death by a group of white males while waiting for a bus one night in southeast London. When the Crown Prosecution Service (CPS) refused to bring murder charges in the case, Giff joined Stephen's family and their supporters at the many protests that followed.

I can still remember going to demonstrations for Stephen in Brixton. One instance in particular stands out because it was the first time I ever saw Giff cry. Getting off the bus, I remember placards everywhere, megaphones and boom boxes booming, a wall of noise and waves and waves of people, as far as my eye could see. The air was thick with tension, rage and grief. A crowd making that amount of noise was incredibly disorienting for me, but I could sense how important it was to Giff that we were there, so I made a momentous effort to keep it together for her sake as she took up her position on the front lines among her fellow activists. People in the crowd were shouting, demanding the CPS bring murder charges. Suddenly, the crowd quieted. Everyone marked Stephen's passing with a moment of silence. I looked to my left and then my right as the tears of a community flowed without words, sorrow etched on the faces of all. It was the first time I'd seen so many adults openly shedding tears. A solitary wail signalled the end of the silence, and then the crowd rose up again, chanting in unison, 'No justice, no peace . . . stop killing our young!'

And that's when I saw a tear running down Giff's cheek. As soon as she noticed me looking up at her, she quickly wiped it away and bit down on her lip to hide any signs of distress. Until then, it hadn't even occurred to me that Giff had a function that allowed water to come out of her eyes. But I had a sense of what lay behind that tear. I understood that she was crying for Stephen's family and mourning a life cut short, while also recognising that Stephen could have been any young Black boy, even one of her own sons.

~

Being around Giff was an ongoing education. Thanks to her, I was able to learn from great Black thinkers and writers, Angela Davis, bell hooks, Stella Dadzie and Audre Lorde – women whose books were strewn all over our house. Even though I couldn't read, Giff told me about what she had learned from these giants. 'Your silence will not protect you' (Audre Lorde), 'All our silences in the face of racist assault are acts of complicity' (bell hooks), 'I am no longer accepting the things I cannot change. I am changing the things I cannot accept' (Angela Davis). These were commonly cited phrases in our house.

What Giff didn't necessarily realise was that I was learning, not only from her words and those of others, but by watching her as well. I studied Giff obsessively, trying to emulate her calm temperament. I became a student of her facial expressions, her mannerisms, her tone of voice, her hand gestures. I saw how she dealt with people who tried to stand in her way – people like my teachers, therapists, social workers and doctors. Giff has the biggest eyes, and when she is faced with someone who is trying to block her or upset her in some way, that's when the long blink comes in. She closes her eyes and then takes a deep breath – eyes still closed – and she stays like that for maybe ten, fifteen seconds. It's only when she opens her eyes again that she'll engage. The long blink gives her the chance to reset and compose herself. A chance to think. Her first instinct might have been to answer someone angrily, but the blink transforms her response into something measured, deliberate and extremely effective. I saw those big eyes shut so many times during my childhood that I started practising the long blink myself. Today, I'm better at it than Giff is – using it to reset my emotions if someone irritates me or I feel incensed – but it took me many years of training to get to that point.

~

The first time I was stopped by the police, I was fourteen years old. I happened to be with a group of white friends. We were walking back from Clapham Common, where we'd just been playing football.

During my teenage years, I started spending time with some white kids I'd met either through primary school or playing sports together over the years. I used to go round to their houses and started getting invited to their parties, which they called 'gatherings'. Their houses were completely different from ours. They were huge, three or four storeys high, with furnishings that their parents had picked out in antique markets when they went on holidays to places like the south of France. My white friends had their own bedrooms; they didn't have to double and triple up with their siblings. They went to a selective school in another district, but despite our differences, for some reason they liked me, and I liked them. I guess I was sort of a curiosity for them – a Black guy who was into guitar music, shook everyone's hand, wore flares and Chuck Taylors and had an impossible-to-identify non-regional accent.

That day, coming back from playing football on the Common with my friends, three policemen with batons in their belts walked towards us. Even with all my training from Giff, it didn't occur to me that they would stop me. I was just on my way home, football tucked under my arm.

'There's been a spate of robberies in the area,' the first policeman said, looking directly at me and not at my white friends. 'One in the last hour. You fit the description. Young man, please can you explain your whereabouts over the last hour?'

I tried to follow Giff's instructions: *soft body language, keep your hands at your sides, no sudden movements.* But it was one thing to practise at home and another to do it face-to-face with the police. I was petrified. For a second, with the officers intentionally inspiring the kind of fear that makes you forget what you did five minutes ago, I even doubted my own whereabouts. But the reality was, I knew exactly where I had been for the last hour.

'I was playing football,' I said.

'What, the whole hour?' one of my friends asked, oblivious to the officer's racism.

'Yes,' I replied to my friend. 'I was with you lot the whole afternoon.'

'Oh yeah,' said my so-called friend. 'You were.'

The officer then asked my other friends to confirm what I was saying, which they did. This satisfied the police because my whereabouts had now been verified by multiple white people. The first officer warned me about staying out of trouble, but since I hadn't actually been causing any trouble, this speech was unnecessary and extremely condescending. I went home that day feeling violated and humiliated, not just by the police but by my friend, who had immediately suspected me. Since then, I have been stopped and harassed by the police almost every single year of my life – a not uncommon occurrence for Black people in Britain.

~

Between Giff's tutorials on how to deal with the police and my own direct experience of being stopped, I began to understand with even greater urgency the principles and necessity of restraint. As a child, I had always been physically expressive. Left to my own devices, I would have been in constant motion: jumping off sofas, crashing onto cushions, rocking back and forth, banging my head, breaking things, wrestling with my brothers. Movement can be a really important release for someone dealing with constant sensory overload; that's why sports were such a great outlet for me – running around helped me to regulate. Even my meltdowns were a form of expression. A meltdown can almost be like a reset for some autistic people. You get it all out – the frustration, the hurt, the excitement, the confusion, the anger – and then you feel better. You get to release the feelings of tension and of being overwhelmed. It's cathartic.

But as I got older, it became clear that I could no longer express myself through meltdowns or other physical behaviours without putting myself in danger – and not just the kind Giff worried about when I'd bash my head against the wall and she'd put my oversized fluffy elephant in front of me to protect me.

This was a more existential threat. As soon as I reached adolescence, Giff knew I was at risk of being adultified, something that happens to Black children in majority-white countries around the world. After about age twelve or thirteen, Giff kept reminding me, I was going to be treated as an adult. It didn't matter that I was small for my age – Black kids aren't allowed to be kids.

It was around early adolescence that the fear of being penalised by the police or others started to paralyse my need to release tension through physical expression. Humming, singing, tapping – my favourite stims – and even head-banging had always been such a comfort to me, but after the age of twelve or thirteen, I stopped doing these things because I knew they could be taken the wrong way. Any sudden movement or noise from me might be interpreted as aggressive or threatening. I had to learn to move differently in the world.

When I was out of the house, I followed Giff's advice, keeping my body as soft and unthreatening as possible. I learned to normalise suppression, to present as calm and temperate, even in situations that were incredibly stressful for me. Still, all of that emotion, energy and expression had to go somewhere. I could channel some of it into playing sports and listening to music, but the rest had to be folded up inside me. I began to internalise, to deny myself external outlets. Any feelings of hurt, any signs of frustration, any desire for sudden movement – all of it had to be swallowed. Not because I wanted to do this, not because it was healthy or right – and not because I was deviously hiding my autism in some way by 'masking' – but because it was necessary for my survival. Without even realising it, I was making myself smaller and smaller in order to become as non-threatening as possible. It's not something I'm proud of – it's something that was forced upon me. After a while, restraint became an automatic response, as natural as breathing.

The problem is, the urge to melt down, to move your body, to let it all out doesn't completely go away. To this day, I still have a version of a meltdown, but it's internalised, completely controlled and never visible to anyone. I've learned to be cruel to myself, biting my hand, making big welts in my skin or screaming under a pillow completely out of view – anything to get some release from the frustration of daily life. None of this happens without consequences, but it's how you have to behave. You have to put in a massive amount of effort to counter the ways that others are going to judge you, even when it's not reflective of how you feel or your natural temperament. As a young man, I had no idea there was a tax to be paid on that level of suppression, and that when the bill came due years later, it would nearly kill me.

~

In the face of such unrelenting judgement, I turned to prayer, as Giff had instructed me to do. Every night as a child, my brothers and I joined Giff in kneeling at the ends of our beds. We'd always start with the Serenity Prayer, reciting each line after her: 'God grant me the serenity to accept the things I cannot change, the courage to change the things I can and the wisdom to know the difference.'

Next, we'd pray for the good of the world, for everyone to be okay and to live well. And then Giff recited the 'Invictus' poem by William Ernest Henley, with the three of us boys repeating each line in unison. At first, this was just a monotonous activity, something Giff made us do every night. But later, when we learned that Nelson Mandela, one of the biggest heroes in our house, recited that poem every day of the twenty-seven years he spent in captivity, it took on a whole new meaning. The poem spoke to the restraint he had shown, the ways he'd had to channel his anger and hate so they wouldn't destroy him.

Thanks to Giff, I can recite the poem from beginning to end. And there isn't a day that goes by when I don't say it to myself:

Out of the night that covers me,
Black as the Pit from pole to pole,
I thank whatever gods may be
For my unconquerable soul.

In the fell clutch of circumstance
I have not winced nor cried aloud.
Under the bludgeonings of chance
My head is bloody, but unbowed.

Beyond this place of wrath and tears
Looms but the Horror of the shade,
And yet the menace of the years
Finds and shall find me unafraid.

It matters not how strait the gate,
How charged with punishments the scroll,
I am the master of my fate,
I am the captain of my soul.

Chapter 11

Hyper-Focused

Growing up, Giff made a lot of our clothing by hand. As a young woman, she'd worked as a seamstress, so she knew how to make a pattern, cut out the fabric and sew everything together. Her mum, my gran, also used to work as a seamstress, and she'd given us her Singer sewing machine and an old slate-topped sewing table with a metal ruler along the side, which we kept in our living room.

When I was very young and still following Giff from room to room, I'd sit next to her, watching as she altered or made clothing for my brothers and me. But as I got older, I started to take note of the intricacies of the work. I saw how straight and perfect the lines of stitches needed to be to make both sides of a garment even. There's something about the way my brain is wired that draws me to symmetrical things; to me, symmetry is aesthetic perfection.

As soon as I started talking, I'd ask Giff questions about what she was doing, the technicalities of it, and after a while, she started teaching me how to make clothes. To begin with, she'd let me try a running seam using two pieces of fabric the size of a shirt pocket. If you want to sew a straight line, you have to get the pressure on the pedal just right, so initially, my lines were jagged. But within a few months, I became very proficient, thanks in part to my decent hand-eye coordination, improved by snooker and sports generally. Giff would cut the patterns, sew some of the parts together, and then give the rest to me to finish, reminding me to keep my lines completely straight like hers and watching that the needle didn't catch. I loved the sound of the juddering machine in my ears and the feel of the pedal underfoot, but most of all, I loved that we could cut out these patterns and transform two-dimensional pieces of fabric into something three-dimensional that you could wear.

The first complete garment I made was a waistcoat. It was a navy-blue cotton number and to be honest, it wasn't much to look at; it had the touch of a fifteen-year-old novice all over it. But it was my first stab at making something unassisted, and I was very proud of it – as was Giff. Next, I altered a pair of dark brown corduroys for myself, with some degree of success. Trousers are notoriously hard to make and can be very tricky to alter. As a teenager, I used to go to second-hand shops and pick up pieces like silk scarves, paisley print shirts and double-breasted jackets, and then remake the garments on the sewing machine to fit me. Years later, in university, people caught wind of the fact that I could sew and came to me for alterations.

But I wasn't just getting interested in sewing – I was developing an obsession with clothes in general and tailored clothes in particular. When I was about fourteen, I saw a poster of Paul Weller, lead singer of the Jam and the Style Council, wearing a double-breasted pinstripe suit, with his mod haircut, sitting on a Lambretta scooter. I remember thinking, *I want to dress just like that.* Another time, about four years later, I was walking through central London, and I spotted this tall Black man walking towards me. He was wearing an orange, single-breasted suit and shining black Chelsea boots. Impressively handsome with perfect posture, he was immaculately dressed and groomed. It was Ozwald Boateng, the fashion designer and self-taught tailor who redefined contemporary menswear in the 1990s and 2000s with his Armani-inspired, sharp, brightly coloured suits. That man – the son of Ghanaian parents like mine – left an indelible imprint on me by the way he carried himself: statuesque, poised, magnetic.

But my favourite era for clothing was the 1930s and 40s. At home, Giff would often have old films on in the background, like *Casablanca*, *The Philadelphia Story* and *Roman Holiday.* That was how I got introduced to the style of old movie stars like Cary Grant and Gregory Peck, men who personified elegance and tailoring at its best. Then there were the suit-wearing Black musicians and film stars of the 1950s and 1960s, like Chuck Berry, Sidney Poitier and Harry Belafonte, along with the activists of the civil-rights era, such as Malcolm X with his skinny black tie and fedora hat, not to mention James Brown, dressed to kill in a variety of neatly pressed suits with his pompadour on point. These men became my style icons.

One day, Giff and I were watching a Cary Grant film, and I told her, 'This is how I want to dress when I'm older.'

She smiled at me. 'You really like classic things, don't you, Jason? To dress like that, you will need a lot of money.'

'Why?' I responded.

'Because those film stars all got their clothes made by tailors.'

Giff pointed out that in those days, all clothing was custom-made, or bespoke. There was no such thing as mass production.

I filed this information away in my mental notebook of tailoring facts, as I still couldn't write anything down.

One beautiful summer's day when I was about fifteen years old, Giff decided she wanted to take me somewhere, telling me it was going to be a surprise. So we jumped on the meandering 137 double-decker Routemaster bus, making our way through Chelsea Barracks and Sloane Square, before eventually arriving at Oxford Circus. We walked down Regent Street, passing the many boutiques of Mayfair, some of the most expensive shops in all of London. Being in the middle of the fanciest part of the city with Giff was unusual enough that I became oblivious to the various street noises that might otherwise have bothered me.

It was then that Giff revealed where we were going: 'Jason, I am going to take you to the most famous place in the world to get clothes made. It's called Savile Row.'

I had no idea what Savile Row was, but Giff quickly explained the significance.

'This is where rich people go and get their suits made,' she explained. 'All the shops on this street are famous for decades of tradition and dedication to the art of tailoring.'

As we turned onto the Row, I could see the awnings of the different tailoring houses, their windows as glossy and immaculate as luxury-car showrooms. We gazed up at the mannequins, dressed in all manner of jackets, shirts, vests (the bespoke tailoring word for waistcoats), trousers and ties, herringbones, tweeds and flannels. All we could afford was a glimpse of what was in the window, and Giff explained that you can go inside only by invitation.

Dazzled, I realised these were like the outfits I saw in Cary Grant and Gregory Peck films come to life. Later I learned that for nearly five decades, Peck actually got all his suits made at Huntsman of Savile Row.

'I would like to get a shirt made here one day,' I told Giff, rightly assuming that a shirt might not be as expensive as an entire suit.

'Jason, it costs nothing to dream,' she pointed out. 'In the future, I'm sure you will make your dream a reality.'

After that visit to Savile Row, I kept sewing and collecting images of besuited men that I stored away in a scrapbook in my bedroom, dreaming of ways to one day be in a position to commission a Savile Row shirt, specifically from Huntsman. I had no idea how I would get there or even when this would happen, but it became part of the impossible dream.

As it turned out, the best way to help me grow and develop was to find the things, like snooker, sewing and tailoring, that really interested me. Throughout my teens, Giff continued to look for ways to play to my strengths rather than my deficits. When I was interested in something, it would often consume me in quite a big way; there was a rigid obsessiveness. I was driven to learn everything. My monotropism – my ability to hyper-focus – would go into full effect, as it did with snooker. Giff decided to continue working *with* my interests – not against them. She told herself, *If he's able to do something that fascinates him, even if that's the only thing he can do, then we need to champion that.*

She recognised that there was limited value in trying to push me to do things that I *wasn't* interested in. There were a lot of things, like reading and writing, that I was forced to do but for whatever reason I couldn't. These failures would make me feel defeated, but my special interests gave me a feeling of success, which in turn gave me confidence to try other things. Sewing was a case in point: the more I did, the better I got. Giff reasoned that even if I didn't become a tailor, this would at least provide me with an outlet or a distraction from some of the monotony of daily life – and this was important. 'If you're not happy or you're upset, you can go and do something that pleases you and makes you happy,' she said.

In the years to come, whenever I needed a bit of inspiration or a mood boost, I'd make pilgrimages to Savile Row to look in the windows. For the price of the bus fare, I could gaze up at the mannequins in their perfectly tailored suits, and they would give me something to aspire to, no matter how difficult things became. Like the champagne glasses that I stared up at for two years before I finally laid my hands on them in the living room at home, Savile Row seemed far out of reach, but as Giff had predicted, maybe not forever.

Chapter 12

The World According to Rocky

As the three of us boys continued to navigate our teens, Giff kept up her habit of using television as a teaching tool, taking concepts that might have been abstract for us and turning them into concrete examples.

'Gather round, boys,' she'd say, 'I've got something for us to watch.'

The TV series and films always contained some kind of lesson that she wanted to impart. I remember as an older teenager watching every episode of the prison drama *Oz* with Giff and my brothers, even though some of the content was pretty graphic and a lot of it went over my head. Giff had figured out that she could put the series to good use as a deterrent. The characters were in prison for all kinds of offences: drugs, assault, murder, drink-driving. Her message to us was clear: 'If you do bad things, this is where you'll end up. And prison is not somewhere you want to be.'

There used to be a video shop in Clapham Junction called Prime Time that specialised in independent films, and it even had a Black movie section, which was unheard of at the time. I remember Giff often borrowed rom-coms like *Brown Sugar,*

Waiting to Exhale and *The Best Man* so that we could learn about Black love, friendships and relationships. When I was about sixteen, she made us watch *What's Love Got to Do with It*, where Angela Bassett brilliantly portrays Tina Turner in her abusive marriage to Ike Turner. After we'd finished seeing how badly Ike treated Tina, Giff said to us, 'If any of you ever force yourself on a woman, lay your hand on a woman, get a woman pregnant and leave her, you'll no longer be my son.' That sunk in, even though I wasn't thinking about women in an intimate way yet. She made the boundaries of consent clear, and I never forgot the lesson.

With Giff, we never watched a film just for the sake of watching a film. Even a fantastical comedy-drama like *Forrest Gump* was mined for its message. Giff sat Joseph and me down after we finished this film and pointed out that the main character was someone with intellectual and physical disabilities who couldn't read or write. 'If you look at your story and you look at Forrest Gump, there are similarities there,' she told us. 'Even though it's a film and it is not based on a real person, there are so many things that disadvantaged Forrest from the beginning. People made fun of him at school; they didn't understand someone who was different from them, so they mocked him. Even though sometimes Forrest would get very exasperated and sad, he had a mum who was very forward-looking, and she would encourage him. Look at all the things Forrest was able to achieve because of his self-belief and his mum's belief in him. If anybody says to you that you can't do something, just ignore them. You can tell them, "According to my mum, I can do anything."'

~

There were a lot of films and programmes that I watched because Giff showed them to me. But *Rocky*, I discovered all on my own. I must have been about ten years old when the original movie from 1976 happened to be on TV. Most of the story went over my head – I was still pre-language, so I couldn't fully understand the plot – but I remember being fixated on the boxing matches, the pure drama of what was happening in the ring.

When I watched the film again after I started speaking, it was a completely different experience. This time, I didn't just watch *Rocky* for the boxing; *Rocky* changed my life.

In the film, Sylvester Stallone plays Rocky Balboa, a club fighter from a working-class Italian immigrant background, living in the slums of Philadelphia. The character is loosely based on Stallone's own life. When the film starts, Rocky's working as an enforcer for a local loan shark, barely making ends meet, but he refuses to be defined by the limitations other people place on him. He's a fighter in every sense of the word. When he gets an offer to go up against the heavyweight champion of the world, Apollo Creed – known as the Master of Disaster – he takes it, even though the odds of beating Creed are a million to one. In fact, that was the original tagline to the film: *His whole life has been a million-to-one shot . . . Now, Rocky Balboa is about to show the world that he's one in a million.*

There's a scene towards the end of the first film where Rocky is sitting on the edge of his bed, talking to his partner, Adrian. He's just been to the stadium where he's going to fight Apollo the next night. Terrified, he says to her, 'I can't do it,', meaning that he can't beat Creed. Adrian asks him, 'What are we gonna do?' Rocky lies down on the bed next to her and tells her: ''Cause I was thinkin', it really don't matter if I lose this fight. It really don't matter if this guy opens my head, either. 'Cause all I wanna do is go the distance. Nobody's ever gone the distance with Creed, and if I can go that distance, you see, and that bell rings and I'm still standin', I'm gonna know for the first time in my life, see, that I weren't just another bum from the neighbourhood.'

Giff had taught me that every film and TV show contained messages that could be applied to real life. Listening to that speech for the first time, I understood that *Rocky* was about much more than boxing. It was about the struggle to make something of yourself. It was about the metaphor of getting to the final round, even if the odds are insurmountable. In my own life, doctors and teachers and therapists had told me that I'd never amount to anything, that I might as well give up before I even tried. I saw the correlation immediately.

Giff recorded *Rocky* onto a VHS for me, and I watched that film over and over again. When I learned there were four other Rocky films, I watched those on repeat as well. There's a scene in *Rocky II* that also had a massive impact on me. Now that Rocky has gained a certain amount of recognition for going twelve rounds in the ring with Creed, he gets a deal promoting aftershave in a TV advertisement. The guy who is directing the ad asks Rocky to repeat what's on the cue cards, but Rocky can't do it because he can't read. He's illiterate. The director tries for hours to get the take, but Rocky keeps fumbling his lines, and the guy becomes furious and accuses him of wasting time and money. After that experience, Adrian starts teaching Rocky to read. Every night before he goes to bed, he tries to read to her. Seeing these scenes helped me feel a lot less alone. It normalised my not being able to read and told me that anyone could be affected by illiteracy.

Before long, I knew every line, every scene, every moment from every Rocky film. When you're neurodivergent, this kind of memorising of films or TV shows is known as 'scripting'; it's similar to but not the same as echolalia (repeating things that other people say). Through memorising lines from *Rocky*, through scripting, I was able to acquire more and more language, as well as information, helping me feel more secure in a world that often seemed chaotic and confusing. Scripting allowed me to express myself when I might not otherwise have had the words. The narrative of the *Rocky* story had a structure to it, a series of patterns, relationships and messages that were clear to me and made sense. As time went on, I could recognise these patterns in the real world; they were familiar to me from Rocky's fictional one. I wasn't a boxer, but I saw aspects of myself in this character: he wasn't a technically great boxer, but he had a lot of will and a huge heart. No one gave Rocky a chance or thought he could do anything, but together with Adrian, he took on the world and won. That's what the film was about: the *will* to win, *the thrill* of the fight and the unwavering *determination* to give it your all. What I took from the story was that even if I didn't have the skills to do something, I had heart, and if I kept going, I could make it to the final bell. This was unbelievably inspiring to me as a fifteen-year-old who had no idea what he would do with his life or what his future would hold.

Chapter 13

Strawberry Hill Forever

'Why can't Jason be more like his brother?' my teachers often asked Giff. 'If Joseph can do it, why can't Jason?'

It used to drive Giff mad. After the funding for the SEN classroom was taken away, and Miss McCann left, my teachers seemed to have very little idea what to do with me. When one of them made the mistake of asking Giff how it was possible that her older child was excelling in school while her younger child was failing miserably, she'd tell them: 'Do not compare them! They are two very different people!'

Giff understood that autism as a label is fundamentally flawed because we all have unique needs, challenges, talents and presentations. Like many autistic people, I also had a range of what are called co-occurring conditions – in my case, deafness, dyscalculia and as I would later learn, dyslexia. That's why it's so important to have a bespoke approach: it's never going to be one size fits all.

Giff wasn't going to sit there and listen as my teachers compared me to my brother and listed all the things I *couldn't* do.

'You're speaking about him like you've already written him off, like he has no redeemable qualities,' she reprimanded. 'But *you* are the educator. You tell me what *you're* going to do to help him. What adaptations are *you* going to make?'

When she came home from seeing my teachers, Giff would often feel very upset because of what they had said about me. She knew that I had my difficulties, but the way that the information was delivered seemed designed to crush her soul.

I did at least do well at sports. I even represented the school – and later the county – playing football. When I was in my third year at Southfields, a new PE teacher arrived. Mr Trace was a recent university graduate with a clean-cut, square jaw, floppy light brown hair and sparkling eyes. He was charismatic, charming and obviously from a fairly upper-middle-class background. There were so many other things Mr Trace could have done with his life, but for some reason, he had decided to devote himself to helping inner-city kids at Southfields.

At this point, I was going to school mostly in the mornings and spending the rest of my day at the snooker hall. But Mr Trace's arrival gave me a new incentive to attend, at least on the two days a week when I had PE. Mr Trace actually cared about his students. When other kids mocked me and called me dumb because I still couldn't read, Mr Trace would protect me, cleverly and wittily pointing out to them one of their own shortcomings. He believed in me, just like he believed in everyone in the class, regardless of their level of ability. We'd talk a lot about snooker together and he would really encourage me to keep going with this particular interest of mine.

It was Mr Trace who signed me up for something called the Junior Sports Leader Award, which was a nationally recognised qualification that allowed me to develop some decent skills around sports, leadership and being a good team member and coach. His interventions allowed me to excel at something at school, which gave me a massive and much-needed confidence boost in an environment where I was always being told I was useless.

~

Thanks to Mr Trace, I also laid eyes on a university campus for the first time at the age of fifteen. The summer after he arrived at Southfields, Mr Trace announced that our class was going to visit his alma mater, St Mary's University, for an interschool sports day. About a dozen kids were invited, all of us piling into a school minibus for the fifty-minute ride to the campus in Twickenham, part of the leafy London borough of Richmond. As we bundled off the bus – a bunch of lanky, rambunctious teens stretching limbs after being cooped up – I couldn't get over how beautiful the place was. There were trees everywhere, lovely green lawns, birds chirping overhead and sports fields for miles, along with a massive white building that looked like a castle. With an actual turret. That overlooked a lake. For a kid from Clapham, this was like landing in a fairy tale. Mr Trace told us that the area was known as Strawberry Hill, and that the castle was Strawberry Hill House. Strawberry Hill! I made the instant link to the Beatles' 'Strawberry Fields Forever', and that further seared the place into my brain.

The next three hours were spent running around St Mary's sports fields, competing against other kids from south and west London. When we climbed back on the bus at the end of the day, sticky and exhausted, I remember thinking: *I love this place. It would be nice to come back here.* I couldn't even begin to conceptualise that one day I might return as a student. After all, I still couldn't read and write, never mind understand the concept of 'university' or what it meant to go to one.

The next time I found myself on a campus, about a year later, Giff had just started training to become a social worker at Brunel University. An extremely learned person who read extensively, Giff had gone to secretarial school and taken various night classes throughout my childhood. Education was extremely important to her, but she had never had a chance to get her degree because she'd been too busy taking care of my brothers and me. Now that we were older, she seized the opportunity.

Her classes were at Brunel's former west London campus, which was in Osterley. The first time Giff took me to one of her lectures, I remember the hall was packed with about 150 other people, most of them mature students and many of them Black mothers who'd brought their kids along. There was a lot of camaraderie in that room, with the mums handing out hardo bread, dumplings, chicken and snacks they'd packed in plastic boxes. Everything was washed down with water and Dunn's River Nurishment drinks, and the fidgety kids did their best to stay quiet while their mothers focused on bettering themselves for the sake of their families. Giff sat with her notebook, diligently scribbling down everything the lecturer said as he shuffled bits of acetate around on the overhead projector at the front. But I didn't pay any attention to him. I was too busy being impressed by Giff, proud that she had gained entry to these hallowed halls. I knew she belonged there. Even so, it didn't even occur to me that university was for me, not in a million years. It seemed sort of otherworldly.

~

Back at school, I was about to start my final year of compulsory education. I was dreading the exams that lay ahead, the infamous General Certificate of Secondary Education examinations, or GCSEs. 'It is vital that you do well in your exams,' our teachers kept telling us. 'These exams will determine what you do with the rest of your life. They determine whether you can move on with your education, and ultimately go on to university. If you fail these exams, you won't have any options in the future.' That was the message we received.

This put the fear of God into us, and even the most lacklustre students from bottom set seemed to be studying and revising. But I remained stuck. I couldn't revise because I couldn't read. When the time came and I had to take the tests, my support assistant was sitting next to me. I was supposed to tell her what I wanted to say, and she would then write it down for me. There were rows and rows of desks in that exam room, filled with students diligently scrawling away, but my paper stayed almost completely blank. I'd spent too many hours struggling to understand my teachers' voices over the din of bottom set, too many hours standing outside classrooms, too many hours playing truant. I hadn't retained any information relevant to these exams. I felt stupid, like people had always said. The teachers had decreed that these tests would dictate what I was going to do for the rest of my life. I'd already figured out that while I was a modestly talented snooker player, I wasn't good enough to play professionally. *I'm going to be the biggest loser*, I thought.

In the end, I failed all my GCSEs except for PE and textiles, both of which had large practical components where I could at least contribute something. This meant I had one and a half GCSEs because textiles only counted for a half. Most other kids – even the ones who were struggling academically – came away with at least six.

By the summer of 2001, it was all over; four years at Southfields and the exams had come and gone. I was relieved, beyond relieved. I could have left school at that point, but thankfully Mr Trace persuaded me to stay for another year to do a BTEC First entry-level qualification in sports, a vocational qualification that could potentially allow me to progress to further education. Mr Trace taught the first cohort and invited me to join.

That year and the next, I really applied myself and ended up doing well, getting a distinction in my BTEC First because it was mostly practical. My qualifications might not have looked like much on paper, but Giff and I knew how hard I'd worked for them, and we were both bursting with pride. Like Rocky had taught me, it wasn't about winning the fight – it was about going the distance and seeing the final bell. And for the first time in my life, I felt like I had done that.

The problem was, what was I going to do next?

Part Three

Sandro and Debs

Chapter 14

CONNEXIONS

It was a miserable rainy day in August 2003, and Giff and I had just left the house, on our way to catch the 345 bus to Clapham Junction. For as long as I could remember, Giff had always bought herself the kind of flimsy, inexpensive umbrellas that you get from the corner shop – the ones that are undone by the slightest gust of wind or drizzle of rain. Everyone in the family tried to persuade her to get a better one, but she always said, 'No, I'm happy with what I've got.' Inevitably, Giff's umbrellas ended up in a mangled mess of metal and black polyester – and the one she was carrying in this particular August downpour was no exception. For the entire walk to the bus stop, she did battle with both the elements and her umbrella, which refused to open, its unbudging, crooked metal spokes sending her into a silent rage. In the end, Giff just put her head down, purposeful and determined as ever, until we reached the bus shelter.

This journey felt different from all our other adventures. On board the bus, Giff's demeanour was sombre, her tone serious. 'Today is a very important day, Jason,' she said, fat grey raindrops gathering on the window behind her, blurry behind the condensation. 'I will always love you and you are my son, but you're eighteen now. You're going to have to learn to stand on your own two feet.'

It was true. I'd turned eighteen in May, officially transitioning into adulthood – quite a feat given the turbulence of my childhood and adolescence.

'I've protected you to the best of my ability your whole life,' Giff went on, 'but the one thing I may not be able to protect you from is people's expectations now that you're an adult. Sometimes these expectations are going to seem unreasonable to you, but this is what being an adult is all about.' She followed this with, 'Jason, the time has come for you to make your mark on the world, and this journey begins today. Do you understand what I am saying to you?'

'Yes, Giff, I understand,' I told her.

My entire childhood Giff had worried about what would happen to me when I turned eighteen. Like any boy transitioning into manhood, I had aspirations: I wanted to get a good job and buy my mum and dad a big house – and help my friends and family. Perhaps these dreams were completely unrealistic, but as Giff always said, it costs nothing to dream. In reality, I had a grand total of one and a half GCSEs and my BTEC First, and I still couldn't read and write. This wasn't a case of Icarus flying too close to the sun but a tale of someone who didn't have the wings to get near to the sun in the first place. I was lucky to have Giff. She had already gone to the job centre in Clapham Old Town and helped me to apply for a part-time position at a local sports chain. But now we had to figure out how I was going to continue my studies, because for Giff, education was a lifelong pursuit, something that didn't end just because you were eighteen years old.

Our destination that day was the now-defunct careers service centre Connexions on Falcon Road, its orange-and-purple logo glowing through the morning's stormy weather. In those days, Connexions was a recent addition to the UK social services landscape, a Blair government initiative set up to offer young people information and guidance about further education and careers. It was supposed to be for everyone, but in 2003, it already had a reputation as the place where kids went after they dropped out of or disengaged from school. In truth, most people went to Connexions when they had run out of all other options, with no distance left to run, so to speak.

At the time, pretty much everyone else in my family was succeeding in their studies. Giff had just finished her BSc in social work, and she was planning her postgraduate studies. Joseph had finished his first year at Kingston University, studying computer science. Simon, at age fourteen, was brilliantly intelligent, the boy wonder. He would have no trouble getting into university when the time came. And then there was me.

Crossing the road to Connexions from the bus, I looked down at my feet as I always did, and dragged them through the puddles collecting on the pavement, completely soaking my shoes and socks. This further increased my angst, and I couldn't stop thinking about the unbearable discomfort of my sodden socked feet.

'Trust you to do that right now,' said Giff, eyebrows raised, her annoyance evident.

Inside Connexions, we joined the other last-chance hopefuls in the waiting area, society's offcuts, desperate for any opportunity to fit into some kind of future. Connexions operated on a first-come, first-served basis, and after what seemed like an eternity (but was probably more like a ten-minute wait), we heard a woman calling out: 'Neeexxxxttt!' Giff nudged me, saying, 'Jason, look alive . . . I think it's our turn.'

Giff picked up her mangled umbrella and grabbed me by the arm as we followed the woman to her desk. It was an open-plan office, one of those spaces with cubicles divided by paper-thin screens for so-called privacy. As we approached, I spotted two chairs, one stationary and one a swivel. Naturally, I made a beeline for the swivel chair and sat down, leaning to the side to get going on a good spin. To this day, even as someone with a relatively senior position at a university, if I go into a boardroom and there's a swivel chair, I'll take the opportunity to swing around on it. That's the great thing about the autistic imagination: a swivel chair isn't just a chair – it's a fairground ride, an opportunity to release tension. I might have learned to suppress a meltdown but not a yearning for a swivel in a chair.

Connexions was clearly not the time or the place for swivelling, though. After less than a full rotation, Giff shot out her hand to stop the chair, bringing it to an instant halt. She widened her eyes and, without uttering a single word, gave me a look that said 'Stop it right now!'

I immediately sat upright, trying to give the impression of being focused and attentive as Giff introduced us.

The woman behind the desk pointed to her badge and told us her name was Kathy: 'Kathy with a K.' Her name might have started with a K, but what I was more interested in was that she was wearing only one earring. A single hoop earring hanging from her right ear. Why was she wearing only one earring? Had the other one fallen out? If so, had she not noticed it? The missing earring was a point of curiosity for me as asymmetry always stands out to my eye. If your glasses are tilted, I'll notice it. If you have one eyebrow higher than the other, I'll notice that. Giff had to teach me to keep my mouth shut about my observations; they'd get me in trouble, she cautioned, if I pointed out to someone that they had a wonky nose or one extra-long earlobe. 'If you don't have anything nice to observe, then don't observe anything at all,' she used to say. That day at Connexions, I noticed that Kathy had yellowing teeth and lipstick drawn outside her lips. Another thing to fixate on – why the lipstick on the outside?

As she had done since I was a little kid, Giff pinched me on the leg, another warning without words, reminding me that it's rude to stare.

Kathy tutted. 'Why have you come here today with your mother, Jason? You don't need anyone to accompany you. You're eighteen now. You're an adult.'

Answering on my behalf, Giff informed this woman that I had some learning challenges, that I'd just left Southfields Secondary School, and that we wanted to find out my options for further study because I still couldn't read and write.

'He does have some qualifications,' Giff proudly pointed out. 'He's got two GCSEs . . . well, one and a half, actually. And he did very well in his BTEC First in sports.'

Kathy sighed a beleaguered sigh. 'This is not unusual, Jason,' she said, turning her attention back to me and tapping her pen on the desk in front of her. 'When someone doesn't pay enough attention in school, they usually end up here. You're not the first, and you will not be the last.'

She continued, turning back to Giff. 'Can you tell me what Jason's skills are? What's his level of literacy and basic arithmetic?'

'No, he doesn't read or write,' Giff repeated. 'He didn't learn to speak until he was nearly twelve. And he can't do maths.'

'Right, so he's eighteen and illiterate and can't do sums,' Kathy pointed out. 'He could *maybe* volunteer at a supermarket for an hour every week and gain work experience that way? Might help him to learn to function in the real world?'

Kathy paused abruptly. We waited for her to suggest something else. She paused a bit longer. It turned out she wasn't pausing. She was finished with her suggestions.

This visit was supposed to be the beginning of a new educational chapter for me, but it was quickly turning into the end.

Giff was not pleased. 'So you're telling me that there's nothing else you can suggest in terms of further education?'

'To be honest with you, it's a rare case where I can't give someone some kind of advice,' said Kathy. 'But no, there's really nothing we can do for *this person*.'

I could see Giff's body begin to stiffen. She closed her eyes. The long blink; a blink that seemed to go on for an eternity. Then she stood up, looking Kathy dead in the eye.

'Let me tell you something, Kathy,' Giff said, grabbing her coat and bag and getting ready to go. 'Your job is to provide people – young people – with hope, not to sit there and demean them. You're supposed to encourage them to maximise their potential, not tell them they are basically worthless. Jason, get your coat. We're leaving.'

Then Giff turned to Kathy one last time. 'You've sat here and basically told me that my son will amount to nothing,' she said. 'But you're wrong. One day he will do something great, unfathomable. You will remember this day, and you will regret not doing all you could've done to help this person. This day will be the most important day in your life because you'll be able to say that you met my son . . . *Jason Arday*!'

Then Giff turned on her heel and marched back through the waiting area, me trailing behind her, before bursting through the pendulum doors and into the street. It had stopped raining by now, but the stormy skies overhead remained an uninterrupted grey.

Catching up with Giff, I smiled happily at her, this woman who was my hero, who had just given Kathy the most brilliant dressing-down. But she didn't smile back. Instead, she grabbed my chin with her thumb and index finger and turned me to face her directly.

'Jason, look at me,' she said. 'I am being serious.'

Wiping the smile completely off my face, I looked into her big brown eyes. I could see that they were bloodshot, that Giff was exhausted. It wasn't the kind of exhaustion you feel after a night without sleep; it was an exhaustion that ran eighteen years deep.

'You have to understand: I won't always be here to take care of you. I know your life has been hard, *very* hard. But you have to make something of yourself. If you don't, people will talk to you like that woman just did every day for the rest of your life. They will talk to you like you're shit on the road. A nobody. Is that what you want? You are my son and I know you better than anyone, so I know you can do something great. Something beyond all our wildest expectations. But you . . . you have to believe you can do something great as well. Do you hear me?'

'Yes, Giff. Yes, I hear you,' I told her.

We walked side by side past the puddles that had soaked my feet, along Falcon Road and under the bridge to the 345 bus.

Giff fell asleep in her seat on the bus, drifting in and out of consciousness, restoring herself however she could, for however long she could, for the next challenge ahead.

Not a single word was spoken the whole ride home.

Chapter 15

One More Round

After our trip to Connexions, Giff needed a moment to revive. She made a cup of tea, sweetening it heavily with evaporated milk. She wasn't impressed with Kathy, but she also wasn't impressed with my inability to recognise the seriousness of the situation. Clearly, she was going to have to take further action, so she dug out a prospectus someone had given her listing all the south London vocational colleges, the kinds of places that might offer a spot to someone with my limited qualifications. Then she sat me down next to her in the living room, picked up the phone, and called them one by one, ticking them off her list as she went. Every time someone picked up, Giff described my 'academic profile' and told them that although I didn't have many qualifications, I still had a lot to offer, that I was really good at sports, and if they had a programme that was sports-related, I would work hard, have good attendance and be diligent. The truth was, I had questionable attendance, I wasn't particularly punctual and I struggled to apply myself. But I *was* good at sports. Richmond-upon-Thames College, Saint Francis Xavier College, Lambeth College, South Thames College, London South Bank Technical College,

West London College and City of Westminster College, every college said no.

Giff had yet to call Merton College in Morden, about half an hour away. By now, it was getting late in the day, but undeterred, she picked up the phone and called the number. This time, she got put through to the sports department, which had an answering machine. She was halfway through listening to the recorded message when an actual person picked up and said, 'Hello?' She repeated her sales patter about who I was and stressed that although some might argue I didn't have a lot going for me, what I did have was the will to succeed. Giff knew that the right person could harness this into something powerful.

'I just need someone to water this seed,' said an exhausted Giff, 'and hopefully it will grow.'

'Okay,' said the man on the other end of the line. 'Can you get to Merton by 10 a.m. tomorrow? We're doing late enrolment then, and there may be places on some of the courses.'

Shocked, Giff replied, 'Yes, I can come tomorrow.'

'Can you bring the boy with you?'

'Yes, I can bring the boy with me.'

'Okay, I'll see you both tomorrow. We'll have a chat, and we'll see. I'm not promising anything, but we'll see.'

Before he could hang up, Giff asked, 'What's your name?'

He said, 'My name's Sandro.'

Call over, Giff slumped back in her chair, but the relief sweeping across her features soon shifted as she sat bolt upright again and looked at me. 'Somehow by the grace of God, you've got this chance now, Jason,' she said. 'We need to convert this tomorrow. Let's pray!' She held my hand, and we prayed … intensely.

The next morning, we woke up at dawn and, fuelled by sweet tea and lightly toasted hardo bread, left the house, getting the 137 bus to Clapham Common station, then the Tube to the last stop on the Northern line: Morden. Finally, we hopped on board the 93 bus heading towards North Cheam, arriving at Merton College at 9.40 a.m., impressively early (which was saying something because Giff is habitually late, and the apple did not fall far from that tree). I'd made sure to wear my smartest outfit: a white shirt with black trousers and black shoes, buffed to a shine with Kiwi Noir liquid shoe polish (if polishing Dad's shoes religiously for many years had taught me anything, it was that you could never polish enough). I knew I had to put my best foot forward in every way possible. Giff was going to give it everything to get me into that college. If ever there was a day I needed to surpass her efforts, today was the day.

We walked through the gates into a paved courtyard, along a walkway, past a big red sign that said 'Merton College' in white lettering. It was a newer building, the bricks freshly minted yellow, and the reception area was full of plush chairs and shiny surfaces.

The first person we met was Maureen, the friendly department head who was handling the intake that day. She explained that there were a few places left on some of the lower courses, and she began to list some of our options. At a certain point, a man with a good head of slicked-back dark hair came into the office looking for something.

'Good morning, Sandro,' the woman greeted him – Giff and I immediately realised this was the same Sandro she had spoken to on the phone the day before. He seemed rushed, like he didn't have much time to spare.

I couldn't guess his age, but he had a barrel chest and a long slender nose, and he immediately reminded me of Sylvester Stallone in *Rocky*, a huge point in his favour. Maureen introduced him to us, saying that he was the programme leader for Merton's BTEC in sports. She asked him if he had any places left, and he immediately told her no, he was completely full, and strode right out again.

Many years later, Sandro explained to me what had happened next. He walked along the hallway and down the stairs, racing to get to the group that was waiting for him in another part of the building. But after making it halfway down, he stopped. Something was troubling him. He was usually someone who was communicative and personable – yet he had left the office without even saying a 'hello' to Giff and me. This bugged him. He felt badly that he had ignored us, and so turned around, went up the stairs and back along the hallway, and came into the office to find us.

When Sandro returned, I stood to attention. He smiled at us, offering his hand first to Giff and then to me. Giff had already given me my briefing before we arrived: 'Make eye contact, shake hands, be respectful. We really need to capitalise on this opportunity and make the most of it. This is our last chance.' Shaking hands was something I had practised doing from a young age, ever since Giff gave me Elephant's trunk to squeeze. I was definitely well-prepared.

As soon as Sandro gripped my hand, I felt my fingers squished like playdough in his strong grip. If a good handshake says a lot about a person, then Sandro's said that he was a man of character.

Right away, I was fascinated by Sandro. All my years of silently observing people before I could speak meant that within seconds of meeting someone, I could tell if they were a good person, if I could trust them. What I noticed most about Sandro was that he had a real presence about him.

'I'm sorry I was too busy to stop before. How can I help?' he asked. I spotted that he had some kind of accent – Portuguese or Brazilian, maybe.

Giff took the lead.

'I just need someone to take a chance on my son,' she told Sandro. 'I know there's nothing to suggest that anybody should give him an opportunity, but the reason he doesn't have the right qualifications isn't because he's been naughty or disobedient. He has learning difficulties. He just needs someone to have a bit of understanding and patience. And I think if he has that, it could ignite something in him that could help him, and he could develop.'

Sandro looked at me intently and then asked me a question: 'Jason, what do you want to do with your life?'

'I want to help people,' I said. 'Especially Giff, for everything she has done for me.'

'Good boy,' he replied. 'On a scale of one to ten, how disciplined do you think you are?'

Giff chimed in, 'Well, he practises snooker every day.'

Sandro said, 'I'm asking Jason.'

'I think I'm sort of disciplined,' I responded, a bit sheepishly.

'I'm going to need you to be more than "sort of disciplined",' Sandro replied, 'because I don't have any places left on this course. I'd have to squeeze you in, and if I do, I'm going to need you to give it everything you've got. Will you be here on time, all the time? Will you apply yourself? Will you listen to me? Will you rise to this challenge? Can you do that?'

'Yes, I will,' I said, nodding. Sandro had an authority about him that I immediately respected.

'Hmm, it worries me that you responded so quickly,' Sandro replied, 'because you haven't thought about how you're going to do these things I'm asking of you. Do you want to put the work in, or are you just saying that to get on the course? I need to know that you're committed to this. Are you committed?'

'Yes, Sandro,' I replied, nodding vigorously. At that point, I probably would have said yes if he'd asked me to follow him to the moon and back.

'You know that I'm already full up on this course. What would you do if you were in my situation?'

This time I paused carefully before replying: 'I would give me a chance.'

Sandro thought for a moment. 'Here's what I'm going to do, Jason: I'm going to put you on a six-week trial. I should probably put you on a level-two course, but I'm going to put you on a level three. I want to see what you're made of.'

Giff couldn't believe it. 'He will not let you down, Sandro. We are beyond grateful to you. I will not forget the kindness you have shown my boy.' She had tears in her eyes. 'Never, ever will I forget.' She got up and hugged Sandro, who smiled and hugged her back.

Meanwhile, I was thinking, *There's no way I can do a level-three course, I'm going to be way out of my depth!*

Sandro must have read my mind because he turned his attention back to me and asked, 'Jason, do you know the film *Rocky*?'

Until this moment, I'd been in a sort of trance, trying to manage the electric feeling of excitement and overstimulation pulsating through my body, while also giving the appearance of being a serious person. But when Sandro asked me about *Rocky*, I lit up instantly. He had broken my trance by referencing the cultural touchstone that meant the most to me.

'Yes, I know *Rocky*!' I told him. 'I love Rocky!' He couldn't even begin to know how much *Rocky* had meant to me and my life.

'There's a scene in *Rocky IV*,' Sandro continued, 'where Rocky's son asks him, "Do you ever get scared when you go into the ring?" And Rocky replies, "Sometimes I do get a little bit scared, and I'm thinking, God, I wish that this guy would hit me on the chin so I don't feel nothing anymore." But then he says, "There's another side that comes out that isn't so scared. It's another side that wants to take more, that wants to go that one more round, because by going that one more round, when you don't think you can—"'

'"—that's what makes all the difference in your life."'

I finished the sentence for Sandro. I knew that scene off by heart. Not many people my age knew *Rocky* – the first one came out in 1976, nine years before I was born. But I knew all of the *Rocky* films from beginning to end.

'Jason, I am going to need you to keep going the extra round, just like Rocky said. Do we have a deal?'

'Deal,' I replied, and although he offered his hand for another handshake, I couldn't help myself and went in for a hug, completely invading his personal space. He hesitantly placed his arm on my shoulder politely, returning my embrace.

'I want you here tomorrow morning, 8.15 a.m.,' Sandro said. 'We're going to do reading and writing exercises before classes start at nine. Don't be late.'

Thanks to *Rocky*, I immediately recognised the relationship

Sandro was establishing. In the film, Rocky's coach is Mickey Goldmill. It's Mickey who sees the potential in Rocky when no one else does and offers to train him to fight the heavyweight world champion Apollo Creed. Just like Mickey saw something in Rocky, Sandro saw something in me and decided he was going to nurture it.

Years after that first meeting, I asked Sandro why he'd decided to take a chance on me. 'I just felt something that day,' he said. 'Something that told me, *I must help this guy.*' As I got to know Sandro, I learned he was someone who liked to take a chance on people, especially anyone who seemed to be a bit of an underdog. He liked to prove others wrong, to show that nothing is impossible if you put your mind to it. He probably thought, *If I can turn this kid around, I can do anything.*

I could see that Sandro had won Giff's admiration with his willingness to let me on the course and give his time to me. She had been coaching me from the day I was born. She was exhausted and ready for someone else to step in – and perhaps she already sensed that Sandro was that person. Giff and I walked out of Merton College hand in hand, and I said thank you to the spirit in the sky, showing my gratitude with an airborne kiss.

Kathy had shut the door, but Sandro had cracked it open.

Chapter 16

Phonics

It was two days after my meeting with Sandro, and my first day at my new part-time job as a sales assistant at Sports World – in the Tandem shopping centre, a short Tube ride away in Colliers Wood – one of those massive mega-chains filled with the biggest sports brands, such as Nike, Reebok and Adidas, often sold at a discount.

About a week before our visit to Connexions and meeting with Sandro, Giff had gone to the job centre in Clapham Old Town and returned with a list of positions I might be eligible for, including one at Sports World. She correctly guessed that anything with 'sports' in the title would attract my attention, so we put together my application – or rather Giff did, as I still couldn't read and write – and sent it off. Four days later, we received a letter with an offer of employment, no interview required. We were both quite shocked I'd got the job, given my lack of experience and qualifications. But Giff explained that this particular Sports World was new, and they were looking to recruit staff immediately. We agreed that because I loved both sports and being around people – observing and learning from them – I'd do well as a sales assistant, where I got to interact with customers. I hoped that not being able to read and write wouldn't be a problem, as long as they put me on the shop floor and I didn't have to operate the till.

The plan was that I would go to Merton during the weekdays, and work shifts at Sports World after classes and at the weekend. On my first day on the job, Giff went with me, as she always did when I went somewhere new, so she could help me find my way. Back then, signs in the Tube and on the street were still meaningless to me, so I would have got completely lost without Giff at my side. As we went along, she pointed out landmarks that I could use to help me find my way home at the end of the day. When we finally reached the glass doors of the shop, the ever-dutiful Giff gave me a big hug and told me to try my best. I gave her my word.

Inside the large, brightly lit space, with its racks and racks of sports clothes, shoes and equipment, I met my new manager, Zain. Short in stature but big on authority, he showed me to the changing rooms, where I put on my new uniform: a pair of too-big-for-me navy-blue Umbro tracksuit bottoms and a red Umbro polo shirt. I didn't mind that the uniform hung loosely off my small, wiry frame; I loved sports gear and couldn't believe that all this kit had been given to me for free. Then Zain took me around the shop floor so I could meet my new co-workers. Mostly they were guys a few years older than me, but when we got to the checkout, I met the girls on the tills, affectionately known as the Tillies.

One of the Tillies stood out from the rest. Other than on television, I'd never seen such a beautiful person before. Her heart-shaped face was perfectly symmetrical, my ideal. She had gorgeous skin, bright eyes and hair neatly slicked back in a high bun. I also noticed that her feet were tiny, and that she was wearing white ankle socks and brand-new white Nike Air Maxes, which added a few inches to her diminutive height. I could barely breathe; I was that taken by her.

'Jason, this is Debs,' said Zain. 'I'm pairing you with her today. She's going to show you the ropes.'

'Hi, Jason.' Her voice sounded like pure silk.

Slightly tongue-tied, I responded, 'My name is Jason . . . Jason Arday.'

Why I felt the need to say my name and surname when Zain had already introduced me, I have no idea, but Debs laughed, endearingly. I offered her my hand to shake, and she placed her small, delicate hand in my bigger one – and I clumsily squeezed it.

She smiled and giggled. 'No one ever shakes my hand, Jason.'

Then she told me to follow her and walked off in front of me, effortlessly gliding ahead, her uniform caressing her slender frame. Debs explained that I was going to be working in the footwear section, the brightly lit back wall of the shop where dozens of single sports shoes – Nikes, Adidas, Pumas and Reeboks – were on display. My job was to talk to the customers and find out their preferred brand and size, before going to the stockroom to collect the right pair for them to try on. Debs showed me how everything worked, taking the time to check that I understood and happily going over anything I was unsure of, even if I was too distracted to pay much attention.

Next, she took me into the stockroom, a storage space that was about five feet wide and stacked floor to ceiling with boxes and boxes of shoes, the smell of new leather filling the air. We were now in a tightly confined space together – my body only inches from hers. I could practically hear her breathing.

'You must be a beautician,' I told her.

'Why do you think that?' she asked.

'Because you're really beautiful, so I'm guessing you must do something that's like that.'

This wasn't a chat-up line. I was being totally genuine.

'That's such a nice thing to say,' Debs replied, smiling, 'but no, I'm training to be a teacher. I've just started a teacher training program at Roehampton.'

If I'd had to guess, 'teacher' would have been the last thing on my list because she didn't look like any of my teachers at Southfields, that was for sure. As far as I was concerned, Debs could have been a model or a singer or a film star.

'Where are you from?' she asked me.

'Clapham,' I told her.

'You don't sound like you're from Clapham,' she replied.

Not only did I have a weird accent, but I also had a backcombed Afro and a voice that hadn't broken yet, and I was only five foot seven. I didn't even have an Adam's apple – and I'd never had a girlfriend. Meanwhile, all the other guys who worked at Sports World were taller, more mature and had a lot more street cred than I did. They all fancied Debs, I later learned, and couldn't believe the new hippie guy had got paired up with her. To be honest, I couldn't believe it either.

The rest of the day sped by as I followed Debs around, enraptured. Before I knew it, my first work shift was over. I thanked her for her help and went to shake her hand goodbye. She laughed again and said, 'Don't!' Then she slapped my hand away . . . and hugged me. I remember her chest against mine and wanting to bottle the feeling. Inhibition completely abandoned, I adopted the mantra 'Fortune favours the bold.'

'When am I going to see you again?' I asked her.

'I'll be back on at the end of the week,' she replied.

As we walked towards the door, Debs turned to me. 'Actually, if you're going to Clapham, we can get the Tube together,' she said. 'I need to go to Balham and get the train to Croydon.'

I was practically tripping over myself to walk in step with Debs, to have extended time with her, thoroughly enjoying the eight-minute walk from the Tandem Centre to Colliers Wood station without having to worry about finding my way, to say nothing of the five minutes it would take to go from Colliers Wood to Balham. I cannot remember anything that was said between us because I was so in awe of her, but I recall thinking that these were the best thirteen minutes of my life so far.

Back home, I came bounding in through the door.

'How was your day?' Giff yelled from the kitchen. The aroma of freshly prepared light soup and chicken stock on the boil was in the air.

'It was great!' I told her.

'I like your uniform, Jason. Look at you!' Even though I looked a bit ridiculous in my oversized garb, Giff was, as always, proud of me. She asked me particulars about the day, but I was still too distracted by Debs's existence to share any worthy details.

I couldn't wait to go to work again to see her.

That Friday, I was back at Sports World. Starting that morning, I had to interact with the customers without Debs's help because my training period was over. I found the shoes for my first couple of customers with no problem – most of the boxes in the stock-room had pictures stuck to the side, so I just had to match the shoe with the photo to find the right pair. It was only later in the day, when a customer wanted to see the more expensive shoes, that I ran into trouble. The expensive ones came in boxes with words and numbers on the side, but no photos. Because I couldn't read, I couldn't find the right pairs. Instead, I just stood there in the stockroom, looking up at the boxes and boxes, knowing that the customer was waiting, and that Zain was watching to see if the new guy was going to screw up. If I lost this job, I wouldn't just be disappointing Giff – I also wouldn't be able to see Debs anymore. Fuelled by a primal instinct and self-interest, I decided to go over to the till and ask her for help finding the right pair. She kindly came back to the stockroom with me and immediately found the correct box, handing it to me with another one of her smiles, saying, 'It is confusing. Sometimes the wrong shoes end up in the wrong boxes.'

From then on, anytime I had to find a pair of shoes without a picture on the box, I'd get Debs to help me. I also discovered that because she always worked on the till nearest the stockroom, I could keep her in my sights through the little window looking out onto the shop floor. When things weren't too busy, I'd often disappear into the stockroom, pretending to look for something, and then knock on the window to catch Debs's attention and wave at her to come and join me, which she usually did. I'd sit on the stepladder, talking some nonsense and keeping an eye on the window to see if Zain was about to bust us for not working or accuse me of being a bad influence on Debs, who was naturally well-behaved and conscientious.

Debs and I got to know each other in the close confines of the Sports World stockroom. She was an August-born Leo, three months younger than me. Leos are said to have radiant and magnetic personalities, and she certainly embodied this. An amazing sprinter, she had competed regionally and nationally, but had decided not to carry on with the sport because she was worried about developing a too-muscular physique.

'What are you talking about?' I said incredulously. 'You look amazing. You should keep doing it.'

I also learned that Debs had a sweet tooth, and her weaknesses were cakes and chocolate. One day, someone gave me a Bakewell tart from Sainsbury's supermarket, and I saved it for her. I also bought her a Galaxy chocolate bar because I'd once seen her pecking at one on the shop floor. I presented her with the chocolate and the tart later in the day.

'That's so nice, Jason,' she said, smiling and happy.

I was so pleased to have done something to make her smile! I couldn't help thinking, *You have definitely earned some Debbie points here, Jase!* The high lasted for the rest of the afternoon.

One day, I was in the downstairs stockroom, organising the new deliveries and putting labels and price tags on the merchandise. Debs was there, along with three or four of the other guys who worked on the shop floor. I was telling her about my love for the band Oasis when one of the guys started mocking me.

'Ohhhh, Oasis,' he mimicked. 'What other music you into, then?'

One thing about me is that I've never cared what other people think about my interests. It was irrelevant to me that the kind of music I liked wasn't what a lot of other young Black guys were into back then.

'I love the Stone Roses. I really love Tracy Chapman, Paul Simon, Jimi Hendrix – a lot of stuff,' I answered, straight-faced.

None of these guys could understand how this little dweeb who looked about thirteen years old and liked weird music was attracting Debs's attention. And because they didn't understand it, they resorted to ridicule, laughing at me hysterically. They kept asking me questions about what else I liked, finding my replies increasingly hilarious. What they didn't know was that I'd been made fun of for being 'offbeat' in school for years, and I didn't care. I liked being me. And I was realising that Debs liked me for me as well.

After less than a minute of this teasing, she decided it was enough.

'Are you really interested in what he's into, or are you making fun of him?' she asked. 'You can sit here and laugh at him, but at least he knows who he is.' Then she stood up and walked out of the stockroom, leaving our now-silenced co-workers in her wake.

I followed her out, seriously impressed. For some reason, Debs seemed to enjoy my quirks; she accepted that I was different and saw it as part of my charm. She wanted to hang out with me because if nothing else, she thought I was interesting, and she enjoyed that I was into stuff like guitar music and tailoring, which wasn't typical for your average teenager living in south London at the time.

~

After the fourth or fifth time I had to ask her for help finding the right shoes, it must have dawned on Debs that I couldn't read or write. But she never let on that she knew. She had this innate kindness about her that meant she wasn't going to make me feel awkward or exposed in any way. Instead, she protected me fiercely. From her position on the till, she could see the whole shop floor, and she would always bail me out. If I couldn't find what I needed or explain something to a customer, she was quickly at my side, asking, 'Can I help in any way?'

But our manager, Zain, began to notice how much Debs was helping me, and it annoyed him. He'd ask her, 'What do you think of Jason?' And she'd say, 'I think he's a good guy. He's good with customers; he's really friendly and super smiley.' Zain was less impressed. The only reason I was able to hold on to my job at Sports World was because Debs always stood up for me. She was single-handedly keeping me employed.

One day, she asked me if I could help her with something. 'I've got this thing to do for my teacher training,' she said casually. 'I just want to see if it works because I'm preparing for my lesson tomorrow.'

She explained that she needed me to be a guinea pig for some phonics exercises, the kind you use to teach little kids to read. So we sat in the stockroom, and Debs took out some worksheets that had groups of letters on them and got me to repeat the sounds to her. The whole time, she pretended I was doing *her* a favour by helping her with her coursework when in fact she was helping *me* without letting on that she knew I couldn't read or write.

Empathetic and patient, Debs was the best teacher I ever had, an exceptional educator. As far as I could tell, except for Miss McCann and Mr Trace, the teachers I'd had at primary and secondary school weren't very well-equipped to deal with someone with complex learning needs. But Debs had a natural gift, and I adored her and really wanted to please her.

Soon, I was taking the train all the way to Croydon with her, walking her home as slowly as possible and extending my time with her from thirteen minutes to more like forty. Debs never asked me to do this – I took it upon myself.

One day, I was getting ready to leave her at her front door when she said, 'Do you want to come in? Can you help me prepare my lesson for tomorrow?'

'Yes, I'd love that,' I said.

Too fixated on being in her orbit, I still hadn't clocked that she was trying to help me learn to read and write.

Going inside Debs's house was a new adventure. She unlocked the front patio door, revealing another door behind that. Then we stepped into a narrow hallway with a staircase. She showed me around: two big living rooms, a separate dining room, and a kitchen. Upstairs there were two floors with six bedrooms, one for Debs's dad and stepmum and the others for her and her sisters. She took me to her room, which was much smaller than the other ones but decorated with posters of R & B singers on the walls, tear-outs from music magazines: Brandy Norwood, Destiny's Child, Asher D. She had a little dressing table, and all her hair products were neatly laid out, including an industrial tub of Let's Jam! hair gel, Palmer's Cocoa Butter and a variety of combs and brushes. I couldn't believe that in just a few weeks, I'd gone from meeting this person to being with her in her inner sanctuary.

'My dad might be home soon,' Debs explained. 'I'm not sure what time, but let's make sure you're downstairs when he gets here.'

We went down to the living room and started going through the phonics exercises she wanted to show me. It's hard for me to remember the particulars of what we worked on that evening because I was so fixated on Debs. I do remember, though, that at some point her stepmother and her two younger sisters came home, and before I knew it, it was past 9 p.m. Giff would probably be waiting for me at home, wondering where I was. Debs and I said our goodbyes, and I crossed the street to the bus stop to wait for the 109 to Brixton.

Spending that entire evening with Debs, the Adrian to my Rocky, was one of the greatest things that happened to me in my life. The next thing that happened was . . . well, not so great.

Chapter 17

Punching Above My Weight

Outside it was dark and cold, and the bus stop wasn't well lit. I was totally alone, with only the gathering steam from my breath to keep me company in the dampness of the October night. Rather than sit down on the bus stop bench, I paced around trying to stay warm and visible so the driver could see me upon his approach. Before long, the number 60 pulled up, which was not my bus. Four boys, about my age or a bit older, got off. Wearing black tracksuits, like most teenage boys in south London at the time, they came over to size me up, two standing behind me, two in front.

The tallest one asked, 'What've you got for me, bruv?'

I distinctly remember thinking, *This is curious. I've never been in this situation before. Interesting.* Even though I knew there had been a spate of muggings in this area, and generally across south London at the time, I remained calm, forgetting that I was an easy target, on my own after dark and relatively small for my age.

'I don't have anything for you,' I replied. This was mostly true. I didn't own a mobile phone yet, and although I had a five-pound note in my pocket, that was my hard-earned cash from working at Sports World. I wasn't willing to part with it unless someone was in great need. These individuals, by my reckoning, were not in great need.

The boys started laughing. Like the guys at work, they found my accent hilarious.

'What ends are you from?' the tallest of the boys asked, referring to the place where I lived.

Enunciating clearly and standing a little more upright as I did, I told him, 'Clapham.'

'Clapham? Doesn't sound like it. Lemme search your pockets, then.'

'I don't think you need to do that,' I told him, *completely* failing to read the room or the seriousness of the situation. My powers of observation were letting me down when I needed them the most.

'Just empty your fucking pockets!' one of them demanded.

'Do you need some money for an emergency?' I asked. 'Because if you do, then I'm happy and willing to give that to you. But if you don't, then I don't see why I should give you anything.'

And that was it. One of the boys behind me swung a punch at the back of my head, and I instantly fell to the ground. Between the double blow of the punch and hitting my head on the pavement, I was rendered unconscious. The next thing I remember, I was waking up in the hospital.

When I opened my eyes, I saw Giff's face coming into focus in front of me. Her expression managed to be both horrified and disapproving at the same time. My younger brother, Simon, was standing behind her, his expression betraying what they were both thinking: *Jason, your face is a mess, and how the hell have you ended up in here?*

'What did you do?' Giff demanded.

I told her I didn't know. In agony, with horrible pain on the left side of my face, I couldn't think straight. My left eye was totally closed up, but my good eye was squinting too – the gleam from the fluorescent hospital lighting was blinding. Even the squinting made the left side hurt. I couldn't move a single muscle in my face, couldn't even grimace without pain. And to make matters worse, there was a terrible ringing in my right ear.

The police arrived and attempted to retrieve details, but I couldn't remember anything beyond leaving Debs's house and talking to the boys at the bus stop. The cops explained that a passer-by had found me, beaten up and unconscious, and called for an ambulance. Someone must have also located my bus pass, which had my home phone number on it, and called Giff, telling her to come to the hospital right away.

She was exasperated. 'If you'd been home at the time you were supposed to be home, this wouldn't have happened!' One of her favourite phrases was *This isn't the time to go to hospital!* I had broken her golden rule by ending up here. She was not best pleased.

At some point, a couple of nurses came in to check on me. I tried to lean forward, to make myself more comfortable on the hard hospital bed, but the pain of moving my head even a millimetre left me dizzy and disoriented. The nurses wheeled me away for a CT scan and X-rays to assess the extent of the damage. As they did so, I felt a weird tingling on the left-hand side of my face. One of them said under her breath, 'Don't let him look in the mirror yet.' I tried to raise my hand to touch my face, and the nurse pulled it down and said, 'No, no, don't touch it.' They kept telling me not to move my face in any way.

The CT scan showed no swelling or damage to the brain, which drew a 'Hallelujah!' from Giff as she clasped both hands together looking up to the ceiling, immediately thanking God. The X-rays did reveal, however, that I had a fractured eye socket and was going to need an operation. What's more, my right eardrum had been perforated and could take up to two months to heal. The doctors told me that I was lucky, that I could have lost my eye. At that moment, I did not feel particularly lucky.

The next morning, I woke up to a vision of Debs's beautiful face appearing around the flimsy curtains surrounding my hospital bed. Even though it hurt to do it, I grinned from ear to ear. She sat down next to me and told me she was so upset that I had been beaten up right after visiting her.

'I feel like I'm responsible in some way, Jay,' she said. She was the first person to ever call me Jay, and I loved it. She frowned in concern, which made the arches of her sharply plucked eyebrows go up on one side. At some point in the visit, she bent over and began stroking the good side of my face. That side was tender to touch too, but I didn't care. I remember thinking, *She feels sorry for me! Maybe this can work to my advantage!* Even though I'd got my head kicked in, Debs was here, so I was winning. Maybe the doctors were right. Maybe I was *lucky*.

After she left and feeling buoyed by her visit, I managed to get up from the bed on my own for the first time. I made it as far as the toilet, where I finally saw myself in a mirror. This was when I realised how deluded I'd been. Debs wasn't going to go out with me! My face was grotesque, unrecognisable, swollen to twice its usual size. The right side was impressively covered in bruises and welts. I looked like a gargoyle.

The police officers returned later that day, having tracked

down the CCTV footage from the bus stop. They had a small laptop that they got out to show me the grainy footage. I watched as the four silhouettes of the boys kicked and punched me as I lay on the ground. My first thought was, *Wow, Jason, you can really take your licks!* But then the gravity of the situation and the residual trauma hit me. They had beaten me up severely, all because I refused to give them my prized five-pound note.

A week went by before the hospital released me. I couldn't wait to get out. I knew I couldn't slack off with my studies in any shape or form, or Sandro was going to think I wasn't committed. Even though I'd finished my six-week trial period at that point, I didn't have the grades to be on the course, and I still had to prove myself. So despite the pain, the bruising and the swelling – all of which prevented me from concentrating for long stretches – I returned to class, determined to tough it out.

That same week, I also returned to work at Sports World – and was back at Debs's side. After the attack, her mothering instinct kicked in and she became super-protective of me. As Sandro said, 'Sometimes good can come from bad.'

About a month and a half later, when the swelling on my face had finally gone down and the bruises had turned from purple to a lighter shade of mauve, I decided to ask Debs to be my girlfriend. She'd come home with me after work, and we were sitting by the side of the lake on Clapham Common south side, still wearing our work uniforms under our coats. Hers was a cropped black puffer jacket. I loved that coat. I had told her a few days before how much I liked it, and she'd promised to wear it for me. It was about eight o'clock on a cold Friday evening right before Christmas. The dark branches of the wintry trees were spidery tendrils against the night sky, and a solitary duck sent ripples across the surface of the pond, scattering the reflected light of the moon. The moon was dancing for me; the moon wanted me to win.

'Debs' – I cleared my throat – 'I don't know how to go about these things, so I'm just going to ask you. Can you be my girlfriend, please?'

She laughed and gently cupped the right side of my face with her small hand. 'Yes, of course!' she said. 'But, Jason, no one ever asks that!'

We both laughed. Inexperienced to an embarrassing degree, I had no idea what you were supposed to say. I just knew I wanted to be with Debs. And then we kissed. It was perfect.

The offbeat hippie kid got the really beautiful, cool girl. I knew I was punching way above my weight. I'd barely completed secondary school and was just about clinging on to my job at Sports World, and yet somehow, who I was seemed to be enough for Debs. This was the win of all wins, especially because she could have had her pick. I was more than happy.

Debs's dad wasn't so convinced. He wanted his daughter to meet someone respectable with good job prospects and a strong academic profile so she could eventually get married, have kids and live in a nice house. I didn't fit his idea of a good match for Debs, not at all. Once I overheard him saying that he didn't think I was 'very serious'. But Debs told him, 'There's something about him that's so special. I can't put my finger on it. One day he's gonna do something, and the whole world will see.' She was like Rocky's Adrian in her unwavering belief in me. I've still got over a hundred handwritten cards that she sent me over the years – all with the same message: 'You're going to be great. You're going to do something, and everyone will see.' She said it from the beginning, when I didn't even believe in myself. She thought I could conquer the world if I set my mind to it.

'I love you just for being you,' she would tell me.

Between Giff, Sandro and Debs, I now had three people who believed in me. It wasn't that I could walk on water, but they made me wonder what would happen if I tried.

Chapter 18

Keep What You've Got by Giving It All Away

Christmas Eve that year found me sitting with my brothers on the sofa in the living room, watching the film *Shanghai Noon* with Owen Wilson and Jackie Chan on the BBC. I was still healing from my fractured eye socket, my face still a bit bruised and battered, but I was on the mend, and very pleased with myself because Debs had agreed to be my girlfriend five days earlier. My parents were big into Christmas decorations, and they had gone overboard as usual: the bright green synthetic Christmas tree was in one corner, loaded with tinsel and hung with the battered painted clay ornaments we'd made in primary school, which Giff insisted on bringing out each year. Coloured fairy lights were flashing everywhere, wrapped not just around the tree but also on the cabinet next to it, and there was a big shiny banner on the wall that said, 'Merry Christmas!' While the Ardays went in for decorations, we didn't have loads of presents under the tree, but the ones we did have were special. If there was something we really wanted, Giff would always find a way. 'Don't ask how I got it!' she'd say.

Personally, I've never been a fan of Christmas. It's too much of a disruption from the usual routine. As a kid, I relied on the days having a predictable order to them because it helped me feel more in control and manage being overstimulated. When your brain is already dealing with a lot of sensory input and you're trying to process it all, any change in the sequence of events destabilises you even more. So it helps when the day follows a familiar pattern. This was why I loved watching soap operas: I knew that if I turned on the television at the appointed time, my favourite programmes and characters would be there. During the festive season, however, the television schedule was all over the place, with Christmas specials and classic movies throwing off the regular programming, and I couldn't rely on any of my usual rhythms and repetitions. At a certain point, somewhere between Boxing Day and New Year's Eve, I'd become completely disoriented, desperate for the usual schedule to resume. Some people might call this rigidity, but I call it a simple need for predictability. And apart from the interruption to the usual order of events, I didn't like the commercial aspect of Christmas and all the emphasis on spending money, rather than reflecting on the spiritual side of things. Shops were too busy, and there was too much traffic, too many gaudy signs and flashing lights. To this day, I could do without it.

For Giff, Christmas has always been a time for reflection, prayer and helping others. And so right around 10 p.m. that Christmas Eve, she hauled herself up out of The Mothership and told us to turn off the television and get our coats on: we were going to midnight Mass. As teenage boys, we weren't particularly happy about switching off Jackie Chan and his dropkicks, but we knew how much it meant to Giff, so we followed her orders.

Our family had started going to Holy Trinity Church, on

Clapham Common, a while back, after Giff decided it was time for a change from Hanley Hall, the church that we had been going to since I was little. Giff was worried that the kids who went to Hanley were 'rabble-rousers' and felt that the Trinity kids would be a better influence on us. Holy Trinity was also closer to home, on the north side of the Common. As we walked over on Christmas Eve, we could see it all lit up and glowing in the darkness, a rectangular building with a white spire and a cross-shaped stone war memorial silhouetted in front of it. We filed inside and took our seats in one of the pews. The place smelled of mince pies and mulled wine and was lit by what seemed like hundreds of candles. The architecture was spartan: walls painted white, with a second-floor gallery made of dark mahogany, and a simple arch in front of the altar. Much later, I learned that the people who had built this place were political radicals and abolitionists. They didn't want a church that was grand or fancy like a cathedral; they wanted something solid and functional, a place where working people could come together, worship and pray.

In his sermon that night, the vicar emphasised turning our thoughts to the less fortunate at Christmastime. He asked us to think about those who were without family or were in need. Then came the carols, with an organist pounding out the notes, filling the space with soaring sound – all of us joining in. 'O Holy Night', 'O Come, All Ye Faithful', 'Joy to the World', 'Silent Night', 'Hark! The Herald Angels Sing'. I especially liked it when the choir sang in rounds, their voices separated at first, then merging together in harmony. The music was a balm to my busy brain. After the songs, we all went up to receive our blessings, and then there was a lot of chat in the aisles as we passed the collection plate around. Then it was time to go home.

Our little council house beckoned in the darkness, the plastic fir and red-tinsel wreath that my dad had put up proudly hanging on the door. The television stayed off: it was time to light the Christmas candle. Every year, Giff's mum, my gran, gave us an enormous pillar-shaped candle that had been blessed. It was as thick as an arm, and it would take ages to burn down. We always lit it for the first time after midnight Mass, then every morning after that until New Year's Day. Giff put the candle in the living room, in a steel pot (her idea of fire safety) and left it burning fifteen hours a day, only to be extinguished at bedtime. That Christmas Eve, we all stood solemnly around the candle as Giff read a verse from the Bible. Then we sang a hymn before she led us in prayer. We prayed to our heavenly Father in his infinite wisdom to please protect our family and friends, to have mercy on those who were vulnerable and needed protection most, to comfort them in their hour of need. We finished with the Lord's Prayer and hugs all around, wishing each other a happy Christmas and New Year. Once we were done, Giff got out the ironing board, and before we went upstairs to bed, we each had to iron our Christmas clothes – shirts and proper trousers – so we were ready for the next day.

In the morning, we woke up to find that both Giff and my dad had already gone to work. They always worked a half-day on Christmas as neither of them could afford to take a full day off without pay. Dad did the Christmas banquets, and Giff had her shift at the mental health unit.

The night before, she had reminded us of how we were going to spend part of Christmas. 'Boys,' she informed us, 'when I get back from work tomorrow, we'll all go over to the local homeless shelter and volunteer.' Giff wanted to teach us to be 'grateful for small mercies'.

As soon as she got home from work, before we made any food for our own dinner or opened any presents, we bundled up in our coats and walked over to the shelter on Cedars Road, laden with big trays of chicken and turkey that Giff had made, complete with stuffing, rice noodles, West African jollof rice, sausage rolls and corned beef patties, as well as shopping bags filled with essentials such as tinned fruit and evaporated milk, toilet paper and disposable cups. Giff was generous no matter the time of year, but at Christmas, she gave away even more that she didn't have in the first place.

'I don't have a lot, but what I have, I'll share with everyone' was one of Giff's mottos. 'Keep what you've got by giving it all away' was another. Her philosophy was that you should always help anyone who was in need because that could just as easily be you. And if you showed love and empathy to someone today, the same would be shown to you in *your* hour of need when it came. I continued to be Giff's diligent student, listening to her every word, taking in everything she said and did. I wanted to copy her behaviour, her compassion, her kindness, her ability to always care for others.

Giff had heard about this shelter through our church. It was run by a local group of volunteers and donors. We knocked on a small metal door in what looked like a semi-derelict warehouse building, and a man came to open it, ushering us into a large open space. Ahead of us, there must have been about fifty men and some women sitting on old sofas and mismatched chairs or on thin mattresses on the ground, many of them clutching their belongings to them in an assortment of plastic bags. A TV was blaring in the corner of the room. About a dozen volunteers were off to one side of the space, preparing food on a couple of electric burners on folding tables. We went over to join them. Giff recognised a few community elders and activists, who greeted her with hugs.

One of the elders, a Black woman with locs beautifully wrapped in a lilac headscarf, explained to us boys what was going on. 'The people here don't have anywhere else to go,' she said. 'They don't have family; they don't have money for food or shelter. And they can stay for only forty-eight hours before they have to move on and find somewhere else. While they're here, we try to do what we can for them.'

Sobered, I stood with Giff, my brothers and the other volunteers behind the hot plates, where big pans of soup were warming. We helped to ladle out a cup full of vegetable soup for each person, handing them a hunk of bread too. I noticed that the other volunteers tended to each person with such kindness, treating everyone with the dignity they deserved despite their circumstances, and I resolved to do the same. Then I watched as the people who'd been served sat and cherished the simple meal and the safety of having a temporary roof overhead.

After we had been there for about an hour, I heard Giff's voice say, 'Boys, time to go.'

My brothers picked up their coats. They wanted to get home to make the most of the rest of the Christmas festivities and help Giff with the cooking.

'Jason,' Giff said to me gently, 'let's go. Well done today.'

'Giff, may I stay a bit longer, please?' I asked, not wanting to leave.

Being here had chastened me. What hurt the most was

knowing that these people could stay at the shelter for only two nights, then they would have to move on.

Giff looked at her watch and then, knowing that ever since I'd been beaten up at the bus stop, I didn't like to be out late at night on my own, said firmly, 'I will come and get you in a couple of hours.'

I smiled and thanked her.

She smiled back at me and winked. 'Do good and be good, Jason.'

Now that the meal had been served, I helped the volunteers clear up the plates and cups. We also handed out clean clothes and linens, and that's when I noticed a man sitting on a mattress over in the corner. He had straggly, shoulder-length brown hair, a beard with a few wisps of grey and piercing blue eyes. I made a point of telling him as much after I went over to hand him the last bundle.

'You have beautiful eyes, sir.'

'Thank you,' the man said, looking up from his spot. 'I've been watching you. You have a good manner, and you've been kind, taking the time to talk to people. Why don't you take the weight off your feet?'

'My job is to help,' I said.

'Just sit and relax,' he said, patting his mattress. 'Everyone's got something to eat and some clean clothes now.'

We introduced ourselves. His name was Alan. I guessed he was in his late thirties, but it was hard to tell. His face was weathered, and he didn't look like he'd had a decent night's sleep in a long time. I noticed that despite the season, he was wearing cargo shorts with combat pockets, for some reason, I randomly wondered if he could have been in the army. He had the kind of face that would have been considered good-looking if a decent barber got hold of him.

I sat down on the floor next to Alan and asked him how long he'd been here. He told me that he had another twenty-four hours at the shelter, and after that, he'd have to leave. I said I was sorry to hear that and wished I could do something to change the situation.

'If you don't mind me asking, sir, how did you end up here?'

'Well, that's a good question,' Alan answered, squinting his eyes for a second before continuing. 'You wouldn't think it to look at me, but I was a man of standing, a man of position once. I was an academic, a professor. I had a beautiful house. I also had a wife and two kids.'

He paused to take a sip of something from a metal hip flask he brought out of his pocket, flipping the cap back on as he swallowed deeply.

Alan explained that his wife and children had been in a fatal road accident about four years earlier. He told me about how the police had come to his house to tell him what had happened, and how he had buried his family in side-by-side graves before returning to an empty home. He described his depression – how he stopped going to work, was eventually fired and could no longer make his mortgage payments. Alcohol became his only solace and his master. After his house was repossessed, he became destitute.

'I just lost touch with reality, Jason. I had a nervous breakdown and couldn't get myself back on my feet. That's how I've been for the last four years. I managed to get myself down to London a couple of years back, but as you see, I'm still homeless.'

Retrieving the hip flask, he flipped the cap back again, this time taking a prolonged swig. Then he went on.

'I want you to promise me something,' he said. 'When you look at someone like me – someone who is homeless – never assume that they're a bad person. Homelessness can happen to anyone. We are all just one bad event away from it. Promise me, Jason.'

With both of us still sitting on that flimsy mattress on the cold, hard floor, I promised. Then Alan's head sank down to rest on his knees, and I wrapped an arm around him in a half-hug, and we sat there side by side.

Whatever happened to me that night, I knew that I had a home to go back to, that I could sleep in my own bed, with my brothers in the beds next to mine and my parents in the room next door. I thought about our humble council house with the Christmas wreath on the door. I'd known that house my whole life. For a family like mine, that council house was our security, our fortress, our very own Buckingham Palace, with Giff as our queen. That night, I really grasped how precarious life is, how close we all stand to the edge of the abyss, inches from the great fall.

Not long after, I looked up to see Giff in the doorway. I told Alan that I had to go, but I'd never forget what he had told me.

'Thank you for keeping me company, Jason,' he said.

I went over to the door, where Giff reminded me to say goodbye and thank you for the opportunity to the volunteers and organisers.

The two of us made the short walk home, me biting my lip and trying not to cry. Christmas Day turned into Boxing Day as we walked in silence along Dorley Road, the drizzling rain reflecting the streetlights off the glossy pavement. The shops were closed, but still a few people were about, coming back from their Christmas outings.

As we stepped in through the front door, Giff took off the beige raincoat she always wore and hung it on its hook, but I was so distracted I went and sat down on the sofa in the living room, my jacket and shoes still on.

'When did we start wearing our shoes inside?' she demanded, hands on her hips. 'No shoes in the house' was Giff's cardinal rule.

Still in a daze, I took off my shoes and stared at my feet. Then it came to me. Before Giff could reprimand me again, I looked up.

'I know what I want to do with my life, Giff,' I told her. 'I want to help people. I'm going to raise money to help people – I'm going to raise as much money as I can and help as many people as I can.'

'Hang on a minute, Jason,' Giff replied, lifting up her hands and raising her eyebrows as if to say, *Slow down*. 'You know you should always try to help people. But don't forget, you're still learning to read and write – one thing at a time.'

'What I saw today, it's not right – it's not fair and it's not right.'

'You know I agree with you, Jason, but . . .'

'I'm going to work with a lot of people to raise money, and I'm going to give it away to people who don't have a home or anything.'

These were the words of a young man who was still a child at heart, who had hardly any qualifications and could barely hold down a job, let alone earn money to give away. But I meant what I said.

'Well, let's see what happens,' Giff replied. 'Focus on today. But I know you, and if you set your mind to it, I'm sure you can do anything.'

'I can do it, I know I can,' I told her. 'Thank you, Giff. Thank you for taking me to the shelter.'

Giff, who never slept much, went into the kitchen to put leftovers in boxes to take to my gran. I didn't sleep that night either. There was too much whirling around in my brain. I knew Giff was right, of course: I *was* only just learning to read and write. Not only that, but I was getting paid minimum wage at Sports World. The idea that I could raise money to give away to homeless people was so far from feasible that I might as well have stopped before I'd even started. But that night, something had shifted. There was a Jason before the visit to the shelter and a Jason after, and they were two different people. Before the visit, my purpose had been to make something of my life so Giff would be proud and I could look after her and my dad. Now my sense of purpose had expanded. It wasn't enough to help my parents anymore. Alan had made me promise never to think the worst of people like him, but I wanted to do a lot more than that. I made a pledge to myself that I would do all that I could to help people in need. It would become a guiding principle of my adult life.

A few days later, the new year came around, and the Christmas candle finally burned down to the wick and went out.

Chapter 19

Mutually Invested

Ever since the beating at the bus stop, I'd had the feeling that something wasn't quite right. A couple of months after the attack, I started having these odd episodes where it felt as if my brain would freeze. I'd just sit there staring into space, my eyelids fluttering, for what could have been seconds or might have been minutes. Later, I found out these episodes were known as absences, or petit mal seizures.

Then, in January, a couple of months after the attack, I had my first full-on seizure. I was in a lecture with Sandro at the time. Suddenly, a ferocious sensation reverberated through me, like an electric current shooting up my body. The pen flew out of my hand as my fingers went into uncontrollable spasms. I remember hitting the floor and lying there, shuddering. It was like a complete unwiring, as if the connection between my brain and my body had been severed. Sandro had no idea what was happening – he just looked up and saw me on the ground, foaming at the mouth and convulsing. He shouted for his colleague, Tom, who called for an ambulance while Sandro put me in the recovery position in trying to ensure my airway was clear. Thankfully he used to teach first aid as part of his sports psychology course. At the hospital, I had a barrage of tests: MRIs, CT scans, EEGs and more. It was the neurologist who gave me the diagnosis: epilepsy. He explained to me that when people have had substantial trauma to the head, they can sometimes experience epileptic seizures as a result.

The seizure was my first, but it wasn't the last, and it marked the beginning of a new and unfortunate period in my life. Thanks to a monumental commitment to suppression, I had trained myself never to have a meltdown in public. For so many years, I had internalised any feelings of being overwhelmed, frustrated or upset, so that I could be safe in the world, so that I wouldn't become a target of the aggression of others, particularly the police. But now, with the epilepsy, I had no control. My body was essentially going into a new version of a meltdown – one that was much more extreme – and there was nothing I could do about it.

When I left the house in the morning, I never knew if I was going to make it back home without having an episode. I had seizures at work, at college, at home. One time, I was stepping out to cross to the other side of the road when my legs went from under me and I hit the ground. When I came around, I was in the foetal position in the middle of the road, a driver shouting at me that I could have been killed and accusing me of drinking or taking drugs. The seizures were scary not only for me but also for everyone around me. Perhaps the worst part was that I'd often lose control of my bowels and bladder, soiling and urinating on myself. A total loss of dignity. The doctors gave me medication, but it took months before we found one that worked, and the side effects made me drowsy and lethargic.

Looking back, it amazes me that Debs stuck with me. She got

me a wristband with a tracking device in it, so that she would be able to see where I was at all times. The wristband had the words 'known epileptic' written on it, and her phone number so people could contact her if I had an episode. It also said 'Professor Jason Arday' on it, not because I even had an aspiration to be a professor yet, but because she thought I was wise.

Members of my family had access to the tracking device as well, in case Debs was unavailable. Unflappable, she never panicked when I had a seizure. Most people would freeze and not know what to do, but Debs would run to find pillows to make sure I didn't bang my head on the floor. She also monitored my tongue so it wouldn't block my airway, and she put me in the recovery position, remaining totally calm. When I had a seizure at work one day, she went and found me another uniform so I could change out of my soiled clothes. Her interventions were all the more remarkable given that she had not dealt with anyone with epilepsy before.

Meanwhile, I'd started having flashbacks about what happened the night of the beating. Out of nowhere, an image would flicker to the front of my mind, as if someone had changed the television channel in my brain, and I'd see myself lying on the ground, a boot heading in the direction of my face. Other times, I woke from nightmares where I was beaten over and over again. I kept these experiences to myself, though, and because I had no access to therapy, there was no one to help me deal with what I can see now was post-traumatic shock. I became apprehensive about leaving the house after dark, and I thought twice about wearing anything that would make me stand out from the crowd. There was a lot of crime in London at the time, so I know I'm not the only one who felt this way, but my fears were exacerbated by the fact that I had been so severely beaten.

Once again, Debs came to my rescue. She told me that I needed to carry myself with confidence when I was out. Ever since I was a little kid, I'd always walked with my head down. Initially, I just liked looking at my feet, watching their rhythm as they carried me along. But it became a habit, reinforced by a lack of confidence, one that allowed me to stay in my own little world, unaware of what was ahead or behind me.

Debs's theory was that my body language was sending the wrong message. 'If you look like you're afraid, attackers will smell the fear on you and you're going to make yourself a target.'

She was one of the most streetwise people I'd ever met.

'Jay,' she explained, 'you've got to walk with your head up or people will pounce on you. Shoulders back. C'mon, man!'

I can remember standing in the hallway in her house while she coached me to walk with confidence. 'Look me in the eye and then walk towards me, no looking at your shoes!' she'd command.

Other times, she'd stand behind me, pushing the small of my back so that I puffed out my chest. 'C'mon, man!' she'd say. 'Walk like you've got someone in you! I want the person I love to walk with his head up. Are you that person?'

'Yes, Debs,' I insisted, wanting to please this woman who could have had anyone.

I practised walking with my head up until finally Debs didn't have to remind me anymore. Even though I was small in stature, she made me feel like I was six feet tall. In turn, this helped me when I was out of the house. I stopped being so fearful.

Throughout this time, Debs continued teaching me to read

and write, as did Sandro. It was like I had two private tutors, one taking the night shift and the other the day shift. They were very different in their teaching styles. Debs would sit with me in the stockroom or on the bunk bed in the room I shared with my brothers, our shoulders and thighs touching. She'd slowly read a line out loud, and then I would repeat it. We'd do that over and over again until it became familiar to me. Then she'd write a sentence, and I'd copy it. Debs was so patient, I don't remember her ever losing her temper or being short with me. I do remember being fascinated by the fact that she was ambidextrous. She was naturally left-handed, but her dad was superstitious about left-handed people and encouraged her to use her right. As a result, she could write perfectly with both hands.

Sandro's bedside manner was not quite so sweet and gentle. A tough taskmaster, he focused on the discipline of practising something over and over until it lodged in your brain. Repetition, repetition, repetition. Before classes even started each day, I'd have to spend over an hour with Sandro working on reading and writing. After classes were over, Sandro drilled me for a few hours. Then I'd spend another two hours with Debs. No time for breaks, no excuses, no time off. He'd been in the military in Brazil, and he definitely had a bit of the sergeant major about him. It was like *Groundhog Day*, but this was fine by me, because I knew what to expect. If I wrote a sentence and it was incorrect, he'd put a massive red *X* through the page and I'd have to do it until I got it right, which sometimes took me multiple tries. His philosophy was that I needed to strive for perfection, even if I didn't achieve it immediately. 'The day will come, Jason, when you will be called upon to be perfect, whether it's for one minute, or one hour. You need to be prepared for that moment.' Sandro could be tough, but I always knew where I was with him. He told me early on, 'There will be many times when you are not going to like me. But remember, everything I do is because I care about you.'

Like Debs, Sandro helped me with my confidence. Because I had regularly been put on the spot by the teachers at Southfields, I had a real sense of trepidation in the classroom and never spoke up unless forced. Not to mention, I was so far behind my peers in terms of my basic abilities, and I didn't want to be ridiculed by them. Somehow Sandro intuited all this.

'Fear of failure and a respect of failure are two very different things,' he said. 'You need to have respect for failure, but you cannot have a fear of failure. You have to fearlessly give everything you have in pursuing a goal, and respect that failure may be the outcome. But fear of it cannot keep you from trying.'

In class, he would deliberately ask me questions that he knew I had the answers to so I would grow accustomed to the feeling of success – something I had never experienced in a classroom to that point. This was hugely important and helped me to find my voice. Even if I got an answer wrong, Sandro wouldn't embarrass me. He'd say, 'That's interesting. I've never thought about it that way.' I've learned so much from him about how to bring out the best in students, and I use this technique to this day in my own teaching.

I was Sandro's student in more ways than one. I studied everything about him and his manner, just as I had with Giff. Personable and magnetic, he was really good at engaging with his students, and he was a great performer, which is one of the most important qualities you can have as a teacher. He won the respect of everyone in the class because he was consistent, clear and ultimately loving. For his students, he wanted only the best.

~

For the first time, I was learning without the pressure of being in a classroom where the teachers seemed to think I was 'stupid' or 'subnormal'. Instead, I was with Debs and Sandro, people I trusted. These people loved me. They actually wanted me to succeed. The going was slow, but I wanted to learn so that they would be proud of me. And this made all the difference. We were mutually invested.

With their encouragement and feedback – and many hours of hard work – I was finally able to pick out a word here and there in children's picture books. It was a slow progression from identifying a single letter to being able to name groups of letters together, helped by the fact that we often read the same books Giff had read to me when I was a little kid: the Biff, Chip and Kipper series, 'Funnybones', 'Flat Stanley' and 'Dilly the Dinosaur'. I knew those books practically by heart. Memorisation helped me solve the mystery of how to connect letters on the page to the spoken word. But even after I began to be able to recognise individual words, it was a long time before I could manage a full sentence and then a paragraph. This was slow, laborious and often boring work, involving hours and hours of repeating the same exercises. Eventually, I could pick out the names of my favourite TV shows in the TV guide, which was a big development. And then one day, I was watching the original *Rocky* film with Debs – for what must have been the fiftieth time – and we had the captions on. I started reading the lines from the film out loud. Of course, I already knew every line, but in that moment, I was putting what I had memorised together with the actual words, and it was like a light bulb went off. It all made sense.

~

While I was slowly advancing academically and learning to manage my epilepsy, the four boys who had attacked me were eventually identified. The police took the case seriously and brought charges. My attackers were all from south London and, like me, they were eighteen – barely adults. I understood what that meant. A conviction for assault and theft would follow them for years, shaping their futures before they had really begun.

I didn't want to make thing worse. When the case went to court, I submitted a Victim Personal Statement explaining the impact the attack had had on me but also saying that I hoped they would be held accountable without being locked away, that I wanted them to focus on their education and move forward with their lives. In the end, the court imposed community sentences rather than prison. At the time, that outcome aligned with what I had hoped for. I didn't yet know that our paths would cross again . . . in very different circumstances.

When I told my dad and brothers that I was advocating for the boys who had beaten me up, they weren't happy about it. With my bruises only recently healed and my epileptic seizures always a threat, they wanted the culprits held accountable. Giff was the only one who understood. 'I'm not happy in some ways,' she said, 'because I don't want you to be hurt by anyone, but I brought you up to forgive, so I can't be angry now.' Ever since I was a little kid, Giff had talked to me about the power of forgiveness. 'Sometimes you have to give those who least deserve it understanding and forgiveness.' This was her belief. Even at age nineteen, I knew that resentment, bitterness and anger are like stones weighing you down. They paralyse you and stop you from being free. I'd had enough experiences with people treating me badly to understand how to forgive. My whole life I had been labelled 'special needs', a phrase that was used as a slur against me. 'Why can't you read?' 'Why can't you write?' 'What's wrong with you?' 'Why aren't you normal?' Thankfully, I had Giff to explain to me that people often mock the things they don't understand, and that, at the end of the day, you must forgive those who have wronged you because it liberates your soul. I'd already forgiven the teachers who didn't seem to know what to do with me, the psychologists who had conducted their cruel therapies on me and all the naysayers who'd told me I'd never make anything of my life.

Besides, as Giff pointed out, I had a lot to thank those four boys at the bus stop for: 'That beating knocked some sense into you, Jason.' My brothers, dad and friends liked to joke, 'Jason owes those guys his life – they beat the literacy into him.'

Chapter 20

Outside of the Box

I had just about learned to read and write, albeit at the level of a five-year-old, but one thing I hadn't learned yet was how to arrive somewhere at the appointed hour. My timekeeping at age nineteen was terrible, as was my tendency to make up silly excuses for why I was always late. When I'd first started at Merton, Sandro told me: 'We're going to learn a lot about each other. I hope you're not the kind of person who always has an excuse in you; otherwise, we're not going to get on very well.' The truth was, I was full of excuses, especially when it came to time management. If I was late for classes: 'The bus ran late.' If I didn't hand in my homework on time: 'It got rained on.' Sandro wasn't having any of it. He'd tell me, 'All your classmates took the bus and they got here on time, and it wasn't raining yesterday.' Central to Sandro's belief system was the idea of personal responsibility – that everyone should take charge of his or her own life ... *without* excuses. He could see that I was making massive strides in all other areas of my development, but this particular shortcoming was going to be a major problem, particularly when I left school and went out in the workforce full-time.

In other words, I might have officially been an adult, but I had yet to start acting like one. My bad habit of always running late was mostly a result of my exceptional ability to needlessly procrastinate and forget to pay attention to the time. This was on full display one particular Friday night in March, when I was supposed to be meeting Sandro at 7.30 at Tooting Broadway station. At 7.45, I was still at home in the upstairs hallway, playing 'Start Me Up' by the Rolling Stones on full blast on the Alba CD player I shared with my brothers, singing along to the music loudly, Jagger-gesturing and vainly posturing in front of the mirror in my Diesel stonewashed flares, battered off-white Chuck Taylors and plain grey T-shirt.

Somewhere in the dim recesses of the bedroom, I could hear a buzzing sound. It was the mobile phone that Debs had given me as a present. My first-ever mobile, a little black Nokia 3610 just like hers, which she had bought for me because I kept running up my parents' phone bills calling her at all hours on the landline. Unaccustomed to having a mobile and too absorbed in my imaginary rock stardom, I forgot that it even existed.

When I finally managed to leave the house to meet Sandro, I didn't even think to look at the phone. If I had, I would have seen the many, many missed calls from the poor man, who was waiting for me outside the Tube station. I'd known Sandro for about six months at that point, and in that time, our relationship had evolved from teacher and student to mentor and mentee. For reasons he'd later explain as part altruism, part intuition, he had taken me on as his own personal *Mission: Impossible.* Not only was Sandro still devoting himself to reading and writing with me every day at college, but he'd also started coming to my football matches, where he'd coach me through the games from the sidelines. He even introduced me to *rodizio* (all-you-can-eat style of Brazilian restaurant service) at the Brazilian restaurants he would take me to after my games – all the while imparting his lessons in life. Back then, almost every conversation we had was about how to prepare myself for future challenges. There was always some sort of instruction to everything he said. 'You learn nothing about yourself when you're winning,' he once told me. 'All the learning is to be done when you're losing.' Sandro was a very philosophical man and he was fascinated by human psychology – the ways that we can use the mind to conquer fears and circumvent disappointments. As far as he was concerned, there was only one thing holding me back from scaling the highest summits of success: my inability to take responsibility for my actions.

In my defence, Sandro's expectations of me – that I show up for my classes and try my hardest every single day – were something new. When I was at secondary school, the teachers didn't seem to expect much of me. I was the kid who couldn't read or write – they didn't seem to care if I even showed up. I could basically do what I wanted because I felt as if they'd already written me off. The only teacher who paid me any significant attention was Mr Trace, my PE teacher, but I had him for just two hours a week, and that was never going to be enough to turn me around. At Merton, lateness and absenteeism were not tolerated. Sandro expected me to be on time and attend classes five days a week. Given some of my previous learned behaviours, this proved challenging.

When I finally arrived at Tooting Broadway station to meet Sandro that Friday evening, I was, true to form, outrageously late. After coming out of the Tube, I spotted him right away, standing by the plinth of the big bronze statue of King Edward VII. As I approached, I wondered what he had planned for me; Sandro had only told me that it was going to be a surprise, and that he wanted to do something to help me build my confidence. Happy to see him as always, I smiled my usual big, idiotic grin in his direction, but Sandro was as stony-faced and unmoved as the statue towering above him.

'Wipe that smile off your face,' he said.

Oh, dear, I thought, as I attempted to process the seriousness of the situation.

'You're ninety minutes late. What happened?'

I shrugged, my face defaulting back to its usual smile, which only further incensed him.

'Do you have nothing to say for yourself?' he demanded. 'I have called you multiple times. Multiple times, and you didn't pick up once! I had planned for us to do something fun tonight – something that would ultimately help you. I've arranged this whole evening, not to mention paid for it in advance, and you're ninety minutes late. And it's not just today – you're late for everything: your job, college, almost every meeting we have.'

'I'm sorry, Sandro,' I told him, the silly smile still flickering around my lips, this time no teeth on show. 'I think the train probably got stuck in a tunnel.'

'The train? Jason, I know you've had a hard life, but you have an excuse for everything! Until you take responsibility for your own actions – your own *life* – you will never amount to anything. You'll never even come close to reaching your potential. People are investing so much into you because we want you to win, but you have to meet us halfway. Showing up an hour and a half late tells me that you are not disciplined and not serious.

With the potential and gifts you have, it's a waste … a waste of life. Call me when you want to take responsibility for your own life.'

With that, he walked away, back into the station. I stood rooted to the spot, staring at the ground and my frayed Diesel stonewash flares covering most of my Chuck Taylors. I'd never seen Sandro angry before. In the past, I'd always managed to smile and bluff my way through my shortcomings, but that wasn't going to cut it in this situation. Everything Sandro had said to me was correct. The worst part was, I'd let him – and ultimately myself – down. On the Tube ride home, I sat trying to swallow the urge to burst into tears having just heard the cold, hard, sobering truth.

'Why are you back so early?' Giff asked when I came into the house.

'I fucked up, Giff. I fucked up with Sandro.' I knew I wasn't supposed to swear in front of Giff, but doing so conveyed the seriousness of the situation.

I explained that I'd arrived late, and that Sandro told me I was wasting my life. Giff didn't say anything at first. Her silence was enough for me to know she agreed it was time for me to start taking accountability for when I slipped up, especially around timekeeping. Then she reminded me that he had given us a chance when no one else would.

'Do not let me – and most importantly, yourself – down, Jason.'

I nodded, agreeing with her.

The next day, I set my alarm and arrived at Merton a full hour early so that I would be waiting for Sandro when he arrived at his office. I was hoping to impress him and show him I was a serious person, but Sandro wasn't that easily won over. When he spotted me sitting behind his desk, already working on my writing exercises, he raised his eyebrows, giving me a look that said *What do you want? An award for being early? You don't get any special treatment for following basic standards of professionalism.* I told him I was really sorry and ready to take responsibility for my life. He nodded frostily and shook my hand.

After that, I started showing up early for class every single day. I put my hand up whenever he asked a question. I picked up all the equipment from the field without being told to do it, in a desperate attempt to show dependability. Sandro didn't seem outwardly impressed. It wasn't that he liked to hold a grudge; he just wasn't going to give me an award for doing something that would ultimately benefit me.

Later that spring, Sandro asked me to come and meet him and his colleague Tom in their office. He said he wanted to tell me something.

'Jason, I've decided to make you captain of the football team next year,' he said.

My immediate response was that I wasn't captain material, that I didn't know how to be a leader, and that while I was grateful for the opportunity, I was going to have to turn it down.

'I'm not asking you, I'm telling you,' said Sandro. 'You are going to be captain next year.'

It turned out, the captaincy wasn't a reward for good behaviour or demonstrable leadership traits. This was another test. Sandro had identified that I had an irresponsible streak and decided the best way to teach me to take responsibility was to put me into a situation where I would be *forced* to take responsibility.

'From now on you will lead, *and you will do it by example,*'

Sandro said, without lifting his gaze from the paper he was marking. Not once did he look in my direction.

When he later announced this news to the team, everyone was just as shocked as I was. The hippie kid from Clapham was going to lead the whole team? But they also knew I was a good player, and ultimately, they learned to respect me because, under Sandro's guidance, I began to step up and flourish in the role. As captain, I couldn't slack off, retreat or go into hiding; I had to get there early to set up before everyone else arrived, and I had to be a role model for my teammates.

The same month I took on the captainship, Sandro told me I was doing well enough in my classes that I should think about continuing my studies at university. My grades were actually good enough to apply. He would write my reference. Debs said she would help me fill out the forms – she was already in her second year of university, so she knew what was required and, as always, gently held my hand through the process. We applied to five universities to do physical education, including my first choice, St Mary's, because I wanted to follow in Sandro's footsteps, and they had a great PE programme. Debs wrote out the entire application for me – including my personal statement, which I dictated to her, and she helped me to polish.

Now that I had set my sights on being a PE teacher, Sandro told me that he would give me another chance to meet him for our evening out. This time, I got there first, arriving so early that I waited by the statue of King Edward VII for over an hour before Sandro arrived. When he turned up, he told me that he'd booked the same activity as last time and said again that it was something that was going to help with my confidence. He knew I was naturally shy and paralysed by the thought of having to get up and present in front of a group of people – something I would have to do if I was ever going to become a successful teacher. And so, he was going to take me to a place that would help me shed my inhibitions. Knowing that I loved music, Sandro was taking me to a karaoke bar.

I had never done karaoke in my life. With trepidation, I followed him down some stairs to a basement room that had a small stage with a disco ball hanging over it. A guy was singing '(Is This the Way to) Amarillo' out of tune into a microphone while a small crowd of people cheered and sang along.

I put my name on the list and waited to be called up. When it was my turn to get up on stage, I had no idea how to use the remote control to select a song on the big television with the lyrics, so before I knew it, 'Loco in Acapulco' by the Four Tops started playing. I started laughing. The crowd laughed back. I started trying to sing the song, but I could only hear my own voice reverberating in my ears, which made me laugh even harder. Soon, my face was aching with laughter and the crowd was in hysterics. I could hardly sing a word. Even Sandro was cracking up. After I got off stage, on a bit of a high from the experience, I signed up for another go.

Next up, I sang 'I Shot the Sheriff' by Bob Marley and then 'Slide Away' by Oasis. Being on stage felt great. I'd already got some practice in singing along to music in the mirror at home, so it wasn't much of a stretch to sing in front of a crowd. I started to pick songs that were longer so I could perform for longer. I sang some James Brown – 'Hot Pants', to be specific – and I even did 'Gimme Shelter', showing off my Jagger moves. As I came off stage, Sandro said, 'Look what happens when you let go of your inhibitions! You've actually got stage presence; you've got a great smile. If you can do this, you can definitely stand up in front of people in a classroom and command their attention.'

Sandro was an outside-of-the-box thinker. He could have taken me to some kind of public-speaking course, but he knew that was unlikely to work. Instead, he found a way for me to gain confidence through the conduit of music, one of my biggest loves. And it had worked.

After that, we started going to karaoke quite regularly, which had an unintended consequence: it helped me with my reading. Although I usually made sure to select songs I had already memorised, I started to enjoy watching the lyrics as they popped up on the screen and being able to match them in my mind to what I was singing. Prior to this, I'd always learned song lyrics by ear, sometimes misinterpreting what was being sung, especially if the singer didn't have the best enunciation. For example, I'd been listening to Pearl Jam's 'Even Flow' for years, singing along to Eddie Vedder's signature growl, without ever knowing that the first word of the song wasn't 'wheeeeeezing' but 'freeeeeezing'.

For 95 per cent of my life to that point, I'd had to guess what things said when they were written down, just like I'd guessed song lyrics by picking things up by ear and pretending that I knew what was going on, even when I was completely clueless. It was exhausting. Now that I could make out words when they popped up in front of me, I felt massively empowered.

Part Four

Purpose

Chapter 21

Eureka Moments

'I've got something for you,' Debs told me, a giant smile on her face, as she produced a fat white envelope with the St Mary's crest in the top left corner from her coat pocket. The letter had been sent to her house because we'd used her address for my applications, and now she had come over to mine so we could open it together.

Debs handed me the envelope, and I turned it over, prying apart the seal, my hands slightly shaking as I pulled out the letter and unfolded it. I saw the words right away: 'Conditional Offer'. I held it up and showed it to Debs, still in disbelief.

'Look what you've done, Jason!' she exclaimed. 'I knew you could do it. I knew it! I'm so proud of you.'

We hugged, both elated. Debs had joyful tears in her eyes.

We sat down on my bed and Debs read the letter aloud to me, every word.

The letter stated that if I passed my course at Merton with three merits, which I was on track to do, I was going to university. Not only that, but I was also going to St Mary's in Twickenham ... Strawberry Hill, the place I'd first visited with Mr Trace when I was fifteen years old and couldn't read or write, when I didn't even know what a university was. Now here I was, almost five years later, holding an acceptance letter to that same institution in my hands. Thankfully, I had Debs there to confirm that I wasn't dreaming.

I had a few months left to finish my course, and I did it, getting eighteen distinctions out of eighteen units, which is called a triple-grade distinction, the highest award you can get. We didn't have a graduation ceremony, but we did have a final dinner for our class, after which Sandro took me to one side and told me that even though I was leaving Merton, he would always be there for me, and I could come to him for advice whenever I needed it. I hugged him and thanked him from the bottom of my heart for all that he had done. If he hadn't taken a chance on me and invested in me, there's no doubt in my mind that university would have remained unattainable. That evening, I gave him a present, a Brazilian football team shirt. He was delighted but said that while he appreciated the gesture, the greatest gift I could give him was to help other students in the way he had helped me. 'Pay it forward, Jason,' he instructed. 'Pay it forward.'

I began to get myself organised for university. My tuition fees were £1,175 a year, so Debs helped me apply for a grant to cover that. I was going to live at home, and most of my other costs were covered by a student loan. Thankfully the Labour government had also just reintroduced means-tested contributions for low-income students like me. When I received the first part of my loan, for just over £1,000, I was blown away. Needless to say, the concept of stretching that amount out for the rest of the academic term had yet to sink in. Even though that money was for my studies, not fashion, I went straight to Carnaby Street and bought a new pair of Diesel flares for myself and a pair of Miss Sixty jeans for Debs to celebrate.

On my first day at St Mary's, in late September 2005, I strode off to Clapham Junction to get the train, wearing my brand-new flares and feeling ten feet tall. When I got off at Strawberry Hill station, the sun was shining, and everything was just as leafy, green and idyllic as I remembered it from my visit at age fifteen. I still couldn't wrap my head round the fact that I was only thirty-six minutes away from Clapham Junction, and yet I was in a different world, with wide, tree-lined streets and massive houses, in one of the most affluent suburbs of London. As I entered through the St Mary's gates that day, I felt so proud to be a university student. It was like floating on air; I felt as if I could walk off a cliff and still land on my feet.

When I set foot on the actual campus, however, it dawned on me that I was in a new educational situation in more ways than one. Everyone else appeared to be white: it was a sea of white faces as far as the eye could see. Walking through the Strawberry Hill campus, I searched in vain for another Black person. I was quite amused by this because I knew that if I got back on the train, I was less than fifteen minutes away from seeing Black people again, so I'd probably survive until then. It was only as I approached a big building with a sign saying 'School of Education' that I finally spotted someone of a similar skin colour. She was wearing a grey polo shirt with the St Mary's crest and the words 'Physical Education (PE)' intricately sewn onto it. I made a beeline for her, said hello and asked where I could please pick up the same uniform.

'What's your name?' the woman asked me sceptically. 'What course are you taking?'

She was slender, about five foot six, with lovely shoulder-length locs and big brown eyes, which were currently looking at me sideways.

I answered that my name was Jason, and I was doing PE.

'Oh my God, I've just met another Jason who's also on this course!' she exclaimed loudly. 'And that's my ex-husband's name! What's going on?! What are the chances of meeting two Jasons??'

Despite being annoyed with me for having the same name as her former spouse, she told me that her name was Angela, and that she would show me the way to the sports hall, having been there the day before. As we walked over, I learned that even though Angela looked like she was in her early twenties, she was actually a mature student, recently separated, with a young daughter. She'd decided to retrain as a PE teacher because she loved sports and wanted a change of direction after working as a freelance textiles designer for several years. I liked her right away. She was kind, funny and blunt . . . to put it bluntly.

I didn't know it yet, but Angela would become my confidant, my trusty guide, the older, cooler, magnificent big sister I never had.

She walked me to the sports hall, where I picked up my new uniform. I'd always loved uniforms. Even though my hopes of blending in had been dashed many times since Heathbrook Primary School, I still yearned for the feeling of belonging that comes from wearing clothing that identifies you as a member of a group. Also, because this uniform was unequivocally St Mary's, I felt like I was now officially a Simmie (a term of endearment used for a member of the St Mary's community). At induction, we learned that there were about 220 students in our course, including a grand total of three other Black students and a large number from Ireland who were drawn to St Mary's because it was a Catholic university with a Catholic tradition.

It was a great first day, but I couldn't wait to get home, mainly so I could try on my uniform. After I bounded in the front door, I raced upstairs, barely saying hello to Giff in my haste to change into my grey polo shirt with the St Mary's crest emblazoned on it. Then came the black shell suit bottoms with the same crest on the top right thigh. And finally, a black rainproof parka with the crest across the chest again. Surveying myself in the mirror, I decided I wanted to personalise my look. The iconic footballer Eric Cantona always put his collars up on his shirts when he played for Manchester United, so I thought, *I am going to put the collar up on mine.* Then I unzipped the bottoms at the ankles so they had almost a flared look. Perfect. As I gazed at my reflection, the pride was bursting out of me.

That night, I took off the uniform and laid it out carefully so it would be ready for the morning. The next day, I leapt out of bed, put on my prized uniform, and practically sprinted to Clapham Junction station, platform 11, to get the 8.36 train to Strawberry Hill. There, I spotted a couple of other St Mary's students on the platform, also wearing their uniforms. They gave me a nod, and I sheepishly nodded back, unsure of the rules of engagement. Even so, that nod of recognition was everything to me; it told me I was a part of something. From that day forth, I kept my St Mary's gear washed, clean and pristine, knowing I couldn't afford to buy a new set. After I left the university and started teaching, I wore that same uniform to my classes. And all these years later, I still have the shirt, trousers and rain jacket, occupying pride of place among my most treasured items; that's how important they are to me.

~

I was in such a state of excitement about attending St Mary's that I don't think it had occurred to me that I was actually going to have to do any coursework. At Merton, we'd done a blend of theory and practical engagement, but the emphasis was on the practical, which was how I had managed to do well. One of the first things we were told at the St Mary's orientation was, 'If you think you're going to be playing sports all week, you're not . . . The majority of the work is going to be theoretical.' *Hmmm*, I thought, *this is going to be interesting. Not sure my strengths lie here.* Then there was a mention of exams. I knew I was paddling upstream, but I thought, *Let's cross that bridge when we get to it. Let's at least enjoy one semester as an undergraduate before you get found out.*

For the first term, we didn't have to submit much in the way of essays, so I managed to coast along. My main struggle was taking notes in lectures. While everyone else was scrawling away a million words a minute, I was a painfully slow notetaker and would often catch only five or six words before the dreaded switch to the next slide. Having learned to read and write only a little more than a year ago, I found notetaking incredibly hard, and the pace felt unrelenting. I was sponge-like in my enthusiasm, trying to absorb everything but failing to transfer that knowledge to the page. It didn't occur to me that there might be accommodations to help with my academic challenges – at that point, I'm not sure I even knew what the word 'accommodations' meant. I simply didn't have the language to ask for what I needed.

Angela is the only reason I survived St Mary's. She could see that I was diligent and trying my absolute best, and she took it upon herself to help me. I made sure to sit next to her at the very front of the lecture theatre, and after class, she'd give me her notes to copy. Other times, she would write additional notes for me that were much more informed and extensive than the ones she'd taken down in the lectures. When we came back from Christmas break for the second term, however, reality set in: I had essays due, and I had no idea how to write them. Although I was at the point where I could string together sentences on the page, this didn't mean I was able to produce a coherent essay at an undergraduate level. Thankfully, Angela once again saw that I was struggling and took me under her wing. After lectures, we'd go to the dining hall for study sessions. 'I'm investing in you,' Angela joked, 'because when you make it big, I'm going to be able to say that I knew you when.'

Sentence by sentence, she tried to show me how to write essays, explaining how to construct paragraphs and use sources to support my views. She'd already done a textiles degree and was a very good writer. We practised and practised, always working together on group activities and assignments. Angela made it all look so easy. I admired her so much. They say you are the company you keep, and there's no doubt Angela's excellence rubbed off on me. She was the most brilliant and talented person on our course by far.

I adored her, but the other students in the PE programme didn't exactly feel the same way. They thought Angela was too blunt, even if she saw it as character-building. She had a habit of calling them 'babies', particularly during practical sessions. 'How am I outrunning all of you babies?' she'd say. 'I'm ten years older than you! Keep up!' I found her lack of tact funny, but that's probably because I was never on the receiving end of her serrated tongue. I just loved that she was determined and uncompromising, and that, like Giff and Debs, she was such a skilled advocate for herself. I learned so much from all three of those women about how to stick up for yourself.

~

Even with Angela's help, my first year at university was a rocky time, and not only because of my lack of academic skills. Back then, I was still having a significant number of epileptic seizures. Once, I had a seizure in a packed lecture hall, falling headfirst onto Angela's lap. When I woke up, everyone was standing around me, including my panicked-looking lecturer, and there was an ambulance waiting.

'I couldn't figure out what was going on!' Angela later told me with her usual humour. 'Why's Jason's head in my lap? Is he coming on to me?'

Towards the end of the first year, we had our initial round of exams. This was the first time I'd ever sat a written test without a support assistant at my side – and even that hadn't gone well for me. As we entered the sports hall, which had been converted into an examination room, my palms were sweating and my stomach was tied in a knot. Everything in my body told me to run away. I knew that I couldn't process information in a setting like this, that I was doomed to fail, but despite these forebodings, I forced myself to sit down. I knew that if I stayed, I was certain to fail spectacularly, but if I walked out, it would look terrible.

The test began, and I did my best to guess the answers to the questions, somehow making it through to the end of the paper.

After the exam was over, I felt no sense of relief – I was terrified of how badly I must have done. I imagined the lecturer on the other end of marking this, laughing and thinking, *This will go down in inept student folklore.* Had I just exposed myself as an impostor? Left myself open to ridicule? It took me back to when the teachers at Southfields used to ask me to read out loud and all the other kids would laugh at me. Perhaps university was a stretch too far after all.

The results were due to come out a couple of days later.

One of the lecturers on our course was a woman called Alison Langstaff. She was small and soft-spoken, with a way of delivering information that I struggled to absorb. To be honest, I usually found my attention drifting to whatever was happening outside the window with the clouds or the trees when I was in her lectures. But I respected that she knew her stuff, and she was an important figure at St Mary's.

The morning that the test results came in, my classmates asked, 'Ms Langstaff, has everyone passed?'

'Everyone has passed – except for one person, who got 9 per cent,' she replied, pausing to deliver the punchline, 'for writing their name.'

Everyone laughed. Except for me. My classmates ran to the door so they could see their scores, anonymised by student ID number, posted on the noticeboard outside the lecture hall.

'Jason, after you've looked at your mark, please come and see me,' Ms Langstaff declared.

Outside, I scanned the board for my ID number. Of course, the lowly 9 per cent was mine. The next lowest mark after that was about 55 per cent. I felt sick to my stomach, not to mention mortally embarrassed.

I went back into the lecture hall to face Ms Langstaff, convinced that I was going to be kicked off the course.

'Is there any reason you got that mark?' she asked. 'Did you just not study?'

That's when I came clean. I told her that I had only just learned to read and write, and that I had real difficulties with taking notes and retaining information.

The only good part of this otherwise horrible and humiliating event was that after that conversation, Ms Langstaff referred me to the disability officer at St Mary's, who asked me questions about my background and told me she felt it was a miracle that I'd managed to get to university at all. She was really understanding and encouraging.

On her recommendation, St Mary's made an application to the Lambeth Education Access office for a disabled students' allowance. Lambeth told me I needed to undergo a needs assessment so they would have a full reckoning of my challenges and abilities. The assessment took place at Roehampton, a university not far from St Mary's in Barnes, southwest London. The man who administered it was named Dr Richard Smyth. I still have the report he wrote which explains that I did very well with verbal responses, but when I was given tasks involving memory, reading and processing speed skills, I had 'marked difficulties'. I was also well below average when it came to reading speed and comprehension, as well as spelling and basic number skills. In this same report, Dr Smyth also noted that I had 'significant underlying difficulties of the type associated with individuals who are described as dyslexic'.

Dyslexia is one of the most common learning disabilities in the world. It means that you have problems with language processing, and you struggle to decode words on the page – something that used to be referred to as word blindness. It's also a co-occurring condition with autism. Dr Smyth's diagnosis went a long way to explaining why it had taken me so many years to learn to read and write. All those teachers who had questioned my abilities or told me I was lazy and not trying hard enough had been wrong about me. I didn't lack intelligence – I just lacked the right kind of support: exactly as Giff had explained to them. In his summary, Dr Smyth described me as someone with 'very complex needs'. I saw now that my teachers hadn't had the training or resources to understand how to help me.

After he'd finished administering the test, Dr Smyth looked up from his notes and, to my surprise, asked me another question.

'Is your mother's name Giff?'

I told him it was.

'I've met you and your mother before. When you were about four or five years old, you came to my office for an assessment. I've never forgotten that day. Your mum was quite the character.'

Dr Smyth told me that Giff had made a big impression on him because of her detailed understanding of autism and developmental delays, my sole diagnoses at that time.

'I remember your mother was formidable, and she was a phenomenal advocate for you,' he told me. 'Even though you were a small child, she was completely convinced that you would go on to achieve something with your life. If someone had told me when I first met you both that you would end up at university, I never would've believed them. I have no doubt that your mother's unwavering faith and strength are the reasons you have made it this far.'

In his report, Dr Smyth recommended that I be given additional time to complete written examinations, and a scribe to write down my answers. I needed to have a laptop and dictation software to help me complete my assignments, and in lectures, I would have a Dictaphone and a scribe to help with my notetaking. Dr Smyth also observed that I was going to have difficulty following discussions in seminars, so this should be 'borne in mind sympathetically by his fellow students and tutors'.

With my new accommodations in place and Angela's ongoing help, I was able to do much, much better in my studies. My second year, I went from getting 9 per cent to scraping 40 per cent, then I went up to 67 and on from there.

During this time, I talked to Sandro on the phone every day, and sometimes multiple times a day. He counselled me to keep going, reminding me 'not to get distracted'. I followed his advice. I knew I couldn't afford to be led astray by the many social opportunities available to me at university. Unlike my peers, I didn't have the luxury of being able to slip up here and there because, quite frankly, I was nowhere near as intellectually adept as them. Every day, I was on time at the front of the lecture hall, dedicating myself to learning, knowing that I had to give it my all.

One of the only distractions I did allow myself was playing American nine-ball pool. My grant and loan only went so far, and I wasn't working at Sports World anymore, so I started playing pool instead of snooker, because at that time, there were a lot more nine-ball competitions nationally offering generous prize money. Although I was never good enough to win a Pro-Am (professional-amateur tournament), I did always make the latter stages. All I had to do was pay my entry fee and get to a quarter-final, and I would leave with some prize money in my pocket. This turned out to be a great way of subsidising my student days, but I had to be careful not to slip back into my old habit of playing six hours in one stretch. Money aside, I couldn't afford to slack off from my degree.

~

Even though I was doing a lot better in my studies, this unfortunately wasn't the end of my challenges.

One day, Ms Langstaff asked me to stay behind after class. As everyone else left the lecture hall, I waited, wondering what I'd done to deserve her undivided attention.

'I've got questions about your coursework,' she said. 'To be quite honest with you, we're trying to determine if you are really capable of this. Your average in first year was 42 per cent and your average this year is 67. We don't think it's possible for you to make that kind of a jump in such a short time.'

Given the drastic improvement I'd made, Ms Langstaff was struggling to believe my progress and was questioning if my work was my own. I explained that Angela had kindly taught me how to write university assignments, and then I had worked really hard over the summer. Ms Langstaff proceeded to drill me on the contents of my essays, checking that I knew what I was talking about. I did as instructed and swallowed my feelings of offence, but I have never forgotten them.

The suggestion that I somehow wasn't worthy of my success would be levied at me again and again in years to come. As I continued with my studies and began my improbable rise through the ranks of academia, people have continually questioned whether I have earned my place. This is common for people who are Black or from other disadvantaged groups. When you succeed against pretty much insurmountable odds, it weirdly makes people question your credibility. 'There must be some glitch in the system,' they say. Or the most recent version of that: 'Well, it has to be a diversity hire.' You recognise very quickly what your accomplishments are reduced to; you're constantly reminded that no matter what you achieve, you will always be 'less than'. To this day, everything I do is scrutinised and challenged in a way that almost never happens to my white colleagues. For every new position I've attained, there has always been someone doubting that I've arrived there on merit. This constant questioning of our abilities is a phenomenon that I and many other Black people seem to have to learn to live with. It is hurtful to be challenged in this way, but ultimately, it has strengthened my resolve. You could say that my early experiences were preparing me for the pain. Sadly, being prepared hasn't made it any easier to bear, but I know that I will never let it stop me because my purpose is greater than my own need.

Although I wasn't Ms Langstaff's biggest fan after she questioned my capabilities, I do have to give her credit for one important thing: it was thanks to her that I first learned about the disability rights movement. One day, I was in a lecture where she was talking about ways to make sports more inclusive, and how to adapt activities for people with physical disabilities. In the course of this lecture, she explained to us the difference between the 'medical model of disability' and the 'social model of disability'.

'These are terms used by the disability rights movement to explain the different ways society views disability,' she described. 'In the medical model of disability, a person's disabilities are seen as a defect, something "not normal" that needs to be cured or fixed. In the social model of disability, society, not the individual, is seen as the problem because it creates barriers and excludes people. Instead of focusing on fixing the "defect" or emphasising the things that the person with disabilities can't do, the social model focuses on what they *can* do.'

This was a real light bulb moment for me. I remember thinking, *I'm learning a lot here.* I may have been somewhat allergic to Ms Langstaff, but I couldn't dispute that on this topic, she knew her stuff. What she was saying also struck a deep chord with me. In talking about 'exclusionary ableism', she was describing something I could relate to on a very personal and visceral level.

That evening, I went home and shared what I'd learned with Giff.

'What they're saying,' I told her excitedly, 'is that people with disabilities feel more included when everyone focuses on the *ability* part, not the *disability* part. It's all about emphasising what people *can* contribute regardless of disability.' As obvious as this may appear now, it was amazingly affirming at the time to hear this language and context, and it allowed me to form a better understanding of my own story.

Giff loved this too, and she went away and read up about the social and medical models of disability. 'That's what I did with you and Joseph!' she told me excitedly. 'I did the social model!'

It was true. Everything Giff had done for my brother and me had been outside the limits of the medical model. She had fought for us to be included in mainstream classrooms, she'd ignored the doctors and therapists who told her that I'd never amount to anything, and she'd always found ways to play to our strengths, not our weaknesses. It was just that until now, we'd never had a language for how exclusion and ableism had affected our lives, even though we'd lived through those experiences every day. St Mary's gave me that framework. It was a powerful eureka moment and a fantastic validation of Giff's approach.

I saw, for the first time, the true beauty of education: that it gives you a way to think about things. I began to wonder if maybe I wanted to be more than a PE teacher – if perhaps one day, I could be part of an institution of learning, helping future students have eureka moments of their own.

Chapter 22

Will Supersedes Skill

Just as I was establishing a firmer foothold at university, life took another dramatic turn. Debs had always told me she didn't want to wait until thirty to become a mum. I was still in my first year at St Mary's when a test confirmed what she'd already guessed. We were expecting. The timing was not great by anyone's standards. I was in my second year at university, and she was embarking on her newly qualified teacher year – one of the toughest periods for any trainee teacher. Even so, Debs wanted the baby. She was apprehensive, of course, but also surprisingly calm. It was one of her greatest skills, this ability to think clearly and pragmatically under pressure.

I knew that Debs would be the most exceptional mother; her maternal instincts were so strong. I, on the other hand, was petrified. I could just about look after myself, and my paternal instincts were non-existent. And the instincts I *did* have told me to run as far away from fatherhood as possible. But I loved Debs, and what's more, Giff had a very strict set of commandments regarding the treatment of women. She would never have forgiven me if I'd turned my back on Debs. 'A good man is a responsible one,' Giff would often say. 'That is the most attractive quality to a woman.' To be honest, I wasn't just fearful of letting Debs down – I was fearful of Giff's disdain if I did.

Debs quickly told her dad, who wasn't best pleased but who decided to support us going ahead and never wavered from that. Meanwhile, I put off telling Giff and my dad what was happening for as long as I could.

My parents were upstairs in bed early one Saturday morning when I took a deep breath and went into their room.

'I've got something to tell you,' I said.

I was assuming that they would be upset and disappointed in me, that Giff would think I had been *sexually irresponsible*, as she described it when issuing warnings to my brothers and me about 'wrapping up' and safe sex. She always told us, 'I am too young to be a grandmother, so make sure you be sensible boys!' I was certain my dad would be furious and would accuse me of ruining my life or making it even more difficult. Better just to get this over with.

'Debs is pregnant,' I blurted out.

The silence that followed seemed to last for an eternity. Then, all of a sudden, my parents started hugging each other, and then they jumped out of bed and hugged me. The Lord was repeatedly praised. Jubilation and rejoicing ensued.

'Our first grandchild!'

Truly, I had not seen this reaction coming. They were delirious with happiness. Meanwhile, I stood there, looking more stunned than ever.

I knew I had to tell Angela next; she had become like family to me. One day, when we were about to leave a lecture, I asked her, 'What's it like to be a parent?'

'It's a labour of love,' she replied. 'Why do you ask?'

Before she'd even finished her question, I spluttered out in a whisper that I was going to be a father. Angela could not believe it. Nor could I. After she got over her shock, she was unequivocally happy for me.

'It's going to be the greatest thing you've ever done, and I will be here to support you,' she told me.

Although I told all the important people in my life about my impending parenthood, I was careful to hide it from Alison Langstaff and the rest of the staff at St Mary's. At that point in the course, we had started going into local secondary schools to deliver practical physical education sessions to under-sixteens, but I hadn't been allowed to instruct the kids directly because of my epilepsy. It was felt it wouldn't be safe if I had a seizure in front of the children, so I was tasked with picking up cones and setting up the activities instead – and Ms Langstaff had mentioned reducing me to part-time status because I was falling behind as a result. Angela, always on my side, stuck up for me, though, and told Ms Langstaff she would pitch in and help me. I felt that if I told Ms Langstaff I was about to become a father, she could have one more reason to drop me to part-time. So I kept that information to myself.

During this difficult time, I remember my dad taking me aside one evening. I'd been telling him and Giff that I was struggling, that it felt like my life was getting harder, not easier. I was about to be a father, and meanwhile, it wasn't certain that I'd be able to stay at St Mary's because of my epilepsy. 'Jason, the only person you can rely on is you. I can sit here and tell you everything will be alright and put my arm around you, but you have no choice, *you* have to make it alright. It's down to you.'

~

Debs had a good pregnancy and no morning sickness. She was so naturally slender that you wouldn't have guessed she was with child if you saw her from behind. Perhaps because of that, the idea that we were having an actual child remained an abstract concept to me – that is, until we were lying in bed one day, and Debs turned over so I could see her belly moving. The baby was visibly kicking inside her. That's when it finally dawned on me: *Oh my goodness, there's really a baby in there!*

From that point on, I started talking to the little baby in her belly all the time. 'You're going to be the greatest person I've ever known,' I'd say.

We found out we were having a girl, and we were delighted. All I wanted was for our daughter to inherit her mother's amazing abilities. I confess, I hoped and prayed that she wouldn't inherit anything from me – that she wouldn't have to struggle with the stigma of having a learning disability as I had done as a child. While she was still in Debs's belly, I sang songs to her, especially 'Dedicated to the One I Love' by the Mamas & the Papas, and played music for her – Santana, James Brown and Jimi Hendrix, everything I'd grown up listening to with my dad – so that when she came into the world, she'd already know some of the best tunes ever written.

Debs went into labour while I was in a lecture at the beginning of my third year at St Mary's. Her sister texted me that she was going to the hospital, and I got there as soon as I could. As our daughter, T., came into the world, she was bawling. The nurse handed her to me, and I rubbed her two cheeks with my index fingers, telling her it was going to be okay, and slowly, she stopped crying. I couldn't believe her size: so small, she nearly fit in the palm of my hand. She was unbelievably beautiful, with a full head of hair and big almond-shaped eyes just like Giff's and a heart-shaped face like Debs's. The long fingers she got from me – the same fingers that had led the midwife at my birth to predict that I was destined for greatness. It was surreal to think that the offbeat kid who got the beautiful girl now had a child with her, and that from this point on, we would always be connected. Still, I could not fathom that I was someone's dad; I still felt like a child myself.

A few days later, I saw Angela in a lecture. She had been sworn to secrecy about my predicament, so I surreptitiously showed her a photo that Debs had developed of the new baby. Angela gave me the biggest hug, overjoyed for me. As we drew back out of the embrace, I asked her if she would do me the honour of becoming T.'s godmother. She replied, 'Yes, of course,' with a tear in her eye – a rare and precious sight, as Angela was cut from the tough stuff. I wanted T. to be Angela, Giff and Debs all rolled into one.

A few days after T. was born, while she was still in the hospital, I remember watching her in her crib, peacefully sleeping and stirring slightly. As I kissed her small forehead, I told her the same thing I'd always told her when she was on the inside: 'You are going to be better than anyone I ever knew. You will do things the world has never seen.' Then I sat back in the chair and grabbed my book, knowing I needed to complete my reading for my lecture in exactly seven hours' time.

~

My academic aspirations shifted dramatically during this time, with one particular lecture at St Mary's in the spring of 2007 being the defining catalyst. Debs was still pregnant, and I was sitting in a lecture with Angela at my side, as usual. Alison Langstaff was at the front of the hall. She had just finished her PhD, she announced to the class, and was now officially a doctor of philosophy. She went on to explain how having a PhD set her apart from her peers at the university. When she finally finished her speech, she declared that henceforth, all students and staff should refer to her by her new title: *Dr* Alison Langstaff.

I'd learned almost nothing during the lecture, but one thing stuck with me, and that was because it was the only thing that she had talked about: her PhD. After the lecture was over, I went up to her to ask her a question.

'If you don't mind me asking, how do you do a PhD? I mean, how do you get to do one?'

Dr Langstaff looked at me quizzically. 'You are just about passing this degree, young man,' she said. 'A PhD is something you will never need to worry about. Focus on scraping through your undergraduate years, Jason!'

There was some truth in what she was saying; I was no academic thoroughbred or prodigy – far from it. But Sandro had taught me that will always supersedes skill. And I had the will and determination of a thousand people.

Angela and I left the lecture hall together, then we walked back to Strawberry Hill station for the 15.08 train. She was chatting away at my side, but she may as well have been talking to herself because my mind was completely fixated on those three letters: PhD. As we got off at Clapham Junction and Angela left to catch her train, I remained in a bit of a trance. I wanted to ask someone what a PhD was exactly, and how I could get one. The only other people I knew to ask were Giff and Sandro. Giff was at work, so I hopped on the Tube and headed to Morden to meet Sandro, who had just finished teaching for the day.

When Sandro saw me walk into his office, he grinned and stood up to embrace me with his trademark bear hug, almost squeezing the life out of my smaller frame. In addition to speaking to Sandro on the phone every day, I visited him at Merton often.

'How was your day, my friend?' he asked.

'It's been interesting,' I told him. Then I asked him my question: 'What's a PhD?'

Sandro smiled. 'It's the mother of all undertakings, Jason,' he replied. 'A PhD is the final rung on the academic qualification ladder. It requires a very high level of academic ability.'

'I want to do one,' I told him without skipping a beat.

Sandro's eyebrow went all the way up on one side.

'It's not to be a doctor,' I explained. 'But I want to do one because I think that's what you need to work in a university, to get ahead there.'

I was expecting Sandro to sit me down and talk me through the process. But instead, his grin widened, and he started to laugh. Uncontrollably. In fact, he was laughing so hard that he seemed to be convulsing, spluttering and coughing, with tears running down his face as he tried to get his breath back.

I was absolutely crestfallen. It was one thing to be dismissed by someone like Alison Langstaff, but to be laughed at by Sandro was a different matter. He and I were 'home team'.

Finally, Sandro collected himself, wiping the tears from his eyes. Then he looked at me.

'Jason, I am not laughing for the reasons you think,' he said, in a perfectly serious tone now. 'I'm not laughing *at* you, I promise. I'm laughing because wouldn't it be one of the most remarkable things the world has ever seen if the boy who couldn't read and write until he was eighteen went on to get his *PhD*?'

Sandro placed his palm on the side of my head. I could feel the calluses there from all the hours I knew he'd spent lifting weights at the gym. Then he paused and looked directly into my eyes.

'I think we can take on the world and win. We can win, Jason.'

No words were exchanged after that. Instead, we just nodded at each other in unison.

That was it. I was resolved to get my PhD.

Chapter 23

When the Purpose Is Greater than the Need

I'd kept T.'s existence a secret from everyone at St Mary's – except Angela and a few other close friends – for almost two years now, but when graduation came around in June 2008, I decided it was time to let the world know I had a daughter. The day of the ceremony, Debs dressed T. in a little white dress with a white headband, and together with Giff, Dad and Sandro, we proudly made our way to Westminster Cathedral, where the graduation was taking place. Westminster is the largest Roman Catholic cathedral in England, an awe-inspiring red-brick building with tall arches and massive domed ceilings inside. Everyone took their places in the pew, with Debs holding T. on her lap. She was such a pretty toddler, her little feet batting up and down in her tiny white socks. I remember Debs had given her a binky, which she wasn't usually allowed, just in case she made noise in the ceremony. When my name was called out, I went up to the front to collect my degree, and then all the graduates filed out into the courtyard to shake hands with the faculty. After that, friends and family came out to join us. Debs found me first and gave me the biggest hug and kiss, passing

T. to me so I could show her off to my friends and lecturers. I took the binky out of T.'s mouth and put it in mine, which made her giggle uncontrollably. Several people came up to me to ask if T. was my sister, and that's when I introduced them to my *daughter.* My friends couldn't believe it, and when Dr Langstaff learned about her, she was flabbergasted.

'Why didn't you tell us?' she asked.

'Because if I had told you, I wouldn't be graduating today with my peers. You would have held me back,' I said. At this point, I had nothing left to lose in telling the truth.

Not only was I collecting my degree alongside everyone else, but I was also finishing university with an upper second-class honours (2:1) – in fact, my final mark was only 0.1 point away from a first class, the highest degree available. Not bad for a kid who had learned to read and write only the year before he started at university. It was a testament to Debs, Sandro, Angela and Giff that I had crossed the finish line – and I made sure they all knew how much this was their achievement too.

Since that day, I've graduated multiple times from other institutions, but St Mary's was my first – and for me, it will always be the most special.

~

After graduating, my immediate goal was to complete a postgraduate certificate in education so I could teach fourteen- to nineteen-year-olds. As soon as I had this qualification, I'd be able to start teaching PE at a secondary school, which would mean I could gain experience as a teacher and earn a living. I had a young family to support now, and I took my responsibilities very seriously. At the same time, I knew I wanted to continue in academia. The next step in my plan was to pursue my master's, the first step to a PhD. I was determined to work in higher education, an environment and intervention that had been so pivotal for me.

Alongside my studies, my special interest in tailoring continued. Thanks to Giff, I knew how to make patterns and sew. I made clothes for T., my friends, and myself. I was reading up about different eras in men's fashion, especially the 1930s and 40s. I even considered taking a night course in pattern-making at the London College of Fashion, until Giff wisely advised me to focus on one thing at a time.

But tailoring and academia weren't my only preoccupations. Throughout my time at St Mary's and after, I remembered the promise I'd made to myself the night I visited the homeless shelter at age eighteen: I wanted to dedicate myself to supporting charities. When I get an idea in my head, I become obsessed with it to the point that I am an absolute pain to be around. Thanks to Giff's moral instruction – that you should always help those in need because you never know when your own time of need might come – it was ingrained in me to devote myself to charity work whenever I could. As a student at St Mary's, I'd taken part in all kinds of fundraising drives. I'd participated in sponsored bike rides from London to Brighton and held clothing sales, getting my friends to donate items they no longer wanted, which I'd then sell to raise money. I joined the RAG (raise and give) committee at St Mary's, and we organised school discos, fancy dress parties and theme nights, with all proceeds going to charity. I volunteered to go to Brazil with the group to install water pumps there. I wanted to do whatever I could to help.

Then, in July of 2009, a year after I graduated, I was hit by a flash of inspiration. The comedian Suzy Eddie Izzard announced that she was going to be running forty-three marathons in fifty-one days to raise money for charity. This really captured my imagination, especially as she didn't have any prior experience of long-distance running and had done only about five weeks of training. There was no rhyme or reason to why Suzy should have taken on this challenge: she wasn't an athlete, and she wasn't particularly fit, but her determination really struck a chord with me. By the time she made it to Trafalgar Square in London, her final destination, she'd run more than a thousand miles all over the UK and raised more than £1.8 million. Her feet were cut to ribbons and her ankles were shot, but she had done it. I was massively inspired. I decided I wanted to be like Suzy and set myself the goal of raising money by running thirty marathons in thirty-five days in the summer of 2010. I started training in the spring of that year.

By this point, I'd gained my teaching qualification and was working as a sports teacher at Richmond upon Thames College. I'd also embarked on my master's degree in physical education and professional practice at St Mary's. My busy schedule meant that my marathon training had to take place at the only time available to me: in the middle of the night. I've always been an insomniac, so I didn't mind this nocturnal schedule. Since the days when Giff used to take me for night-time walks around Clapham to help calm me down, I've loved the hush of the city after dark, the stillness you find in those hours a familiar friend. As I ran through deserted streets, free from the constant drone of traffic noise, other sounds became accentuated: the rhythmic slap of my running shoes on the road, the rustle of a fox behind some rubbish bins, and if I stayed out late enough, the chorus of birdsong that arrived just before dawn. It got to the point where I was running about eighty miles a week, mostly in the dark. The idea was to get 'miles in the legs' so that my body could become used to the discomfort of running long distances over consecutive days. I put myself on a strict diet too. To be honest, this gruelling regime wasn't a lot of fun, but I was highly motivated. As Giff had always told me, 'If the purpose is greater than your own need, God will always help you to deliver because your cause is *just*.'

The reality was, I'd set myself an ambitious goal, in terms of both distance covered *and* the fundraising target. A friend of mine created a JustGiving page and put the link up on Facebook, explaining that I was raising money for two charities: Shelter, which helps homeless people, and a children's hospice called Shooting Stars, where I'd volunteered while still a student at St Mary's. I had high hopes, but sadly, the JustGiving page didn't show signs of much activity. After about three months, we'd hardly raised anything. My friends were all recent graduates who didn't have a lot of cash. They were donating £5 or £10 each, which was very generous given their circumstances, but it wasn't getting me anywhere near my target.

I remember talking to one of my friends about it, and he told me, 'To be honest with you, Jason, the problem with your charity stuff is that it's like paying rent. It comes around every month! You're always raising money for something – a tenner here, a fiver there. If it's a choice between that and a pint, I'd rather have the pint! No offence, brother.'

'Understandably,' I replied, laughing. 'None taken.'

My friend had a point. I was always doing some kind of fundraiser, and I was going back to the same small cohort of people over and over to ask them to donate. But what was I going to do? The challenge was starting in a few days, and I needed to make it worth it.

Desperate times called for desperate measures. I was going to have to *borrow* the money to donate to my own fundraiser. I was so focused on my goal of raising money to help others that it didn't occur to me that this was . . . completely bonkers.

The next day during my lunch break, I made my way down to the NatWest bank on Twickenham High Street to ask for a loan. Debs had set me up with a bank account when I was a student, but needless to say, I didn't have a very good understanding of finance or how banks or borrowing worked. So I just walked in there and said to the woman at the counter, 'Hi, I'm doing a fundraiser for charity, and I need to borrow £1,000 to help kickstart my fundraising goal.' The woman was extremely sweet about it. She entertained me for twenty minutes, patiently explaining interest rates and credit scores. I told her, 'I don't know what any of that is – I just need £1,000.'

She couldn't have been any kinder to the hapless twenty-five-year-old standing before her, but in the end, she had to put it in plain English: 'Look, Jason, I can't give you a loan. You wouldn't be able to pay it back.'

She did wish me all the best with the challenge and asked me to send her a link to my JustGiving page so she could donate, which she later did. I walked out of the bank feeling dejected. I'd assumed they would simply say yes if I asked nicely. Wasn't it that easy? My naivety at this point was far greater than my real-world experience.

But as luck would have it, the very next day, I got an email from two people who ran a PR and marketing agency. They'd seen a small article about me and the marathon challenge in a local newspaper and had found my email address at the bottom of the JustGiving page. Their names were Paul and Keith, and they told me they wanted to support me in my fundraising efforts. I had no clue what PR was (or marketing, for that matter), but Paul and Keith said they wanted to help and it wasn't going to cost me anything, so I thought, *Why not?* They just asked me a couple of questions about how I got interested in charity work and what my story was, and then they said, 'Leave it with us.'

Three days later, on 19 July 2020, it was time to run my first marathon, a feat I knew I was going to have to repeat another twenty-nine times. I chose as my starting point Piccadilly Circus, right by the statue of Eros, the winged god of love, perched on top of the fountain in the middle of London's busiest junction. Piccadilly Circus is iconic – bright neon lights at all times of the day and night – so it seemed like the perfect place to start and finish, as I would be running in a loop. It was a very hot summer that year, so I made sure to set out at six in the morning because I didn't want to get too dehydrated, and there would be less traffic earlier in the day. I took off running along Regent Street, past Hyde Park in the direction of Sloane Square. From there, I ran across Battersea Bridge, through Clapham to Putney, then all the way to Twickenham, Strawberry Hill and Teddington.

Along the way, I was surprised to see people waving at me and stopping me to shake my hand. I hadn't realised that many people knew about what I was doing. At some point, I slowed down to check the time on my phone and saw a text from a friend linking to a two-page spread about me in one of the London papers. Paul and Keith at the PR company had secured it. All along my route, people who had seen the article were stopping to cheer me on. 'What you're doing is amazing. I've donated!' Some people even started running with me. After I got to Teddington, I turned around and headed back in the direction of Picadilly Circus. I was determined to finish that first marathon in good time, and I made it: four hours and forty minutes. A respectable time.

After I got home that day, I clicked on the JustGiving page and found that we had received a whole rash of donations. And this was just the beginning. In the coming days, Paul and Keith built a website, and then I got a sponsor, which meant I got free running gear and shoes. Everything was going really well. Now I just needed to finish the challenge.

As the days went on, the running got harder. It's not that I thought it was ever going to be easy, but I hadn't factored in how much my body was going to fight running for four or five hours every day. At a certain point, every muscle in my being screamed for me to stop, and I was feeling heavier and heavier with each step. I lost my appetite. I wasn't getting enough nutrients. The only thing that kept me going was knowing that so many people were depending on me.

Then, on day twenty-one, something happened that really should have derailed the whole endeavour: I had a seizure in the middle of running. I'd known going into the challenge that this was a possibility. Ever since my head injury, I could no longer rely on my body to do what it was supposed to do; I was just trusting to luck that I would somehow get through the marathons without having a seizure. Instead, I had a bad one. I fell to the ground on the roadside, and when I came around, a dozen people were standing above me and I had intense pain in my right leg. Someone called an ambulance, and I was taken to the nearest hospital.

The X-ray showed a small hairline fracture in my fibula. The doctor gave me a soft boot and told me I could not continue with the marathons – any physical activity would only make the barely visible fracture in my leg much worse.

'But there are so many people who've donated,' I told him. 'They're relying on me.'

This doctor had read about my marathon challenge in the paper. 'I think what you've done is great,' he told me. 'But you've got a fracture in your leg. People will still want to donate to you. They'll understand.'

'It's only a hairline fracture,' I countered. 'Giving up is not an option. It's a risk I'm willing to take.'

Anything I start, I have to see through to the end. People had donated a lot of money, and I had to honour that. There was no way I was giving up now.

Paul and Keith also tried to talk sense into me. 'Jason, you don't need to finish,' they told me. 'You've done enough. Your health is more important.'

Giff and my dad didn't want me to continue either. But I wouldn't listen to them. Out of desperation, Giff appealed to Debs, believing that I would listen to her.

'I know that you're telling the doctors no, and everyone else no,' Debs said. 'But I'm begging you: please, will you stop now?'

Up to this point, I had never said no to Debs. I loved, respected and appreciated her, and I always took her side of things on board. I knew she always had my best interests at heart. But this was different. I'd come this far, and I wasn't going to give up now and let the two charities down and all the people in need of these funds. I could still walk, and I could just about run. I was determined and I wanted to continue.

I told Debs I was sorry, but I was going to finish what I'd started.

That was the day Debs realised, probably for the first time, that she was with someone who was completely stubborn, and that once he had set his mind on something, he wasn't going to give up an inch, even if it was to his own detriment or the detriment of those who loved him.

The next nine marathons were truly an ordeal. It took me well over five hours to complete each one. Even though I used painkillers, I was in agony throughout. My right leg ballooned to twice its size. To this day, I don't really know how I did it. What I do know is that I'm someone who will always push things to the absolute limit, to the point that I don't even acknowledge that there *is* a limit. I'm not saying it's a good thing; I'm saying this is who I am. There's a sort of belligerence in me, a mental toughness, a refusal to accept defeat. It could be that I was born with it, or maybe it's something I learned through having a hard life; it's impossible to know. Much later, I would learn about the phenomenon of interoception, which is your ability to register and understand internal states in your body. If you're neurotypical, your body likely sends regular signals to your brain to say, 'I'm hungry, I'm tired, I'm in pain.' But for some people who are neurodivergent, those signals can get muddled and take longer to reach their target, and for me, that resulted in an extremely high tolerance for pain and discomfort.

As I ran the final nine marathons, Giff's words of wisdom, the ones that live inside my head, kept me going. Every step of the way, I could hear her comforting and encouraging me, reminding me that there were people in greater need, that my own suffering was a short sacrifice that would give others relief in the long run. Just as she had taught me to do, I visualised the goal: the statue of Eros, where I would hold T. up in celebration when I finally finished.

Eventually, the last day of the challenge dawned. Sponsors arranged for a stretch of Regent Street leading up to Piccadilly Circus to be cordoned off. A local news programme was going to cover my run at different times of the day. My sponsors had made banners and T-shirts.

When I got to Sloane Square, about two and a half miles from the finish line, exhausted and limping, I got the most incredible boost. Thanks to Paul and Keith, hundreds of people were waiting for me wearing orange T-shirts that said 'I'm following Jason' on the back. In case anyone was in any doubt, I was wearing a red T-shirt that said 'I'm Jason'. From Sloane Square to the finish line, I had hundreds of people running along behind me, buoying me up with their energy and enthusiasm. When I got to Regent Street, the street was lined with people cheering me on, everyone holding signs and banners that said 'Go Jason!' and 'Come on, you can do it!'

I'd always pictured what the final mile would be like, and I had promised myself that no matter what state my legs were in, I wanted to run it in under ten minutes, finishing with a flourish. Just like the famous scene in *Rocky II*, where Rocky sprints away from the pack and up the steps of the Philadelphia Museum of Art, I forced myself to speed up to a sprint and break away from the rest of the runners. I'll never forget the crescendo of cheers as I turned the corner towards Piccadilly Circus, like I was being carried along by a wave of sound. I could see the statue of Eros. I knew Giff and my dad were waiting there, as well as my brothers, Sandro, Debs and little T. So many of my friends and the general public. And then there was the tape and a massive banner saying 'FINISH'.

There must have been about two or three thousand people waiting at the statue. When I broke through the tape and completed the challenge, I fell to my knees, relieved it was all over. I might have cried. I looked around and saw Debs, and she handed T. to me. Just like I'd visualised, I held T. up and kissed her.

I had far exceeded our original fundraising goal, but running those marathons came at a cost. Although I didn't do any permanent damage to my leg, there were days afterwards when it hurt so much that I couldn't make it upstairs without Debs's help. She would literally have to carry me up the stairs and help me on and off the toilet. I also ended up doing temporary damage to my kidney, and I lost a lot of weight. Did I mention I was stubborn and a pain in the proverbial rear? The most important thing was I did it. It was always about helping those in need. Nothing else mattered.

Chapter 24

THE QUIET PART OUT LOUD

Before T. was born, I had worried about whether she would experience delays similar to my own, and if so, what they would mean for her in a world that stigmatises and even punishes neurodivergence. Now, as she grew from a baby to a toddler, Debs and I watched her closely for signs, knowing there was every chance that she could inherit some of my neurodevelopmental issues. T.'s first smile, her first time rolling over, waving hello, clapping hands, pointing: everything seemed to be progressing according to the textbooks. Would she have delayed speech? We didn't have to wait long to find out. At seven months, our daughter said her first word: 'Dada.' From there, the words flowed out of her, and by the time she was a year old, she was happily chatting away in complete sentences. It was surreal for me to watch T.'s rapid language development – the opposite of my own experiences when I was her age. In fact, she hit all her baby milestones effortlessly and exceptionally early.

And then T. learned to read.

From the time our daughter was an infant, Debs had kept the house full of children's books – some from her work as a primary school teacher, and others that we had used when I was learning to read, like 'Anancy and Mr Dry-Bone' by Fiona French and 'Pig-Heart Boy' by Malorie Blackman. She read to T. every day, often multiple times a day. I was a much less skilled reader, not so adept at the various flourishes that Debs deployed, and T. tended to furrow her little brow at my monotone. Thanks to my dyslexia and dyscalculia, I also still sometimes muddled the words and numbers on the page.

One night, I was snuggled up to T., reading her a story wondering if I might just fall asleep myself. Initially, Debs and the baby stayed in her childhood home, and then for a while, they'd lived with Giff, my dad and me in mine. But I'd now moved into Debs's two-bed flat in Thornton Heath, the first place we'd ever lived on our own as a family. T. had a crib, but at a certain point, she started climbing out of it, sometimes hitting the floor with a thud, so we took the railings off to make it into a toddler bed. Our daughter was an incredibly easy child, except that she hated bedtime and sleeping in general. She was an active and inquisitive kid who never wanted to miss out on anything by closing her big eyes. At bedtime, she'd usually ask for another book, then another, and then another, delaying sleep as long as possible.

That particular night, as I started reading the fourth or maybe fifth book, I decided to skip some of the paragraphs in the story so we would get to the end a bit quicker. As always, I read T.'s storybooks in a slow, uneven monotone, often misreading words. (Again, to say I was not the best reader would be a kindness.) My daughter would often ask, 'Why don't you sound like Mummy?' Debs was a masterful reader, superbly fluid and able to change pitch and cadence, using different voices to portray all of a book's characters. To be fair, this was a big part of her job.

'Daddy,' T. said after a few pages, looking up at me with her big brown eyes, 'you're not reading all the words.'

Caught out by a three-year-old, I did what anyone would in that situation: I lied.

'Yes, I am!' I protested as I shamefully tried to gaslight my sharp-as-a-tack toddler.

But T. wasn't fooled.

'Daddy, you're naughty,' she insisted. And then she took the book away from me and read it aloud, complete with the different voices for the different characters, just like Debs did.

She was word-perfect.

'T., can you read?' I asked her, blown away.

'Yes, I can write too.' She climbed out of bed and got her Peppa Pig notebook and wrote down her name in big bold letters.

At first, I didn't believe her. I pointed at words on the page and told T., 'Say that word!' and 'Say that word!' And she did. For someone like me, who had struggled with reading and writing throughout my life, this was like watching a magic trick!

Obviously, I wasn't supposed to swear in front of a three-year-old, but I couldn't help myself. 'Mate, you're fucking brilliant!' I told her.

She looked at me disapprovingly for the second time that night. 'That's a naughty word, Daddy.'

I immediately apologised. We had somehow swapped roles, with T. as the adult and me as the child.

Over the next few months, T.'s reading and writing continued to progress, far exceeding her age level. This little person rapidly mastered phonics and the relationship between sounds and the letters representing them – a process that had taken me eighteen years. She had a natural facility, a total gift. Even Debs, who taught kids to read for a living, had never seen anything like it. There were times when I wondered if T. was even related to me.

Debs knew exactly how to support a gifted child like T. As a mother, she was naturally compassionate, considerate and nurturing, whereas fatherhood was an unexpected challenge for me. Even though I knew I'd never be half the parent that Giff was – they broke the mould when they made that woman – I'd been a bit overconfident about my parenting abilities. I thought that because I was good with people, I'd be good with a little kid. Somehow, though, it didn't translate. Although I could learn how to give T. her bottle, I couldn't figure out how to engage or establish a wavelength of understanding with a baby. It took a long time for T. and me to connect, and initially, she gravitated much more towards her mum. Where Debs was majestic, always engaged, always present, I started to overcompensate, trying too hard rather than letting it come naturally. When I put in the effort with my career and the fundraising work, I could see the margins gained, but it didn't feel like that with parenting.

Some people say that children pick their parents. I don't know if that's true, but if I could have picked a child, it would have been T. Brilliant, independent-minded, precocious T. Everything I did was for her now. I just wanted her to be proud of me.

~

Throughout this time, I kept my sights set on my goal of obtaining a PhD. By the end of 2011, I'd completed my master's in physical education, with an emphasis on teaching and making the discipline more inclusive. Once that was under my belt, I started to apply for PhD programmes. To my dismay, I was turned down flat everywhere I went, told that my master's wasn't at a high enough level, and that I didn't have the rigour or the research background needed for doctoral work. I was still operating at an undergraduate level, they said, and should undertake further postgraduate study to get up to speed.

To this day, many people assume that because I'm autistic, I'm some kind of prodigy or savant who sailed into my academic career. But the opposite is true. I actually process information at a very slow pace. Anything I learn, I have to work incredibly hard to absorb and retain it. And this wasn't the only factor standing in my way. As I tried to find my way in academia, I was sorely lacking role models. In 2011, when I was coming up, there were only fifty Black professors in the whole country (out of a total of fourteen thousand). From the day I started at St Mary's until I was thirty years old, all my lecturers were white; I wasn't taught by a single person of colour, not even once. As a result, I didn't benefit from the kind of guidance or mentorship that might have been offered by someone who had a similar background to mine. There was no blueprint. It quickly became apparent that the master's I completed wasn't going to adequately prepare me for doctoral work at all, but how was I supposed to know that? I thought all master's programmes were created equal! Sandro was still doing his best to guide me – to inject me with enough self-belief to pull it off – but he was from Brazil. This wasn't his world either. I was making my academic career up as I went along.

If my master's wasn't adequate, this meant I was going to have to undertake further postgraduate study to bring myself up to standard, which would be both time-consuming and expensive (I knew I wasn't going to be offered any kind of grant). In the meantime, I'd started applying for jobs in academia, submitting over a dozen applications and getting turned down as many times as I applied.

The first of these was a graduate assistant post, which I applied to during the first year of my master's. I got as far as the interview stage, and I felt confident that I was a competitive candidate. Not only that, but I also felt I did really well in the interview. Even so, the job went to another candidate. When I asked the selector in charge why I hadn't been successful, his exact words were: 'Sometimes your face just doesn't fit.' He said the quiet part out loud.

I was absolutely gutted. I was a young dad, desperately trying to support my family and already in arrears on nursery fees. Losing that job vexed me a lot, but it also made me beyond hungry and determined to harness the injustice of this feeling. I remember thinking, *In the future, I am going to have to make myself undeniable. If I lose, I don't want it to be on the basis of my 'face not fitting'.* I reluctantly accepted the result and then let it sharpen my focus.

After applying for a dozen other jobs, I did finally get shortlisted for a university lectureship in PE. Looking at the description of the position, I could see that I was completely qualified. But I'll never forget walking into the room and seeing the looks on the faces of the three white men and two white women on the panel. Nothing in my name or application had given away that I was Black, and from their expressions, I could see that they were taken aback. In the first part of the interview there were a lot of questions that had nothing to do with my professional abilities: 'Where did you grow up?' 'Where is your family from?' 'Why are you even interested in this subject?' I felt they were trying to figure me out. I left with a very bad feeling. When I heard I didn't get the position, I wasn't surprised. Later, I learned that the job had gone to someone who had recently qualified as a PE teacher in a secondary school and had decided to change tack and teach in higher education.

With my usual stubbornness – and Sandro's encouragement – I kept sending off the applications, preparing for the breakthrough to come.

Chapter 25

Show Them Who You Are

One thing that Giff had instilled in her sons was the importance of manifesting the things they wanted out of life. Long before this was a fashionable concept, it was something she taught us to do. She used to say, 'Speak it into existence!'

The same summer that I was working towards further postgraduate study, I was spending time with my younger brother, Simon, at our parents' house when we decided to do a bit of manifesting of our own. Simon had recently graduated from university, and he was completing postgraduate qualifications in mental health.

We'd always been close, but as we got older, our bond had grown stronger, and I considered him not just my brother but my best friend. The two of us had promised to help Dad and Giff by repainting the bedroom we had shared as kids – it probably hadn't had a lick of paint in twenty-five years. As we cleaned the walls, we talked about how our parents had lived in this house our entire lives, and yet they couldn't do anything to the place without permission from the council. The walls in our bedroom were a sort of off-white, so that was the colour we had to repaint them: the same council-approved off-white. Then we got out the rollers and began splashing the paint on the walls, talking about the future. Like me, Simon wanted to transcend our humble beginnings, earning enough money to one day get on the property ladder or even be able to throw away a fiver on a triple cheeseburger from McDonald's with extra bacon, ketchup and mayo without having to think about it.

At lunchtime, we were sitting on the bunk bed eating our twenty chicken wings from the local chicken shop – or as we called them, our 'walking and talking wings'. That was our thing. Whenever we were together, we'd order a box of wings and go for a walk, chewing on chicken and putting the world to rights. On this particular day, we sat in our old bedroom, with paint on our fingers and clothes, so the wings became our 'thinking wings'.

That's when Simon asked me a question: 'What do you want to achieve in the next ten years?'

'What do *you* want to achieve?' I asked him back.

'I don't know,' he said.

'Well, you must have some idea because you just asked me!'

A classic brotherly exchange.

'Okay,' he said. 'Let's write down our goals on Post-its and then we'll show each other.'

We wrote down our goals, smearing the ink with our greasy fingers, and then showed each other what we'd written.

Simon's goals were to have a really good job, find someone to be with, travel a lot and be happy.

On my piece of paper, I wrote that I wanted to help as many people as possible and make sure that all my family and friends were financially secure. I wanted to buy Debs a house. And then the final goal – because it was an audacious and unrealistic dream – was to be an academic at Oxford or Cambridge.

Simon started to laugh at that last one, shaking his head and saying, 'Mate, if there's anyone on God's green earth who can make that happen, it's you, man. You operate on a higher frequency to the rest of us normal people.'

I laughed too. 'No way that's going to happen,' I told him. 'I teach PE. I don't think you can even do PE at Oxbridge!'

But as Giff had always said, 'It costs nothing to dream, and sometimes, the dreamer can even outrun the dream.'

Simon and I took the Post-its and stuck them to the freshly painted wall, where they stayed for a very long time.

~

All in all, that summer of 2012 was a pretty joyful time for me. In my entire adult life to that point, I could count on one hand the number of days when I could've said I'd experienced anything like joy: the day Debs said yes to being my girlfriend, the day I first held T. in my arms and the day I graduated from St Mary's. Beyond that, I had lived most of my life carrying a feeling of sadness inside me – something I always disguised with a grin. But that summer of 2012, dare I say it, I actually felt good.

This was the summer I was asked to be one of eight thousand Olympic torchbearers who carried the flame across the UK and Ireland as part of the lead-up to the 2012 London Olympics. It was a massive honour in recognition of my fundraising work, even if I ran for only about three minutes before passing the torch to the next runner. Crowds of people turned out to cheer on the other torchbearers and me. My family, Sandro, Angela and Mr Trace, were there to support me, with T. on Simon's shoulders holding up a personalised Coca-Cola banner that read 'That's my daddy!'

But this was just one of the experiences that made this summer so special. A lot of it had to do with the concerts I went to during those months. Ever since I was a little kid, when Giff used music to calm me and help me feel connected to the world, music has been my therapy. When I was fourteen years old, Giff took me to one of my first concerts, Ladysmith Black Mambazo at the Royal Albert Hall, and after that, I went to see live music whenever I could afford it. Now that I was involved in raising money for charity, I'd sometimes get free concert tickets through the various causes I was supporting. At home, I kept a running list of every gig I'd ever attended and put the ticket stubs in a box so I'd never forget them.

The next gig – Bruce Springsteen and the E Street Band at Hyde Park on 14 July 2012 – was outstanding. Simon came with me, and although neither of us are obsessive Springsteen fans, there's no doubt the Boss is unparalleled as a live performer. This experience was made even more memorable when Bruce brought out Sir Paul McCartney for the final few songs. I'd never seen McCartney perform live before, so this was truly mind-blowing. They played the classic Beatles songs 'I Saw Her Standing There' and 'Twist and Shout', with Springsteen taking John Lennon's harmonies.

If this wasn't incredible enough, I went back to Hyde Park the very next day to see Paul Simon perform the entire *Graceland* album for its twenty-fifth anniversary. *Graceland* is possibly my favourite album of all time. When it first came out, I was a year old, and it became part of the soundtrack to my childhood.

Whatever you want to say about the politics of that album – whether Paul Simon should have broken the cultural boycott of South Africa to make it – there's no disputing the power of the music. Just the sound of the accordion on the first song on the A-side, 'The Boy in the Bubble', stirs something in me; it penetrates my soul.

When the 1987 *Graceland* concert from Zimbabwe was broadcast on British television, I was two years old, and my dad had the brilliant idea to record it onto a VHS tape. I must have watched that tape almost every week growing up. I knew every chord, every moment of that concert. As I grew older and acquired language, Giff explained to me that the people playing on the record were township musicians who lived in the stranglehold of apartheid, and that this was an album that fused Western songwriting with beats and melodies from our home continent of Africa. This was powerful – a positive, vibrant representation of the Africa that Giff had always described to me.

If the Bruce Springsteen show was impressive then the 2012 *Graceland* concert in Hyde Park is definitely the greatest gig I have ever attended. Debs and Simon came with me. It was supposed to rain, but instead, the sun came out and the whole stage and everyone in the audience was bathed in a warm golden light. Not only was I seeing Paul Simon and legendary South African musicians such as Hugh Masekela, Ladysmith Black Mambazo and Ray Phiri, but there was a surprise guest: Jimmy Cliff. My dad idolised Jimmy Cliff. At one point while Jimmy was on stage, duetting with Paul Simon on 'Many Rivers to Cross', I lay down on the grass and closed my eyes, just like I used to do in those rare moments of freedom as a kid on the

Common, letting the sunshine and the music wash over me. I was dazed with joy.

Later, when the band struck up the chords of 'Diamonds on the Soles of Her Shoes', I felt as if I was experiencing the music within the chambers of my heart. That song meant so much to me. Maybe because of the music, maybe because of the age of the performers – many of them were elderly and unlikely to perform all together again – I was filled with the feeling that comes from knowing that a moment will be fleeting, that it can't last and won't be repeated, so you have to appreciate it in the here and now.

I turned to my brother Simon. 'I don't know if there will ever be a day that will be better than this,' I told him. 'We won't see the like of this day again. It's just about as perfect as a day could get.'

Now and then, Paul Simon would throw in a few Simon and Garfunkel songs. Late in the evening, after the sun had gone down, he played 'The Sound of Silence'. Alone on the stage, with just his acoustic guitar, he sang the legendary first line of the song, greeting the darkness. This was a song about emotional emptiness, loneliness and alienation that Giff had gone to for consolation and support when we were little kids. Darkness was a familiar companion for me too, and in that field in Hyde Park, under the moon and stars, never had the words felt more meaningful. As Paul Simon approached one of the great lyrics in the song, it was as if the crowd recognised themselves in the same ten thousand people he was singing about, and they roared with collective appreciation.

I felt like I was living inside the song as I stood between Debs and Simon, holding them so tightly, the pads of my fingertips in their shoulders, biting down on my lip as I mouthed the lyrics without sound, attempting not to cry. Simon knew exactly how I was feeling and squeezed my hand; Debs, rubbing the back of my neck, understood as well.

~

I didn't think that summer could get any better. But it did.

When I first heard that I'd got an interview for a lecturer position at Liverpool John Moores University, I assumed that it was unlikely to go my way, based on prior experience. I'd been applying to be a lecturer for quite a while now, getting turned down left, right, and centre. There were eighteen candidates including me going up for four posts at Liverpool – the competition was steep. Professor Phil Vickerman was a director in the faculty at the time, and he led the interview, along with his colleagues. A mild-mannered northerner with a side-of-mouth grin, he was someone I warmed to as soon as I met him. He would become a very important person in my life.

It may be hard to believe, but I've always felt that my cognitive delays help me in job interviews. Most people get nervous responding to questions in this setting and answer too fast, tripping over themselves. But because of my slow processing times, I have to absorb each question bit by bit. I'll often repeat it before answering, a lot like I did as a kid with echolalia. Then I'll process the question rather than race to answer it. This ends up working to my advantage, as my answers tend to be very well considered. On this day, the interviewers asked me a lot of technical questions, but I remained composed.

Towards the end of the interview, Phil asked me something off the cuff: 'What have you done that you're really proud of?'

I'd prepared extensively for the interview, scripting it out in my head, but not for this particular question. My first reaction was to think it through and try to guess what he wanted me to say, but instead, I decided to be honest.

'Well, I'm twenty-seven years old, but I've only been reading and writing for less than ten years. Being here in this interview is something I'm very proud of. In some ways, it doesn't matter whether you think I've done a good job today. For me, I feel as if I've won just to be sitting here.'

The people interviewing me looked at me, not sure they'd heard me right.

'What do you mean?' asked Phil.

'I couldn't read or write until I was eighteen, and I didn't learn to speak until I was eleven.'

There was a visible softening in the room.

Then I told them the story of my three-year-old daughter reading the same books that I had learned to read only a few years earlier.

The interview came to a close, and I went around the table and shook everyone's hand, exchanging warm smiles. I felt I had done well, but I didn't necessarily think I'd get the job. As I left the interview, I heard Sandro's advice ringing in my ears: 'Just show them who you are.' I thought to myself, *Well, if nothing else, I've shown them who I am.*

Two days later, I got a phone call. I didn't recognise the number, but I knew it was the area code for Liverpool, so I picked up. It was Phil.

'As you know, Jason, we've had a lot of excellent candidates going up for these positions,' he told me. I braced myself for bad news. 'It was hard to make this decision, and in the end, we decided to give the PE lecturer job to . . . you.'

What?

'You have tremendous potential – we wanted the person who we felt the students would best respond to, and that's you.'

I screamed, 'No way!'

I kept saying thank you to Phil, over and over. After I got off the call, I realised there was a thunderous downpour going on. I was so overjoyed, I ran outside and stood in the rain, letting the water soak me to my skin, arms in the air, thanking God. I started dancing barefoot in the puddles. To have this dream of working in higher education and then to get offered my first position in academia during the best summer of my life was an amazing thing. Once again, I remembered one of Giff's favourite sayings: 'If the dreamer can outrun the dream with the cause being greater than their own need . . . then anything, if not everything, is possible.'

The Olympic torch, the concerts, the job offer. All of this happened within a couple of weeks. But even if none of these events had taken place, I think I still would have experienced a feeling of invincibility that summer, like everything I touched was going to turn to gold. Things were going my way, and I felt I wasn't going to have to struggle and fight, at least for now. Even at the time, I knew it wasn't going to last. It may sound pessimistic, but I also understood that my greatest lessons had been learned in adversity. To paraphrase Bruce Springsteen, glory days will pass you by. The summer would soon be over, and soon enough, the good times would be over too. Maybe you're supposed to have just a sip from the bottle of joy, not take multiple swigs at a time.

Part Five

The Robin

Chapter 26

Strength to Get Through

My life as a university lecturer – my dream job – began. Not only would I be teaching at Liverpool, but I was also going to start my PhD there. Of course, as with anything in my life, the job came with complications. The first major problem was that it wasn't logistically possible for Debs to uproot to Liverpool. Her dad, her sisters and her friends were her world, and more pragmatically, they helped out with the baby. Proximity to them meant everything to her. So we decided that I would commute from London to Liverpool, leaving on Sunday night and coming back home on Friday evening.

I really hated being separated from Debs and T., but what choice did I have? PE within the context of higher education is sort of a niche academic subject; there aren't a lot of universities in London with PE courses, as most of them are in the north of England. During the week in Liverpool, I stayed in a tiny, dingy flat in the Sefton Park area, sleeping on a blow-up mattress. Before long, I was able to move to a much nicer house on Penny Lane, the road made famous by the Beatles song. A few nights after I moved in, however, the police knocked on the door because they'd had a report from the neighbours that a Black man had broken into the building.

The National Express bus from London to Liverpool took five to six hours each way, and because I made that journey once a week, it became an all-too-familiar slog. I could have taken the train, which would have been much quicker, but the bus was an economic necessity. My salary was decent, but between rent on two places, student loan debt, living expenses and nursery fees, there wasn't a penny to spare. National Express buses are cheaper than the train for a reason: rarely do you get to your destination on time (usually because of a pile-up en route). The journey often felt like it would never end, and it usually featured a crying baby at the back and someone next to you breaking wind into the already stale air. To give myself something to look forward to, I'd always treat myself to a cheeky Burger King double XL triple bacon cheeseburger and a bottle of water at the much-anticipated service station stop on my way home on Friday nights.

As the countryside unfurled itself outside the window, I used the hours of travel to work on my PhD thesis. I had a small ThinkPad laptop that I would place on the little plastic table that drops down from the seat in front, and I'd peck away at the keyboard with two fingers, the slowest typer in the world. My thesis was on the subject of reflective practice and peer mentoring among student teachers. I'd been a student teacher myself and had written about this area a bit when I'd done my master's at St Mary's. The topic was a strategic choice, selected to play to my academic strengths given my modest levels of ability at that stage.

The best part of this new adventure was that Liverpool was my kind of place: full of hard-working people, a city built on love and community. I'm a big fan of the music that's come out of the northwest as well, not just Oasis, but obviously the Beatles, the Verve, Cast, the Stone Roses, Inspiral Carpets and the Happy Mondays, to name a few. Meanwhile, the students I taught were great: mainly white, working-class people who seemed to be fascinated by me and my manner. I think for nearly all of them, this was their first experience of being taught by a Black person. We got along really well. Some people feel they need to perform in front of a classroom, but I saw teaching as an extension of myself; I didn't put on any airs and graces, and the students responded well to that. At Liverpool, I got into the habit of learning three to five things about every student in my classes. What was their favourite breakfast cereal? What was their middle name? Which area did they grow up in? I have an excellent memory, and when I dropped these details about their lives into the conversation, it showed them I cared and endeared me to them. The people – the exchange of knowledge and construction of ideas with students – remains the best part of academia for me.

If it were just about my students, I would have stayed at Liverpool a lot longer, but after thirteen months, I had to come back to London. My father's chronic neck problems paired with sciatica and other health ailments finally caught up with him. Though he was only middle-aged, he was in agonising pain. Giff was also experiencing some health issues, and it scared me. I needed to be closer to them to take care of them.

~

Soon after I came back from Liverpool, I got a job teaching at a local university as a lecturer, when something happened that can be described as either coincidence or fate, depending on how you think about these things. It was an otherwise ordinary day at the beginning of the academic year, and I walked into the lecture hall to teach a class of about eighty students. This was a PE elective module, so there were people there who were studying all kinds of sports-related subjects. Right away, I thought I recognised two of the students seated in the third row. Who were they? Had I taught them before? I racked my brain. Then I went through the class register to familiarise myself with their names, and that's when I realised who they were. They were a bit older than the last time I'd seen them, but their faces were ingrained in my memory.

I was about to teach a cohort that included two of the four people who had brutally beaten me at a bus stop when I was eighteen years old.

I did my best to start my lecture, but it takes a lot of effort to concentrate on speaking while being reminded of the time you got the living shit kicked out of you. After the class, I stood in the door, shaking the hands of each student before they left, something I've always done. As the two men approached, I asked if I could talk to them now that the lecture was over.

'Have we met before?' I began.

'Do you know who we are?' one of them asked in return.

'I think I do,' I replied.

The two men had recognised my name when they signed up for the module, and they knew exactly who I was. Since the last time we'd met, they told me, they had completely turned their lives around. When I made my impact statement, appealing for leniency, they explained, this had changed the course of their lives. They had continued with their education, as I had hoped they would, and they had also started coaching and mentoring other young kids who were at risk of getting involved in gang crime or violence.

'After the case was closed, we weren't allowed to contact you,' one of them said. 'But we really wanted to say thank you for your forgiveness, so maybe it's fate that we're getting to meet you now.'

Both of them gave me a huge hug, which I returned.

The two men remained in my class for the rest of that semester, proving themselves to be brilliant and diligent students. After that, we stayed in touch, and over the years, they often asked me to write job and character references for them, and I would happily oblige. About three or four years after we met in the lecture hall, one of them became a father. He asked me to be the godfather to his child, and I gratefully accepted. That beating had a profound effect on my life, in that it gave me my epilepsy, but it also had a profound effect on those two young men. It set them on a path to redemption, giving them a second chance. And meeting in that lecture hall, in much sweeter circumstances than we had at the bus stop, gave me the kind of closure I didn't know I needed.

Chapter 27

Night Shift

After I returned to London, I looked at our finances and realised that what I was making as a lecturer just wasn't enough. Money was a constant worry. We had our housing costs, our student debts and childcare, plus the expense of my doctoral studies, and the price of admission for professional conferences and to do research, both part of being an academic. This all had to come out of my own pockets – there was no financial support to be found. Debs and I also wanted to get married, so we needed to save for our wedding. In the past, I would have gone straight to Rileys to make some extra cash playing snooker or pool, but the entry fees to tournaments had gone up substantially, and it had become a much riskier prospect. I couldn't afford to pay sixty pounds or more to enter a tournament and then potentially lose in the first round – we wouldn't be able to put food on the table. Once, I decided to 'borrow' the two hundred pounds that Debs and I had saved in a kitty in the kitchen, thinking that I could double it by playing for money at Rileys. I lost big time. By rights, the guy I was playing should have given me the opportunity to win my money back, but when he decided not to do that, I had to come home empty-handed. I remember walking around the block for almost an hour before I got up the courage to go inside and tell Debs what had happened. When I did, she was beside herself. Two hundred pounds was a small fortune to us at that time. Needless to say, I slept on the sofa that night. Rileys was not going to be the answer to our financial woes.

I was going to have to get another job to close the gap. Because I was already working five days a week, I knew that if I wanted to earn additional income, it would have to be at night. My parents had both worked night shifts over the years – my dad on boats as a chef, and Giff as a residential nurse. Conveniently, I've been an insomniac since my late teens, so my body was used to going without a lot of sleep. I got a job at Sainsbury's supermarket working the night shift, starting at 11 p.m. and finishing at 5 a.m.

I've never suffered from being proud – I'd learned how to work hard and survive from my mum and dad – but even so, working at Sainsbury's was a humbling experience. As it turns out, a bustling daytime supermarket feels very different under strip lighting in the early hours of the morning, when its empty aisles are eerily quiet. Many of my co-workers were also struggling to pay bills and keep a roof over their heads. We were all exhausted.

One of those co-workers was a man called Sam, and my conversations with him kept me going through the long hours of the night. He was a Black mixed-race man with a heavy beard and a wiry, triangular torso. Well over six feet tall, he was very good at putting stuff on the top shelf for me. Sam had lived a hard life. By his own account, he'd made mistakes and abused alcohol, which had cost him his children, his family and his marriage. Working at Sainsbury's was part of his rehabilitation;

he was trying to make something of himself so that he would be able to see his kids again. Like me, he worked around the clock, stocking shelves by night and as a refuse collector by day (or as he put it: 'I collect the bins, Jase'). Working with Sam, who was funny and wise, made the time go by quicker. In the middle of the shift, we were entitled to a short break, and we'd go and help ourselves to some of the food past its sell-by date in the stockroom. Sam would often talk to me about the regrets he'd had in his life, and about how he'd always been too afraid to chase his dreams. He wanted to be rich, to be his own boss, with his own company. Sainsbury's was very far from his ideal, but it was still a step up from the dark hole he'd been in before embarking on his journey to sobriety.

'Necessity arrests ambition, my friend,' he told me. 'Never let fear or necessity be your master, or you'll end up like me – full of regret and sometimes bitter.'

Sam's words struck a chord, perhaps because he reminded me a bit of my parents whose lives were also dictated by necessity and hard work, and who had to do what they could to survive in a sometimes hostile environment to get me and my brothers ahead.

'Jason, I want you to listen to me,' Sam said. 'Do you know the difference between you and me?'

'No, Sam. Tell me.'

'I have to do this out of necessity, to put bread on the table. I've put my dreams aside in order to make ends meet. I'm paralysed by fear. But I see something in you: you're fearless. Yes, you're having to do this job now, but one day you'll scale Mount Everest, whether anyone thinks you can or not. Because the difference between you and me is that you genuinely believe you can make it, while I didn't always believe I could . . . That's the fear, mate.'

For as long as we worked together, Sam insisted that the supermarket job was just a temporary stop along my path. He encouraged me to keep going, not to give up. At a time in my life when I felt tired, physically weak and vulnerable, he helped strengthen my resolve.

While I was putting in my hours on the supermarket floor, I also managed to get an extra job with a private cleaning company, working a shift from 5.30 a.m. to 7.30 a.m. This job paid marginally more per hour than the Sainsbury's gig, which was minimum wage. After I finished at Sainsbury's and the cleaning job, I'd come home, shower, and head over to the university to start teaching at 9.30 a.m. Sleep became something that took place in transit between jobs (and sometimes in my office at the university for the briefest of intermissions). Three to four days a week, I worked day and night. I rarely saw my family and friends. Often, I was on the verge of collapse because of sheer exhaustion. As long as I kept moving, I could stay awake, but the worst situation for me was sitting down in meetings, because my head would start nodding, and I'd have to fight to keep my eyes open. My body was crying out to be allowed to rest. At least I could sleep a bit on weekends, but not for long because that was when I helped my parents, worked on my thesis, graded papers and if I was lucky, spent some time with Debs and T.

~

In the midst of this schedule, on 9 May 2014, my twenty-ninth birthday, Debs and I got married. The ceremony took place on a beautiful spring day at a hotel in Guildford. T. was six by then and served as our bridesmaid. Somewhere in her mind, she saw this as *her* wedding, as if she were getting married to Debs and me, which was very sweet and made me chuckle. Sandro and Ben, aka Soulman (a dear friend), were my best men, and my brothers and three close friends of mine, Amrit, Matty and Mark (known as Vicar), were my groomsmen. Mr Trace from Southfields did one of the readings: the lyrics to Jimi Hendrix's 'Little Wing'. I wore a custom-made navy double-breasted mohair suit from Peckham Rye, a tailor that used to be on Newburgh Street just off Carnaby Street. I had told the guys there about my passion for tailoring, and they had seen that I was a working-class lad with a dream, so they let me pay for my suit in small instalments over an extended period. Debs wore a beautiful white sequined wedding dress.

But this major event in our lives was quickly outdone the following day, when Debs revealed that she was pregnant with baby number two. When we found out we were having a boy, we were over the moon. One boy and one girl. It felt meant to be, a complete set.

To add to the milestones, on 15 May 2014, I went up for a job interview as a PE specialist at Leeds Beckett University. I was ploughing through my PhD thesis by then and expected to finish by mid-to late 2015.

During the interview for the Leeds job, they told me they were only supposed to hire people who already had PhDs. Fortunately, they were willing to make an exception for me, but only if I could complete my thesis within my first year of employment. That meant submitting my PhD by August 2015. Before I knew it, I was back on the National Express, this time for a five-hour journey from London to Leeds, followed by a five-hour journey home at the end of the week, my two fingers pecking away at the PhD on the ThinkPad.

Being a university lecturer had been my dream, but to be honest, the reality was becoming more of a nightmare. T. would get so upset whenever I left to go up to Leeds. Debs – with a swelling belly – would stand on the doorstep with T. perched on her hip and watch me walk down the hill until I disappeared around the corner, both of them waving through tears as they said goodbye. I had a family, but during the week, I was totally alone. I missed them all the time. On the bus, I'd often have to hold back tears of my own. Every day meant pushing myself beyond the limit, physically and mentally, like Rocky biting down on his gumshield and going one more round. In Leeds, I started working at a local Sainsbury's branch, relieved to be on nights so that my students didn't have to see their lecturer stacking shelves during the day. The cleaning company had an outpost in Leeds as well, so I was able to pick up some more shifts there too.

Often, I found myself praying to God for an easier life. But when I told Giff about my prayers one weekend, hoping to find a sympathetic ear, she had a very different reaction.

'Jason!' she told me, in a tone that betrayed her dismay. 'Never pray for an easy life! Always, always pray for the strength to get through it. Do you understand? God doesn't give you what you can't handle. A difficult life is a blessing. Nothing good lasts forever, and nothing bad lasts forever. Don't take the coward's way out and say that prayer ever again.'

So I stopped praying for an easier life and continued working day and night, getting the bus to Leeds and then coming back to London again, week after week after week. Survival mode and precarity were all I'd ever known, so I just kept putting one foot in front of the other. I was a street fighter, a scrapper, someone well-practised at holding on for dear life. I'd find myself muttering the lyrics to the Queen song 'The Show Must Go On' under my breath, reminding myself to never give in and face adversity with a grin.

Once again, my co-workers on the night shift came to my rescue whenever I was losing my morale. At my cleaning job, I worked with an amazing woman named Marcela. She was Colombian, in her twenties, and by day, she was studying for a business degree, using the money she made from cleaning to help pay her fees. Her ambitions were to finish her degree and have her own company. She was diminutive in stature, but her presence filled every room, whether we were cleaning a massive open-plan office or a tiny toilet stall. The funniest thing about Marcela was that she always came to work in power suits with pencil skirts or smart dresses with high-heeled shoes. This puzzled me because obviously those nice clothes were going to get ruined on a job that used industrial-strength bleach. So one day, I took it upon myself to ask her why she wore such nice outfits on the job.

She laughed and said, 'Do you like them, Jason?'

'Yes, you look amazing. But I'm worried your clothes will get ruined – and you're wearing heels!'

'Do you want to know why I dress this way?' she asked.

'Yes, I do,' I replied.

'The reason I wear them is because I won't do this job forever. I'm going to be a CEO of a major company one day, so I will dress like this every day until I am one step closer to my destiny. I am honouring my ambition by dressing this way.'

Marcela had so much confidence that she would achieve her goals. That, for me, was powerful; her outlook had a profound effect on me. Our job was in many ways unglamorous – we were cleaning toilet bowls on our hands and knees, me in overalls and Chuck Taylors and Marcela in her dresses and heels – but she had a vision that was embodied by the clothes she wore. After that, I followed Marcela's lead, buying one item of clothing a month to honour my ambition and present myself as a good academic. The only difference was that I didn't wear my clothes to the cleaning job – I kept them in suit bags in London. Even so, both Marcela and Sam left a profound and indelible imprint on me at a time when I often struggled to find the will to go on. It was a period that lasted for two and a half very long years.

Chapter 28

Feed the Faith, Starve the Fear

Our son, N., was born in January 2015, a healthy, beautiful boy. We asked Sandro to be one of the godfathers, and he accepted, honoured and delighted to be asked. N. was such a funny, smiley baby, a real character from the beginning and great with people. Our family was complete. I was a much more confident parent with N. than I had been with T., Debs having already coached me on the mechanics of parenthood. The rest I left to feeling and instinct. Even so, there was no doubt that our son came into the world during a time of intense pressure for me.

The clock was ticking. I needed to submit my PhD thesis in May in order for it to be reviewed before August 2015, the deadline for it to be approved so it could go to the oral defence, commonly referred to as a viva (short for 'viva voce'). In a viva, you have to sit in front of a panel of examiners and answer questions about your contribution to the field, after which your thesis is judged. The deadline had been made clear to me the year prior; I had to pass my PhD by the end of September 2015 if I wanted to keep my job at Leeds. I had told myself I wasn't allowed to shave until I got my PhD: This was a big incentive for me, because I much prefer to be clean-shaven. By the time

N. was born, I had less than nine months to finish my thesis and my beard was already quite impressively long; meanwhile, I was still teaching during the day, working night shifts, travelling back and forth to Leeds and writing my thesis on the bus. My lifelong insomnia continued, as always, but with one significant change. Whenever I was home with N. and he fell asleep on my chest, snuggled up in my ever-growing beard, I'd fall asleep too. I'd never been able to nap before, so this was quite the development. My weekends in London were busy, however. Giff had recently been diagnosed with glaucoma, and her impaired vision meant that she needed more help with appointments and day-to-day life; I was there for her as much as I could be, sometimes at the expense of time with Debs and the kids.

Then, in the months leading up to my deadline, I began to notice problems with my own sight. I was finding it difficult to focus – my vision was blurry, my balance was affected and to exacerbate it all, something was off with my hearing. My good ear wasn't working as well as it had in the past. Initially, I dismissed these symptoms as the result of exhaustion and lack of sleep. But then a friend of mine at work noticed that I kept losing my balance and jumbling my words. At first, she thought I was coming to work drunk, but I don't drink and she knew that. So what was going on? I contacted my doctor, who referred me to a neurologist. I got an appointment right away, which was a sure sign that the symptoms were serious. When I went back to find out the results of my MRI and CT scans, the doctor's stiff body language was a giveaway that all was not well.

'The problems you have been experiencing are because of a small tumour near the base of your brain,' he told me, a pensive look on his face. 'The tumour is pressing against your pituitary gland. This seems to be why your balance is slightly affected, and why you are having a bit of trouble with your sight.' I didn't know what to say and may have even laughed. For everything I'd been given, for everything I'd had to give up and as hard as I'd tried, here I was, facing another test of my mettle. I desperately needed things to go my way, and instead, I was getting a diagnosis of a brain tumour while on a temporary contract for a job. I felt I could not afford to take time off work. Not only that, but I would lose my job altogether if I didn't make my deadline and gain my PhD by the end of September.

Thankfully, the doctor did offer me what felt like an injection of hope: 'This kind of small tumour can be removed through minimally invasive surgery.'

We didn't know yet if it was cancerous, but the doctor cautiously emphasised that this type of growth is very often benign. And he pointed out that I was young, fit and healthy, which gave me a reason to remain optimistic. I decided to focus on that. The most important thing was to stay calm and positive.

I decided not to tell my family about the tumour until I knew exactly what was going on; it would only worry them. But even though my preference was to keep things to myself, I knew I had to tell someone, so I called up Sandro and asked him to meet me for lunch. He immediately guessed something was wrong because he was usually the one who initiated our get-togethers. Without asking another question, he picked me up in his grey saloon car and drove me to our favourite Italian spot in Tooting. When I told him about the tumour over lunch, he just looked at me. 'Oh, Jason,' he said, getting up to give me a giant hug.

After a second consultation, the specialist reassured me that the tumour was 'almost certainly' benign, and I was able to breathe a giant sigh of relief. The doctor explained that while this was a manageable situation, some standard postsurgical tissue analysis would be done to ensure that all was definitively well. The tumour would have to be removed soon or it may continue to affect my visual function. The neurosurgeon wanted to schedule the surgery immediately, but I asked for a little more time so I could complete my thesis. We collectively agreed to wait.

Once again, I remembered Giff's words to always pray to God for the strength to get through it. I prayed feverishly, I'll admit, with a tiny bit of anger and annoyance directed at God, muttering under my breath in the hope he wouldn't hear me. A futile exercise, given the omnipresent nature of the Almighty.

At the end of July, I submitted the thesis, hoping it was good enough to get me to the last round. I just wanted to hear that final bell. Whether I was going to win or lose, it would be enough to know that I had taken it to the limit and given it my best. To extend the Rocky reference, there were times when I just wanted someone to punch me on the chin and put me to sleep so it could all be over. But in the absence of that knockout blow, I had no choice but to fight on.

The priority now that the thesis had been resubmitted was to have the endoscopic transsphenoidal surgery to remove the tumour. I needed to recover in time for the oral defence in September. The viva had to take place by 29 September to meet the deadline of securing my full-time employment. In August, the surgery went ahead and was successful, and the tumour was confirmed to be benign. Now I had less than five weeks to recover and prepare for the viva. Generally, it takes four to six weeks to recover from a surgery like this one, so yet again, my back was up against the wall.

Ten days into my recovery, I was gingerly going about my day-to-day business at work when I definitely should have been resting. Suddenly, I collapsed in a heap on the office floor. This wasn't one of my usual seizures. I couldn't move my face or arms; it was terrifying. I was taken to the hospital, where the doctors told me I'd had a transient ischemic attack (TIA) – a 'mini-stroke'.

There were only three weeks until the viva, and now I was dealing with a new problem: I couldn't access my short-term memory. When I'd try to recall something I'd read or written, I'd draw a blank. To be able to defend your thesis in a viva, you need to remember everything that went into it – all your sources, the statements you've made and your reasons for making them. You have to justify every word. That's the point of an oral examination. But I couldn't remember anything. I knew I wasn't going to be able to sit there in the viva, leafing through the hundreds of pages of my thesis trying to find a particular reference or sentence; I'd look like an idiot. I needed to somehow commit everything to memory again, and I had only three weeks to do it.

I'd worked on my thesis for over thirty months, and now I was reading it as if for the first time. I kept trying to memorise the information it contained, but my brain wasn't responding properly. I spent the three weeks before the exam studying, cramming, writing copious notes, trying to prepare for every line of questioning, but I couldn't make the information stick. After all this effort, was this how it was going to end? The one thing Sandro and I had kept at bay for over a decade was fear.

'Feed the faith and starve the fear' was one of Sandro's favourite mantras, borrowed from the legendary hall of famer boxer Marvelous Marvin Hagler paraphrasing the Bible. But I was all out of faith, and my fear was getting fed day and night, to the point of gluttony. I was becoming terrified of failure. It was the worst time to have a crisis of self-belief, but that's exactly what was happening to me.

Sandro and I had been focused on this goal since 2006. It had been nearly ten years since I'd first told him I wanted to get my PhD, and he wasn't going to give up on me now. In the week before the viva, he kept encouraging me to focus on the aspects I could control, which meant being as prepared as possible. 'Failure to prepare . . . prepare to fail.' Another one of his mantras.

I had started my PhD at Liverpool John Moores University, so that's where the viva was taking place. Sandro was going to go with me. I knew that I couldn't get through it without him. We drove up a day early because Sandro insisted that we needed extra time to prepare. That morning, I decided it was time to shave off my extensive beard, relieved to be clean-shaven again after nearly twelve months. Sandro picked me up after work in his car and we hit the road. At this point, it felt as if Sandro and I had lived a thousand lives together. I considered him a father figure, even if he preferred to think of himself as my cool older brother. No matter what, we brought out the best in each other, although Sandro did sometimes get the short end of the stick when it came to me.

The next day, we went for a walk down by the docks, Sandro taking in the city that had taken me in. The sun was shining as we passed the Liver Building with its two mythical liver birds looking out across the city and the River Mersey. I showed him around some of my old haunts: the Albert Dock, the International Slavery Museum, the Cavern Club, and the British Music Experience. After we finished our tour, we made our way to Liverpool John Moores, where I'd arranged for us to meet with my other mentor, Phil Vickerman, affectionately known to me as Big Phil. We met up at Big Phil's office, where my viva was going to take place the next day. It was a good chance to get myself accustomed to the setting. As I'd predicted, Phil and Sandro got on like long-lost friends, with Big Phil exuding his usual warmth. Like Sandro, he's someone who believes in harnessing the potential of people, and my two mentors recognised that quality in each other.

I suggested that we take a walk over to Liverpool Cathedral because Sandro had never been there before. I knew that this was where my graduation ceremony was going to be held, should I somehow manage to make it through the viva the next day. Everyone agreed that going there for inspiration was a great idea, so we made the short walk over.

Liverpool Cathedral is the largest cathedral in Britain, and stepping inside truly takes your breath away. The stained-glass windows cast shadows across the nave thanks to the sunlight streaming in from the outside, and the arched ceilings reach to impossible heights. Looking up almost gives you vertigo, the place is so enormous. As the three of us entered, a cordial priest with a thick Liverpool accent welcomed us, telling us about the sermons that were scheduled for later that day. Giff had always told me, 'If you ever meet a person of God, ask them to pray for you,' and so that's what I did.

'If it's not too much trouble, Father,' I asked, 'could you bless me with a prayer. I have an important exam tomorrow, and to be honest, I could do with all the help I can get.'

The priest asked Sandro, Phil and me to join hands, then he placed his hand on my head, asking the Lord above to bless me in all my endeavours, but particularly the challenge I would be facing tomorrow. He finished with the Lord's Prayer and then said, 'Amen,' to which we collectively replied, 'Amen.'

Later that night, Sandro and I lay in our beds at the hotel. We were sharing a room with two separate beds so that Sandro could keep an eye on me in case, heaven forbid, I had another TIA or seizure or God only knew what. After we switched out the lights, I could sense that something was happening that hadn't happened before. For some reason, I could tell that Sandro was scared for me.

'How do you think it will go tomorrow?' I asked him.

'As your mother always says, Jason, I don't have the gift of knowing what tomorrow will bring.'

I lay there, unsatisfied with his answer, until Sandro spoke again. 'But whatever happens, I could not be prouder of you,' he told me. 'It's incredible – from where you started when I first met you to where you are today. No one would believe it. We're all proud of you, and I love you. Now sleep well.'

In the twelve years I'd known Sandro, he'd praised me only a handful of times (you really had to earn his praise) and he'd certainly never told me he loved me before. His was the school of tough love, where love is implicit in the expectation of greatness, because that's the bare minimum you should expect of yourself.

His words meant so much to me as a result. 'I love you too. Thank you for everything,' I told him. 'Okay, I'll try to sleep.'

Instead, I was awake all night, thinking about everything. Giff and all her words of wisdom occupied my thoughts. I thought about how hard she'd struggled for me to make it to this point. I remembered the first time I met Debs and the first time I held my kids in my arms, not to mention all those hours writing the thesis on the National Express bus. I recalled all the people who had absolutely no belief that I would amount to anything, and Giff's uncompromising certainty that I would do something great. I was trying to drum up a sense of pride, but the overwhelming feeling was fear again. Not for the first time, I thought of the woman in Brazil who had prophesied that my life would be filled with great things, but difficult ones as well. If I failed the viva, I would automatically be made redundant, which would be very difficult indeed. I didn't sleep a wink.

In the morning, I found an iron and pressed my brown herringbone trousers and the light blue-and-white Ralph Lauren twill shirt that Debs had bought me for my birthday some years back. I may not have felt the part, but I certainly looked it. Then I packed my bag and read through my thesis and notes one last time, terrified that no matter how hard I tried, the words just wouldn't lodge in my head. Also into my bag went a copy of the prayer that Giff had given me before I left London, to give me strength.

Sandro and I went down for breakfast. I don't usually eat during the day, so I just drank apple juice. Sandro had eggs, bacon, sausage and horribly burnt toast. Then we made our way to John Moores, getting there an hour and a half before the viva because Sandro didn't want us to be late. Just as we were arriving, Big Phil texted me to say that, sadly, he was ill and wasn't going to be able to attend the viva. I took this as a bad omen, even putting it down to accidentally walking under a ladder the day before. My fear and anxiety increased. Sandro and I sat down in the lobby, and Phil's assistant, Anne, who was a wonderful human being, brought out some tea and biscuits as a kind of consolation prize. Even if I drank tea, which I don't, I wouldn't have been able to swallow it. I couldn't sit still. Instead, I walked up and down the lobby, palms sweating, horrible knots in my stomach. Like a little kid, all I wanted was to go back to Clapham to be at home with Giff. I was already anticipating the catastrophe of failure. I chastised myself: *Why did you dare to dream in the first place? If you don't dream, then you don't fail!* My usual positive mindset had vanished, replaced by negative thoughts. It was so unlike me.

'I have a bad feeling about today,' I told Sandro. 'Body on fire, head in the fridge,' he reminded me.

Another favourite saying, this one borrowed from the English Rugby World Cup-winning player Will Greenwood. 'Now is the time to draw on your legendary cool, calm and collected temperament, Jason.'

The defence of my thesis became an even greater challenge than I could have ever imagined. And it wasn't only because of the memory loss.

The two examiners – I'll call them Professor 1 and Professor 2 – were sitting on the far side of the conference table as I walked in. As I remember it, they barely looked up from their notes. Neither of them got up to greet me or shake my hand. In fact, they hardly managed a nod to acknowledge my existence. Two people, about to decide my fate. I took a seat opposite them, clasping the twenty-five pages of notes that I had brought with me to compensate for the memory loss, plus Giff's prayer. I smudged the ink with my sweaty palms as I smoothed them out on the table in front of me. I hadn't told the examiners about my brain surgery only weeks before because I feared that the viva could be postponed.

The examination began. There was no preamble, no chit-chat – just immediate questioning of my work. For a PhD thesis, it's critical to make an original contribution to the field or meaningfully advance existing research. My offering fell into the latter category. While I didn't expect my belly to be tickled, I wasn't prepared for what appeared to me to be immediate hostility. This set the tone for what would be an excruciating afternoon.

I'd brought a glass of water with me and had finished it within the first five minutes, but even so, in my nervousness, my hand kept reaching for the empty glass so I could take imaginary sips from the remaining beads of water.

I can only imagine how out of my depth I looked. I'd been told that if a viva lasts more than ninety minutes, it's generally not a good sign. We were seventy minutes in, and after more than an hour of verbal jousting, my brain was dead. Nothing was registering. I asked for a toilet break so I could gather my thoughts. When I went back through the lobby, where Sandro was waiting, he could tell immediately that I was in a bad way. He told me to go and splash some cold water on my face. 'And don't forget to read Giff's prayer,' he said.

The prayer Giff had given me is very important to me; it appears in the last scene of one of our favourite films, *The Greatest Story Ever Told*. It draws on several Bible verses, and here's what it says:

> Go now and teach all nations. Make it your first care to love one another ... Without the asking do not fret then over tomorrow, leave tomorrow to fret over its own needs. For today, today's troubles are enough. And lo, I am with you always, even until the end of the world.

She'd also included a line from Philippians, which read: 'I can do all this through Him, who gives me strength.'

After I splashed my face with water and said the prayer, I stood leaning on the sink and looking in the mirror for what seemed like an eternity but was probably a matter of minutes. The water and prayer had not helped; in fact, I was now in the middle of a full-blown panic attack. I could barely catch my breath, terrified.

Sandro who had been waiting for me outside, came into the room and immediately saw that I was hyperventilating. 'I'm going to do something to you now because I love you,' said Sandro sternly. 'I'm going to slap you across the face to calm you down.'

And that's what he did. I felt his hand land across my cheek with a loud slap. Stunned, I reached my hand to my stinging face and found myself miraculously able to breathe again.

'I know you're scared,' Sandro told me taking me by the shoulders, 'but I also know you can do this, Jason. You have already achieved the impossible by being here. One last push, and then we go home.'

He embraced me. I looked back at him, knowing he was right. Something in me shifted. My frantic thinking stopped, and I managed to come back to a place of calmness. I told myself then, *All right, if you're gonna fail, you won't fail because of fear.*

The viva became a tale of two halves. In the first half, I'd allowed myself to be flattened, my efforts minimised; I hadn't trusted myself. But I went back in for the second half completely focused and determined. I reassured myself with positive self-talk: *No fear, no fear, no fear.* It was as if I felt an angel beside me, holding my hand. I remembered that I was the expert in the area I was researching, as is the case for most people in this situation. When I most needed it, my self-belief came back. I was more assured in my answers and more engaged in the cut and thrust of scholarly debate. Nearly sixty minutes later, the viva came to a close. The examiners asked me to leave the room while they deliberated. I met Sandro back in the lobby, and he gave me the biggest hug and kissed my cheek.

'I am proud of you no matter what. No matter what.' We waited for what seemed like a very long time. Eventually, I was called back in. Sandro accompanied me. 'Congratulations, Dr Arday,' said Professor 1. 'You have passed with minor amendments.'

I burst into tears out of sheer exhaustion and relief. I had been in this viva for over two hours. And to this day, I don't know exactly how I got through it. Even with Sandro's encouragement and Giff's guidance through prayer, I had been in that room on my own. There were moments when I let fear get the best of me, but I had found a way.

I had three months to make the changes they'd asked for, and I finished them within no time. I had done it, but instead of feeling relieved, I was left with a horrible, hollow sensation, as if I had only barely crossed the finish line. I was so disappointed with how the viva had unfolded. Sandro kept reminding me, 'It doesn't matter whether someone gets over the finish line by an inch or a mile, the most important thing is to cross the line. You have done that, Jason.'

When my PhD certificate arrived in the post, I didn't even open it. Weeks later, Debs sat down with me and opened it for me. She talked to me about the person she'd first met, who couldn't read or write, and about this same person who was sitting in front of her and had just earned his PhD. How far I'd come. She showed me the certificate and reminded me of my achievements. I sobbed on her shoulder. The pressure and strain had been intense; there was never any margin for error, just a lot of sacrifice. I'd thought I would feel overjoyed at achieving a goal I'd had since I was an undergraduate, but it was the opposite: I didn't feel like I'd achieved anything. I only felt a sense of emptiness about the whole experience.

Debs made a big deal out of my graduation, booking a hotel in Liverpool and bringing our families together for an amazing meal the night before. The next day, I stood in the cathedral for the ceremonial collection of my PhD. With my job at Leeds Beckett secured, maybe we could move on with our lives.

Chapter 29

Snakes and Ladders

Now that I had my PhD, I'd naively assumed that things would get easier for me. When I mentioned this to a colleague, he laughed. 'The PhD gets you to the door of academia, but it doesn't give you the key.'

As it turned out, he was exactly right. I still had to publish, bring in grants, get my work out there and have a public impact so that I could get invited to conferences and deliver keynotes, making a name for myself and my work. But how to pull this off? I didn't even know my stripper from my paint, to paraphrase Peter Gabriel. Trying to navigate the world of academia was a confusing thing, to say the least. Most of the time, it felt like all my colleagues had a map and directions that no one wanted to give me. I'd ask questions like, 'So how do you become a professor?' 'Which grants should I apply for?' 'How do you get funding for your research?' And they'd tell me, 'Oh, it's different for everyone,' or offer some other vague response. I'd later come to learn that this was referred to as 'gatekeeping', and I was finding out the hard way that academia is competitive, and people tend to withhold the secrets of how to advance.

Despite this, I was determined to figure out where I fit in

the British academic landscape, what my contribution would be and how I could make a difference. I knew I wanted to create a body of work looking at access to higher education for Black students. I wanted to study the mental health impacts facing Black academics trying to move forward in their careers (a subject that was obviously deeply personal). I also knew I wanted to do solutions-focused work. One of the things about most academic disciplines is that they tend to be founded in theory and sometimes neglect the practice element. But because I had a PE background, I'd been taught from day one about praxis: the practical application of theory. As a result, I was constantly asking myself, *What are the practical implications or interventions that we can use to make a difference here?* I didn't only want to highlight how things were broken – I was motivated to fix them.

While my PE background was the source of many insights, it also posed a problem: the research into race and education that I wanted to explore fell squarely within the study of sociology. The mandate from my department was that they wanted me to focus on sports-related research – anything I did outside of that would have to be on my own time. But I wasn't going to let that directive, or my lack of training as a sociologist, stop me. After all, I had expertise born of lived experience. I knew what it felt like to try to navigate an educational system that I didn't understand, and that wasn't designed for me. And now that I was trying to make a career for myself as a young academic of colour, that experience could also feed into my research.

Even without the 'right' background, I had a hunch that I already thought like a sociologist. People fascinated me. As a non-verbal child, I'd learned to be hypervigilant, alert to all the ways that people conceal and reveal themselves in their interactions. I had been quietly observing for years, banking a lot of information, and now that could be put to good use in my new field of study.

I soon learned that one of the key tools in the discipline was the interview. Sociologists use interviews to conduct research, collect data and understand why certain groups of people – and the individuals within those groups – behave the way to do. The interview format suited me really well because I was good at asking people questions and adept at listening to answers. I was able to glean information not just from their words but also their entire demeanour, everything from facial expressions to gestures and posture. As I began to do sociology research, I realised that when I was interviewing people, I already had the skills I needed. It was about finding out what made people tick, the personal meanings behind their actions, and I could do that.

Like many people who are dyslexic, however, I still had to work very hard to find ways to compensate for my shortcomings as a reader and a writer. Sometimes it could take me as much as an hour to read and absorb a single page of academic text, so I started looking around for other ways to fill in the gaps in my understanding. Remembering that Giff had used the television successfully when I was a kid, I began watching lectures online, as well as documentaries that were relevant to my field of study, and this worked well for me in terms of helping me to acquire additional knowledge without having to deal solely with the written word.

When it came time to dip my toe in the water of publishing sociology reports and papers, I'd often work on my drafts and apply for grants at night, racing through my shelf-stacking duties at Sainsbury's so that I had time to do my homework in the back room before my shift ended. Sam would often cover for me on the shop floor so I wouldn't get into trouble as I sat tapping away on my ThinkPad. Writing has never come easily to me, and I don't expect it to ever get easier, but I found that starting with a lyric from one of my favourite songs helps me click into gear. During this period of intense study, my monotropic thinking style aided me as well. My brain, with its ability to hyperfocus on a single subject (or a handful of subjects), allowed me to stay in a state of studious flow for hours, pouring all my intellectual energies into my chosen topic.

That was the plus side. The negative side was that my brain never seemed to want to process information as quickly as I needed it to, and this frustrated me as I tried to put together academic papers, and in my professional interactions in general. The feeling of not being fast enough permeates my work life to this day, and it makes things really difficult in a modern world that's all about instant communication and gratification, and that wrongly values speed over process. Most people do not make time for process, and they're not very forgiving when you don't run at the same speed as they do. When you can't respond instantly, you are seen to have 'deficits'. I wish my brain would work quicker than it does, but that's just how I am wired. In spite of all the strategies I've developed over the years to compensate, I can't change my brain and have to manage the frustration of that so I don't take it out on other people by losing my temper, even if the irritation remains simmering underneath. Many times, I have to apply Giff's 'long blink' to ensure I maintain my composure. At others, I'll come home from a day at work and have to scream into a pillow or bite down on my hand, internalising my meltdowns in the way I'd learned to do as a teenager, when I first started suppressing any outward signs of my distress.

~

As time went on, I continued in my mission to ascend the academic ladder, except that for me, it wasn't a ladder that went straight up. Instead, it was more like a game of snakes and ladders, where in order to move forward, I was sometimes falling down snakes. Needless to say, the first papers I submitted as a self-trained sociologist got violently rejected. I was so bad and found writing impossibly difficult, but I kept going, straddling my two different lives – Jason the PE practitioner by day, and Jason the aspiring sociologist by night.

I decided that I would be more intentional and would keep seeking better positions at other universities. In 2017, I took a job as head of department at a university in London. This was a major step up for me. Not only was I going to be able to live in London full time, but I was also going to gain forward momentum and a bigger salary, which meant I could finally leave my night job at Sainsbury's and quit my cleaning job too.

In my new position as head of the sports department, I was given a big office with my name and title on the door, a first for me. But the glory was short-lived. On my second day, I got called into my boss's office. She was in tears as I listened to her explain that my position was being cut because the university was in a precarious financial situation partly because of an unforeseen shortfall in student numbers.

'I just bought a sofa on a buy-now-pay-later plan,' I told her. 'How am I going to pay for it now?'

My joking tone provided a moment of comic relief for both

of us, but my worries about paying for the sofa were genuine. It occurred to me that maybe this was karma for the time that my brothers and I had broken our parents' sofa as kids.

After being let go, I ended up having to take a temporary contract at the University of Roehampton until I secured something more permanent. I had gone from being head of department to another precarious contract, which in many ways was no different from working at Sainsbury's or cleaning. It was a tough pill to swallow, but I had bills to pay. It was around this time that I decided to set myself a new challenge. Not only was I determined to find a permanent job, but I wanted to go even further than that: I decided that I wanted a university professorship by the age of thirty-five, which was just a couple of years away. The problem was, that particular rung on the academic ladder was so far out of reach as to be laughable.

After a year at Roehampton, I managed to convert the position into a permanent job, securing my first lectureship in education. I was immensely grateful. Now I could say, 'I'm an academic in education' rather than a PE specialist, which was a significant leap forward in how I was perceived by others in the sector and most importantly myself. Determined to advance even further, I kept applying for jobs at some of the UK's leading universities. I saw this as the next step, particularly in terms of job security. Although I was getting a lot of rejections, I soon realised that by applying for these jobs and going up for interviews, I was essentially conducting my academic research, trying to figure out, for myself and others, exactly how the world of higher education functioned. At the time, I was also interviewing lots of other Black academics as part of my research and finding out about the challenges they faced. Their responses to my questions fed into and informed my path. Too often, I learned (and experienced) that Black academics were given a bigger workload than their white colleagues. They were made to feel as though they were lucky to have their jobs and should be grateful. They were made to feel afraid and inferior, and were continually threatened with the prospect of losing everything they had worked so hard for.

At the suggestion of Sandro, I began keeping a detailed notebook documenting my journey and all the things I was doing to progress at each stage of my career, fully aware that if I pulled off the impossible dream of scaling the summit that is academia, I would be asked how I did it. I called this notebook 'The Roadmap'. Again, I put my observation skills to good use, watching how other aspiring professors got things done. I listened carefully to 'corridor conversations' and chatter in staff rooms, where my colleagues talked about the grants they'd applied for, what to say and not to say in interviews, publications to pursue, and techniques for organising your time. Besides discovering how intentional these people were, I realised that they were strategists of the highest order. According to them, the first, second and third most important things to focus on to succeed in academia were research, research and research. So that's where I put my energies. I also wanted to focus on being a really good educator (because that's me at my essence, a teacher, enamoured with the process of knowledge exchange), while providing a ladder for and supporting other Black and minority ethnic academics as much as I could.

As I began to forge a path for myself as an education specialist, people started inviting me to give more lectures and keynotes. I travelled to the United States, South Africa, Brazil and New

Zealand. This was an arena of academic life where I could definitely thrive. Thanks to Sandro's training and all those hours at karaoke, I was becoming a good orator. I'd also spent a lot of time in the early days of my academic career studying Barack Obama's delivery. I would watch his speeches, observing how he used cadence, diction and body language to captivate and inspire a crowd. I wanted to communicate complex ideas in interesting and simple ways as he did, to make things informative and entertaining, to put on a good show.

~

After going up for many, many interviews, I finally secured a position at one of the UK's most prestigious universities. But the move to this particular university ended up being a bad one. When I arrived there, my boss informed me that I was responsible for bringing in more Black and minority ethnic students from across the region, which meant that I had a second job to do that my colleagues did not, leaving me with half as much time for my research and taking me away from my goal of being on a research and teaching contract (the contract I had at the time was teaching only). As I knew from my research on race and education, you cannot advance in academia as a Black person by doing unremunerated diversity labour. There has always been an institutional expectation that your participation in such endeavours is compulsory, and most academic institutions are unaware of the burdens they place upon Black students and faculty as a result. But I hadn't fought so hard to get where I was only to have my research compromised. So I decided to trust my intuition and have the courage of my convictions, as Giff had always advised. I resigned.

Around the same time I left the job, I began having problems again with my balance and equilibrium. My vision became blurry, and I found myself mixing up my words. I went back to the doctor. A routine MRI showed a slight regrowth on my pituitary gland – known as a recurrence. The doctor explained that a recurrence can happen even after a tumour has been completely removed and successfully treated. With another surgery and regular monitoring, he said, it was something they could manage, and that I should be fine.

Soon after this, fortune finally smiled on me. I heard about an assistant professorship in sociology at Durham University, England's third oldest after Oxford and Cambridge. They were looking for someone who specialised in race and higher education. So I interviewed for the job and got it. This was the academic jackpot: a full-time, permanent research and teaching contract. In the space of a year and a half, I'd gone from a temporary contract at Roehampton to being an assistant professor at one of the top universities in the country. From the outside, I was riding the highest of professional highs.

But when it came to my personal life, my mid-thirties were not an easy time. Not at all.

In late 2019, Debs and I sadly parted ways. We had met and started our relationship at such a young age, when we were just teenagers. We'd had two incredible children and many wonderful years together. Debs was – and will always be – a phenomenal mother and someone who unfailingly believed in me. But in trying to climb the very steep hill of academia, I'd sacrificed a lot, including time with her and the kids. While my monotropic brain had been my secret weapon at work, allowing me to focus all my attention on the task of propelling myself forward professionally, it wasn't so helpful when it came to my personal relationships. I could be uncompromising with those close to me – and maybe more importantly, with myself – and I never gave myself an excuse or a day off. In my mind, I was doing all of this for them, to secure my family financially, but it came at the cost of my marriage.

It was a painful period; I had lost my right hand in separating from Debs. We had been through and fought every war together, and I had broken rank. She knew that I would always support her and the kids in every way possible, but for now, I was going to move back in with my parents while I figured out what came next for me. This part of the journey, I would have to walk alone.

Chapter 30

Nature's Tiny Therapist

As 2019 ended and 2020 began, I was four months away from turning thirty-five. I'd defied the doctors, psychologists and therapists who told Giff I'd never live a meaningful life. I'd come back from a serious head injury and a diagnosis of epilepsy. I'd somehow scraped together the qualifications to get myself to university, working all the hours of the day and night just to stay in the academic rat race. I'd survived a brain tumour. And perhaps most improbable of all, I'd secured myself a position at Durham. It felt like at last there was some forward momentum.

I'd begun to suspect that after everything I'd been through, things would somehow work out for me, no matter how unfavourable the odds.

Then the Covid-19 pandemic hit. On 23 March, Prime Minister Boris Johnson issued the order: 'You must stay at home.' Lockdown began. I'd already moved out of the house I'd shared with Debs and the kids and was living at home with Giff and my dad, both of whom needed help with day-to-day tasks because of health issues. Simon was a mental health nurse and immediately began caring for people with Covid as a frontline worker. My older brother, Joseph, was living in Essex and working as a schoolteacher. So taking care of our parents naturally fell to me. Simon instructed me to keep Giff, who suffered from respiratory issues, in a total bubble. 'Do not let her get infected,' he warned me. 'People with respiratory issues are not surviving this.'

My kids were with Debs, but I couldn't risk seeing them and potentially exposing Giff and my dad to Covid.

After about a week of being locked down, I woke up one morning and realised I couldn't get out of bed. Not only that, but I didn't *want* to get out of bed. Instead, I spent the entire day horizontal, without even getting up to pee or feed myself, just sinking further and further down into the pit of my mattress. Ever since childhood, I'd seen colours floating in my mind like the ones in a lava lamp, fluid and moving, and I would turn to these for entertainment or consolation. But now the colours were gone, and in their place was a pervasive darkness. At some point that day, I tried to call out to check on Giff and my dad, but to my dismay, I couldn't make the words come out of my mouth. I could hear in my head what I wanted to say – I just couldn't make the necessary noises. Had my speech been taken away from me? At that point, I had been talking for twenty-four years; I didn't want to go back to being non-speaking. That first day, I simply lay on my side, wordless, not listening to music, not picking up my phone or laptop. Completely immobile. My parents must have assumed I had Covid and left me well alone. I wondered if I might have caught it too, but I didn't have a temperature or even a cough.

My hope was if I could sleep and rest, I would wake up the next day feeling a bit stronger, but the next morning, I still couldn't get out of bed and I still couldn't talk. I didn't want to eat. I didn't want to do anything. My survival instincts had left me. I had no clue what was going on or what I should do about it. I was lost to myself.

For every problem I had faced, there was always an answer, but for the first time in my adult life, I had no answer. I literally had no words.

My employers at Durham were still figuring out the necessary tech to transfer all classes and meetings online as the world continued to remain in a state of flux, so thankfully I could avoid having to interact with anyone professionally. After a couple of days confined to my bed, I managed to reach out a hand from under the covers to check emails in the hope that no one would suspect something was amiss. Somehow I also managed to drag myself upright, putting one foot in front of the other, so I could go downstairs and make myself some food and check on my parents. I even forced myself to speak a few words as I didn't want them to worry about me. After about ten days of barely functioning, I learned that university was resuming virtually, and I had to get back to work. In the weeks to come, I showed up for classes and meetings without leaving my bedroom. I kept the camera off so that no one could see me. I did the things I was supposed to do: answered emails, gave lectures online, interacted virtually with students and other faculty. I didn't tell my bosses or colleagues that I was struggling. Not wanting to burden my parents, I didn't even tell Giff or my dad what was going on with me. I didn't want anyone to know, and to be honest, I didn't think anyone could help.

Work took up about ten hours a day and taking care of my parents another couple of hours, but after my duties were complete, I'd crawl back into bed, and everything would go dark again. Listening to music has always been my therapy, something I've done as religiously as prayer, but during this period, I stopped altogether. To pass the time, I started playing quizzes on my phone, joining global quizzing leagues where there are tens of thousands of people playing against each other. If you want your ranking in quizzing leagues to go up, you have to play for hours and hours a day. So that's what I ended up doing. During this time, I stopped shaving again and grew out a beard that eventually reached my chest.

Autistic burnout is something that happens to many autistic people at some point in their lives. It's a state of overwhelming physical and mental exhaustion, brought on by stress and the daily challenges of living in a neurotypical world, where in order to survive, you continually have to suppress your natural tendencies. From a young age, I'd learned to suppress not only my stims, which might have helped me to regulate, but any negative emotion, from sadness and hurt to frustration. I prided myself on always facing adversity with a grin. I felt I didn't have the luxury of allowing negativity to overwhelm me or slow me down. Giff had always warned me not to abuse my remarkably calm-on-the-exterior temperament, and never to take it for granted. But that was exactly what I had done. I had spent decades pushing myself and refusing to give in, but I had never taken time to rest, reflect and care for myself. As a result, an entire ocean of sadness, hurt and frustration had built up within me, just waiting for its moment to break down the dam.

Burnout is different from depression in that it's not a mood disorder – although it can certainly lead to depression. During burnout, people can find that they lose skills, just like I'd temporarily lost the use of my voice. This is not something a doctor is going to diagnose you with because it's not listed in the *DSM*. Instead, like so many other aspects of being autistic, it's a phenomenon that is understood mainly by the people who have to live through it.

Thankfully, all this was happening to me at a time when I was out of the public view, when I could be confined to my bed without anyone realising what was going on. I continued to work to the best of my ability; it was perversely impressive just how normally I could present to the world when I had to. A master at masking, I could still give the appearance of control, revealing very little emotionally and hiding behind a smile. But the reality was that when the workday was over, I was continuing to sink, and nobody was aware of what was happening.

The dominant feeling I experienced during those weeks was that I didn't want to feel anything at all. In the words of the Pink Floyd song, I just wanted to be comfortably numb. Every morning, I experienced a paralysing disappointment when I opened my eyes and saw the early morning spring sunshine filtered through the curtains of my bedroom again. I prayed for the sun to stop coming up, but nothing else. My faith had left me. Over the years, I'd always felt God's presence, even as I fought with him at times. But I'd never lost my faith. I'd never even questioned God's existence. Now, for the first time in my life, I stopped believing in him. If there was a God, I felt that he had forsaken me, and I was no longer interested in fighting my way back to the light.

I desperately wanted it to be over. I wanted to feel at peace – something I had experienced only fleetingly in my adult life. There had to be somewhere beyond 'this place of wrath and tears', as William Ernest Henley had written in 'Invictus'. My birthday was just a few weeks away, and I decided I wanted to do it before then. I planned it out meticulously, researching which bridge would be the best to jump from – the one where I was most likely to succeed and least likely to be stopped. I don't want to give the name of the bridge or too many other details because I don't want anyone to follow in my footsteps, but suffice it to say, I made my way there late at night, headphones on, listening to every song I'd ever loved for what I assumed would be the last time. When I got to the bridge, I climbed over the guardrail and sat on a ledge with the river flowing beneath me. I felt a calmness. I had done my best, made the most of my life, helped many people, kept all my promises and stayed faithful to my mission. As I closed my eyes, I felt the lightness of a person who knows it's all over.

The peace I craved was close. As I prepared to propel myself forward, I knew I wanted to listen to one more song – my favourite: 'Take It to the Limit' by the Eagles.

As Randy Meisner sang about dreams burning out at the end of the evening, the song I loved took on a different meaning, the midnight blue of the river flowing below me, the long lines of smudged reflections from the traffic and buildings on the riverbanks. Everyone has their song, and that has always been mine. I had taken it to the limit over and over again – and now it was time to rest.

But before I could jump, I heard another voice, one that I recognised immediately. It was a family member, calling for me. I turned around and saw the familiar face looking over the barrier, completely horrified.

This person, who has asked me to not include their name, had received the notification from the medical bracelet that I wore that I was on the bridge, and when they couldn't get hold of me, they rushed over.

In all my careful planning, I had forgotten about the wristband with the tracking device inside it, the one Debs had given me after my epilepsy diagnosis, in case I had a seizure and fell unconscious. My family member had received an alert saying that I had been near the bridge for a while. After calling me several times with no answer, they rushed to the scene, expecting to find that I'd had a seizure. Instead, they shouted and shouted for me until they located me on my precipice.

I had never been so disappointed to see anyone as I was that night. In the end, my decision to listen to the Eagles likely saved my life. The song is four minutes and forty-eight seconds long, which gave this person just enough time to race to my rescue. They were eventually able to grab me by the shoulders and pull me to safety as I collapsed, crying like a small child.

We went back to my parents' house and I got into my bed. I probably should have felt relieved to be rescued, but I was devastated that I had failed in my carefully planned mission. I'm ashamed to say that I felt nothing but resentment for the person who had pulled me back from the brink.

Giff was distraught. She had no idea what I was going through. I'd kept it from everyone, even those who were closest to me. After that, my family called in a mental health crisis team, and for the next three weeks, the counsellors and nurses visited me twice a day, once in the middle of the day and again in the evening. I dreaded those visits. The people they sent were well meaning, but they didn't know what to make of me. I wasn't unhinged, I hadn't lost my mind and I didn't need to be sectioned, sedated or put away. I was completely in control of myself. I think I left them at a loss as to how to help. They offered antidepressants, which I did not want to take, and suggested therapy, which I did not feel would help.

During this time, Giff spent hours sitting at my bedside as I lay there in silence, my head welded to the pillow. She'd stroke my brow, talking to me in the familiar tones that were usually a source of such calm and comfort. Giff's faith in God was unshakeable, and her faith in me had been the wind in my sails, always propelling me forward. But now I had lost my faith, not only in God but in myself. As Rocky says in *Rocky III*, 'Nothing is real if you don't believe in who you are.' He had always been my inspiration, but I didn't want to fight my way back to belief anymore. I just wanted everything to be over.

'Look at your fingers, Jason,' Giff said, repeating something she had been telling me since I was a small child. 'God made your fingers different lengths for a reason. Every day is different, just like your fingers. Yes, you may feel bad today, but tomorrow will be different.'

Mostly, I didn't respond, but at some point, I asked her the question that was most on my mind: 'Why has God forsaken me?'

Giff drew in her breath and stood up. She left the room and returned with a book in her hands, and she began to read. She recited a poem for me – one that she had been reading to me since I was a child. 'Footprints in the Sand.' It's about a man who has a dream that he's walking on the beach with the Lord. When the man looks behind him, he can see two sets of footprints in the sand until he experiences a very difficult time in his life and then he sees only a single set of footprints. The man feels that God has forsaken him.

Giff continued to read. The man asks the Lord why He has abandoned him in the darkest period of his life. And the Lord says, 'I never left you during your times of suffering. When you saw only one set of footprints, it was then that I carried you.'

Giff had always been my spiritual guide, more than any priest or other religious leader. Now I listened to her as she recited the familiar poem, but nothing was getting through.

~

That dreadful spring passed with me continuing to teach remotely and not taking as much as a day of sick leave. As summer began, my brother Simon decided it was time for another restoration project at our parents' home. This time, he wanted us to tackle the garden at the front of the house. Truthfully, this was less of a garden and more of a weed-filled, overgrown jungle. Gardening is not my thing at all. I don't like getting grime under my nails, and I don't like insects, which Simon knew very well. But he was also aware that making me do something outside that involved manual labour and wasn't related to my work or usual duties was important for my recovery. Simon's plan was for us to cut back all the overgrown plants and then replace the topsoil with fresh fertiliser and a new lawn in time for the summer. This was proper, back-breaking work, involving spades, a wheelbarrow and a lot of digging. As we worked, we listened to music on Simon's portable mini-speaker. I hadn't listened to music for months, not since the night on the bridge, but this was also part of my brother's plan for me. He was cleverly integrating all the things I no longer enjoyed back into my life: listening to music, watching television and eating our 'walking and talking' chicken wings together while setting the world to rights.

People in the throes of despair will often look for a sign, whether it's random words on the side of a bus, clouds in a certain shape in the sky, a butterfly landing on a flower or anything else that might offer a sense that there's some kind of plan or higher purpose at work. The first time I noticed the robin perching on top of the fence in the garden, I didn't think anything of it, but when it came back the next day and the day after that, always around the same time – midday – I was so desperate to find an omen in anything that I decided that the robin was a sign. I started talking to the robin. I told it about the garden and what I was doing that day, about everything that had happened to me in the past weeks and months. The robin would put its head to one side, as if it were listening intently, its beady eyes fixed on mine, as I convinced myself that it could understand everything I said. After staying for about ten minutes, stoically putting up with my ramblings, the robin would fly off. In the coming weeks, I spoke to this robin every day, revealing the contents of my brain and my heart to nature's tiny therapist.

Meanwhile, Simon and I continued to plant and dig, and I slowly found my way back into the light, aided by the garden, my brother and the little robin. Simon was masterful in redirecting my energy and focus, getting me out of the house and forcing me to do something physical that would ordinarily have been of no interest to me. As we transformed the garden from a total mess into a well-kept lawn with neatly trimmed hedges, complete with new garden furniture and a barbeque, my capacity to appreciate the little things returned to me. My favourite soap operas, *Home and Away* and *Neighbours*, soon became staples of my day again. I began to enjoy music once more, with the album *Ten* by Pearl Jam becoming my first musical indulgence in a while.

It wasn't that the barely suppressed sadness that had brought me so low had gone away, but I was learning to walk alongside it. After years of trying to ignore darkness, a familiar companion to me, I had paid the price. Maybe that first lyric of the Simon and Garfunkel song had contained the secret all along – rather than shut the door to darkness, I resolved to stay on nodding terms with it in the future.

By the time we finished work on the garden, I knew I was going to miss being out in front of the house and having this project to focus on. I wanted to thank the robin for helping me to feel better, but it had stopped visiting. Every day, I went to the garden at noon, only to find, to my disappointment, that the robin was no longer on its perch on the fence. Maybe its intervention was temporary. Maybe the robin knew I was feeling better and decided that it was no longer needed. A few weeks later, however, as I stood in the garden, the robin appeared again, right on time. Elated, I raced to tell my little friend everything that had happened since the last time I'd seen it, barely pausing for breath, rushing and swallowing my words to get them out before the bird flew away again. The robin listened patiently and then flapped its wings and went. Somehow, I knew this would be the last time I'd see it. To this day, I believe the robin was my reminder that God is always present, even in my most desperate moments.

But that isn't the end of the story of the garden. A few months after we finished our impressive renovation, there was a sewage blockage in the underground septic tank for the housing estate. This tank, it turned out, sits directly under our garden, which meant that the backed-up sewage leaked out and seeped up into my parents' lawn and flower beds. Not to put too fine a point on it, but I woke up one morning to the smell of shit, and when I went outside to find the source of the disgusting stench, I realised it was coming from the front of our house. Animal excrement is supposed to be a great fertiliser, but I can categorically state that putting human sewage on your garden will destroy it almost immediately. When Simon came round to take a look, the lawn was saturated with brown water, and the plants and grass had dramatically wilted. He was as upset as I was. All that hard work and all the money we'd spent on soil, fertiliser and plants was for nothing! But then the breeze blew a disgusting waft of sewage directly into our nostrils, and we looked at each other and couldn't help ourselves. We burst out laughing. We laughed for so long that we were both crying; we couldn't stop. It was the first time we'd laughed together in many, many months. It was cathartic, healing.

Eventually, we composed ourselves for long enough to order a delivery of our favourite 'walking and talking' chicken wings, and then we pulled out a couple of folding chairs and sat in our stinking garden, eating our wings and still laughing.

Chapter 31

Self-Care

As lockdown restrictions started to ease in the spring of 2021, Londoners began emerging from their mole holes, blinking in the sunlight. Like so many people, I remember feeling ambivalent about the end of the lockdown. I didn't want to go back to my old routine, commuting to work every day, travelling up and down the country. Since the pandemic, I'd been able to work from home, which was a novelty for me. Being in one place had given me time to rest, to both break down and recover – and in many ways, I didn't want it to end.

But there was *one* advantage to lockdown being over: I could finally do something that I'd been dreaming about and working towards since I was fifteen years old, something that I knew would lift me up like nothing else. I was finally going to get myself a bespoke shirt from Savile Row, just as I had promised I would when Giff took me there as a teenager to look in the shop windows.

Audre Lorde famously wrote, 'Caring for myself is not self-indulgence, it is self-preservation, and that is an act of political warfare.' Going to get that shirt was my version of Lorde's self-care: a reclamation, something that I knew would bring me joy for months or even years to come. Of all my special interests, tailoring is the one that means the most to me, that brings me the deepest satisfaction, that fulfils and sustains me. During the pandemic, one of the things that kept me going was promising myself that as soon as lockdown lifted, I was going to get myself my shirt. Over the years, I'd managed to amass quite a few tailored items, relying on my friends from Peckham Rye (who had made my wedding suit) to create custom pieces for me: a coat here, a pair of trousers or a full suit there, all of which they let me pay for in instalments. But Peckham Rye had recently closed down. It was time to graduate to the Premier League of tailoring. The guys at Peckham Rye knew about my long-standing dreams of frequenting Savile Row, and they had often told me, 'If you're going to go anywhere, go to Huntsman,' which they considered the best in the business. Huntsman had been around for over one hundred and seventy-five years, and its clients included Clark Gable and Gregory Peck, the same impeccably dressed film stars who had inspired my love of 1930s and 1940s tailoring. Some of my favourite rock stars were also partial to a Huntsman suit, including Charlie Watts, the drummer from the Rolling Stones; legendary guitarist Eric Clapton; the Thin White Duke, David Bowie; and the Modfather, Paul Weller.

Having recently completed a couple of consulting jobs, I knew I could likely afford a Huntsman shirt, an entry-level bespoke item for a Savile Row first-timer. I'm not someone who has vices or spends a lot of money on myself. I don't drink, smoke or do drugs. I don't drive a car, eat out or take fancy holidays. Every day, I wear the same pair of battered Adidas Gazelles that I've worn for the past six or seven years. Most of my money

I give away, either to charity or to my family and friends. I make sure the people I love have everything they need before I spend anything on myself. Tailoring is my one and only vice, if you want to call it that – and I was about to scratch that itch.

On a bright day in early March, I got the Tube from Vauxhall to Oxford Circus, and walked the short distance through Mayfair and some of London's fanciest streets to Savile Row. As I approached Huntsman, with its smart red awning and royal seal in the window, I half-assumed I'd get turned away at the door, as Giff had told me that these establishments were by invitation only. I was thinking that I could at least peek in the windows, though, and get a sense of my options. To my surprise, the Huntsman door was unmanned that day, so I decided to poke my head inside.

Right away, I was greeted by Michael Cheng, the sharply dressed store manager. I was expecting him to eject me, but instead, he welcomed me. I told him that I had been dreaming of coming here and having a shirt made since I was fifteen years old, but that I'd always assumed that Savile Row was by invitation only. Michael explained that they'd done away with the invitation part a long time ago. We fell to chatting, and I told him all about my lifelong love of fine tailoring. He must have appreciated my enthusiasm because he invited me to meet the head cutter, Dario Carnera. I already knew all about Dario, aka the Man with the Golden Shears, from watching videos of him online. I was properly starstruck. Dario is widely regarded by his peers on the Row and his colleagues in-house as one of the best cutters in the world. That day, he was wearing his trademark single-breasted waistcoat, with trousers and a neatly trimmed beard and round glasses perched on his nose. Like Michael,

Dario was incredibly personable and kind to me, even though I was ostensibly a nobody who had strolled in off the street.

Again, I explained my love and appreciation for tailoring. I also made it clear that I didn't have a huge amount of cash, but that I thought I could afford a shirt. Michael told me, 'We can always come to an arrangement. Let us work with you.' And before I knew it, I was agreeing to a full tailored suit and a white shirt, which I could pay for in instalments. This was beyond my wildest dreams. Next, I was introduced to the rest of the team, including Sean O'Flynn, who is known as one of the finest bespoke shirtmakers in the world. I met everyone from under-cutters to client managers to trouser- and coat-makers. After that, Michael, Dario and I looked through the cloth books. I knew exactly what I wanted: a nod to the 1930s and 1940s (in my opinion, the greatest era for men's fashion). I had an image in my head, the same one I'd had since I was a teenager: classic, timeless, like the most stylish jazz musician imaginable, maybe at the end of the night, his tie a little undone, his sleeves rolled up, but his suit still immaculately suave. That was how I wanted to look. Heavy flannel cloth was the order of the day in the 1930s and 1940s, so I made a beeline for the Fox Brothers' clothbook. Most suits of that era were double-breasted (DB), with a high fastening on the coat and fishtail trousers. I wanted a Fox's DB navy-blue flannel, sixteen ounces, with a simple white poly shirt in cotton, double cuffed. Dario took meticulous measurements of my chest, waist, hips, shoulders, arms, inseam and neck. My thirty-five-year-old self could hardly believe it – never mind my inner fifteen-year-old self, who was screaming with joy.

I returned to Huntsman three times after that day, first for the basted fitting, where the suit is put together using a special kind of stitching that can easily be undone as refinements are made. Then there's a second fitting to refine alterations and amendments, and a third and final fitting when everything is finished inside and out. When I tried on the completed suit for the first time, it felt as if I were putting on the skin I was always supposed to inhabit. The high waist on the trousers encircled me, and the beautifully sculpted lines of the jacket extended across my shoulders and arms, down my back and over my chest. Everything fit like a second skin, a sensory dream. It was more than just having a suit made. This was the ultimate expression of my individuality, made for me and me only, and a recognition of the fact that I had got to a position in life where I could have clothes made on the Row at Huntsman. This was a source of immense pride and accomplishment. I could not fully express to Michael and Dario how grateful I was.

As with every Savile Row piece, everything was personalised with a special name tag. Mine had the words 'Dr Jason Arday' printed in an old-fashioned typewriter font, with the date the garment was made and the Huntsman branding: my name tucked like a beautiful secret on the inside of my suit. If I may contradict George Michael, sometimes the clothes *do* make the man.

After I brought the wine-coloured Huntsman hanging bag home, I laid it on the bed next to me before I went to sleep that night, with the top of the bag resting against the pillow. I slept blissfully for more than five hours, which is unheard of for me. When I woke up, I wondered if it had all been a dream, but then I stretched out my hand and realised to my delight that my suit was still lying next to me.

I was already planning my next commission. But these weren't the only thoughts of the future on my mind.

~

For over two years now, I'd been thinking about what it might take for me to become a professor. When I first set myself that goal, I was barely moving alongside the heavyweights of academia, carrying their spit bucket, but now I felt I could spar with them. I just had to figure out how and when I was going to close the distance on that particular ambition, understanding the importance of timing it just right. I was careful to seek advice from other professors, and I had attended workshops and seminars about academic promotion, how to be competitive and the boxes you need to tick. I had a clear idea about what being promoted to professor would entail. The only problem was bringing this to fruition.

Then, towards the end of March 2021, a job came up for a professorship in education at the University of Glasgow. I applied and was invited to interview via Zoom. I knew I was good enough and ready for a new challenge. All my failures applying for jobs had taught me how to manage the moment, and I was unfazed by the big occasion of the interview, reminding myself that the preparation had been in the sacrifices I had already made. As Giff and Sandro would often say to me: 'Show them what you are about. Show them what you can do.' So I did.

As the interview drew to its conclusion, the panel indicated that the successful candidate would be informed within the next five working days. A week later, the head of school told me via video conference that the panel had reached a decision. My appointment as Professor of the Sociology of Education at just thirty-five years of age made me one of the youngest professors in the UK.

It took a while for the news of this feat to sink in, but one freezing winter's day in Durham, as I was walking towards the train station to go home, the scale of the achievement finally slapped me in the face. I stopped in my tracks, arrested by the following thought: *I'm a professor. Whatever happens, that's the salutation that I will carry with me for the rest of my professional days. That's mad.* I remember writing the words down in the notes on my phone: Jason Arday, Professor of Sociology of Education at the University of Glasgow.

The job started in January of 2022, and right away, I came face-to-face with the main drawback of the position: the commute. Getting to Glasgow involved setting my alarm for 3 a.m. so I could catch the early flight from London City airport to Scotland, then return on a 4 p.m. flight the same day, two or three times a week. I knew flying back and forth in a single day was going to be incredibly draining, but I didn't have a choice. Giff and my dad needed me at home, and so did the kids.

Thankfully, fate provided me with someone who was going to make this feat just a bit more bearable. The first time I booked a cab from the airport to the university, I got in and the driver and I immediately started chatting. His name was Callum, and he was in his fifties, with a beanie on his head and a goatee on his chin. That morning, in his thick Glaswegian accent, Callum ended up telling me about his life – what he was going through at that time, and his relationships with various family members, which were complicated, as most relationships are. I enjoyed talking to him so much that when the ride was over, I asked him if he'd consider picking me up and taking me back to the airport every time I came to Glasgow, which was going to be multiple times a week. He accepted. And from that point on, whenever I flew into Glasgow, Callum was there waiting for me. Without him, I doubt that this insane commute, which took five hours each way door to door, would have been sustainable. Our conversations kept me going, along with the chocolate-covered cashews that I'd buy for myself at Marks & Spencer in Glasgow airport and then eat right before my first lecture, to set myself up for the day. Callum and the cashews: small acts of self-care (thank you, Audre Lorde). Just knowing they would be there when I landed brought the comfort of routine to the long and arduous journey.

Chapter 32

Go the Distance

After around a year of teaching at Glasgow, a quite remarkable sequence of events began to unfold. In April 2022, I received an email from an elite university in London asking to have a conversation. I'd often been headhunted in academia, both domestically and abroad, but this was my first time being sought out by an elite British institution. I hugely respected this university and thought in some ways that it was a hand-in-glove fit. Not only that, but it was also a short bus ride away from my house. As talks progressed, I began to embrace the idea of being in London. Seeing family and friends more regularly seemed like a massive luxury to me; in fact, it was something I longed for. I had been on the road now for almost ten years, commuting across hundreds of miles. I was indebted to Glasgow, especially the kind, forward-thinking, exceptional senior leaders and decision-makers who were the main architects behind my appointment. They had provided me with an opportunity to realise my professional ambition, and it moved me that they believed so much in my potential. But if my breakdown had taught me anything, it was that I needed to achieve greater balance in my very unbalanced life.

As we were nearing the end of negotiations with the London university, I received another email. This was from Professor Rajani Naidoo, then at the University of Bath, who I'd recently met, someone I greatly admired and who had become a much-needed, supportive, new presence in my life. She attached a note to a job advert, saying simply: 'Dear Jason, you are perfect for this. You must apply. Best wishes, your friend Rajani.' Intrigued, I clicked on the link, which redirected me to the University of Cambridge website, where I found a link welcoming applications for the 2002 Professorial Chair in the Sociology of Education. I read the job specifications and criteria. Fortunately, I had everything needed for the post, which had been established in 2002, and a little bit more. At the very least, I could put together a competitive application.

I looked up from my laptop. There, on the wall of my childhood bedroom, was the Post-it note I had written ten years earlier, when Simon and I were repainting the walls. The ink had faded a little, but the greasy finger marks from the chicken wings remained, along with the words 'In ten years, I want to be an academic at Oxford or Cambridge.'

I sat on the knowledge of the Cambridge job for a few days, unsure of what to do. I was so close to accepting the London position, but as the days progressed, I received multiple emails from friends and colleagues encouraging me to apply for the other job. They all said some version of, 'You are literally the perfect fit for this post; you are exactly what they are looking for!' Cambridge is only an hour and a half from Clapham on the train. It wasn't a short bus ride away, but it was still a manageable commute compared to Glasgow.

As always, I spoke to Giff to get her advice. She reminded

me how important it was to trust my instincts and judgement. I reminded her that the Cambridge job was one of the most coveted chairs in global academia, and that a lot of people from all over the world were going to apply. Giff said to me: 'Jason, has it occurred to you that maybe this is your destiny? After everything you have been through, maybe you were supposed to end up here all along? I think you are ready. Do not be afraid. God would not bring you all this way to fail. Apply, and let's see. Once you are shortlisted, then we can plan through prayer.'

As I wrote the application, I tried to avoid thinking too far ahead, but questions were definitely rattling around in my brain: *What if I get rejected? What if I have completely overestimated my capabilities? What if my story ends up being a cautionary tale like Icarus flying too close to the sun?* Then I remembered the way Rocky told Adrian that it didn't matter if he lost the fight with Apollo Creed because all he wanted to do was 'go the distance'. That had always been the goal: to go the distance. Get to the final bell, no matter what. The offer from the institution in London was still on the table, so I had that as a fallback.

After three days of putting together my Cambridge application, I had a final read-through. With a click and a prayer, the application was in the lap of the gods. I promised myself that once it was sent, I wouldn't think or worry about it. Mid-September came around, and so did an email. The subject heading read 'Invitation to Interview: Professor of Education (2002).' Here was my opportunity to stand in front of them and show them who I was.

Whenever I'm in a challenging situation, I always try to find the right sports analogy to help me, and this time, the analogy was tennis. The Cambridge interview was going to be my Grand

Slam, my Wimbledon final, my Centre Court, the biggest arena of them all. The interview dates were set for 2 and 3 November. A two-day process. I told myself that concentration was going to be the most important thing; I had to focus for every second of every minute of every hour that I was on that court. This would be the factor that would give me the smallest of edges against my very distinguished and exceptional opponents. *Play each point, one point at a time. Do not even think about the trophy lift.* This was the mantra; this was the mindset. I prayed: *should things go my way, please let me take it with good grace, and should things not go my way, please let me take this with good grace.*

Mentally I was ready, just wishing away the days until November.

~

I arrived in Cambridge the night before the first interview, a bit after 7 p.m. The candidates had been booked into separate hotels. At the reception of my bed and breakfast, a woman behind the counter greeted me by insisting she couldn't find my booking. Was this her way of saying, *you don't look like you belong here?* But I knew I did belong, and I told her to look again, until she eventually figured out that the booking was under the name of someone at the university. After finally getting to my room, I pulled back the curtains, only to be greeted by a band of moths that flew out from within the folds. Carefully placing my bag down, I decided to shake off any negative energy by ironing my outfits, including my underwear and socks. Why I decided to iron my underwear, I have no idea. Perhaps it was nerves and being on autopilot. I had never done it before, but ironed they were.

My outfit for day one consisted of my navy-blue Peckham Rye tailored trousers with a two-inch turn-up, a beautiful navy-blue merino wool roll-neck, and canary yellow socks with burgundy Italian penny loafers. I gave everything a quick spray of travel-sized Febreze so that nothing would smell of the damp B & B for my interview. After that was done, I watched the latest episodes of *Home and Away*. *Neighbours* had recently been cancelled, but thankfully I still had some old episodes saved on my phone. So that meant two hours of TV total. This was my version of Zen meditation, a temporary escape from the task at hand.

Predictably, I lay awake most of the night. At 4 a.m., I forced my eyes closed and finally fell into a fitful sleep, only to be woken up a couple of hours later by the alarm on my phone (Pearl Jam's 'Even Flow', my preferred song for shocking myself awake.) All I wanted to do was press the snooze button. My eyelids felt like they were glued together. It was a pathetic start to a momentous day.

Eventually, I stumbled into the shower with a mix of songs playing very loudly: 'Supersonic' by Oasis, 'Turn It on Again' by Genesis, 'The Changingman' by Paul Weller, 'Pali Gap' by Jimi Hendrix, 'Pinball Wizard' by the Who and 'Silver Springs' by Fleetwood Mac. I was hoping that one of them would spring me into action. In the end, Dodgy's 'In A Room' snapped me into gear.

Outfit on and freshly twisted locs flowing, looking every bit the part, I took a short cab ride to the Donald McIntyre Building, Faculty of Education, Hills Road. Unlike many buildings in Cambridge, some of which date back to when the university was founded in the thirteenth century, the Faculty of

Education building is a very modern combination of red brick, buff-coloured wood and glass. Through the double electric doors I went. To the left of me was a plaque memorialising the opening of the building by Prince Philip in 2005, and a few yards further along on the same side, there was a huge bronze head of the influential Brazilian educational philosopher Paulo Freire, the author of *The Pedagogy of the Oppressed*, a book that talks about education as a vehicle for liberation. Freire is someone who has influenced me since my early days of thinking about education in an academic context. I took this as a good omen.

I sat in the foyer and waited for my chaperone for the day, Sophie, to arrive. She was talkative, distracting and very kind, introducing me to the chair of electors, Paul Ramchandani, who had the coolest professorial title I had ever heard: the LEGO Professor of Play in Education, Development and Learning. Like Sophie, he was welcoming and kind, which in a high-stakes situation like this one can be quite rare and went a long way to making me feel at ease.

After Sophie took me back to the foyer, I texted Giff to let her know that I had arrived safely. *Whatever happens today*, I told her, *we have already won. We have nothing else left to prove.* Giff replied: *Don't forget the Sankofa bird, Jason.* She was reminding me of the mythical Ghanaian bird that flies forward while turning its head backward, looking to the past to carry itself into the future. The image of the Sankofa had helped Giff so much when she was at her lowest point, told by the doctors and therapists that I was a lost cause. *Draw on your ancestors and everything at your disposal today*, Giff wrote. *You are right – we have already won, and I have asked for victory in Jesus's name.*

This first step of the interview process involved giving two presentations to the panel. Outside the interview room, I jogged determinedly on the spot, Rafa Nadal-style, releasing any nervous energy before entering. I knew that a strong first half would set me up for a tilt at the big prize tomorrow. Feeling fearless, I gave my presentations, executing everything just as I had envisioned. The day was over. I'd earned something greasy to eat. Twenty chicken nuggets from McDonald's, with three barbeque sauces, sorted me out, along with another instalment of *Home and Away* on my laptop back at the hotel.

That night, I actually slept, and in the morning, I got out of bed feeling energised. I blasted 'Morning Glory' by Oasis, putting on the same navy trousers as yesterday, but this time with a green merino wool roll-neck, green socks and my burgundy penny loafers. I prayed again for grace and dancing feet, and for me to be at my swashbuckling best. In the cab on the way over, I texted Giff to let her know my progress. She sent more love and prayers. Then I texted Sandro, who replied, *I love you and good luck.*

This next interview was being held at the Old Schools, a magnificent fifteenth-century white stone building in the centre of Cambridge, home to the university's administrative offices. I definitely felt a little bit of awe going in. This was my opportunity to experience the pressure of Centre Court under the lights, with the roof closed for added drama. Inside, I waited to be called into the interview room, which lay behind two imposing dark oak doors. Once again, I jogged on the spot, Rafa-style. The last thing I said to myself in preparation for the most important interview of my life was the same quote Rafa Nadal told himself in the fifth set against Roger Federer in the

2008 Wimbledon Championships men's singles final: *somebody is going to have to beat you, because you are not going to lose it today. You are not going to choke or bottle it. Make it difficult for them. Let someone be better than you, but do not fold, Jason.*

The head of HR opened the doors and ushered me in. I walked through the long oak-panelled room for what seemed like an eternity, passing by giant oil paintings of old white men in gilded frames on either side of me, until I reached the seven interviewers waiting at the other end. To start, I gave a five-minute presentation explaining my reasons for wanting this most sought-after of posts. I kept it succinct and crisp. Then the formal interview began. I stayed calm and focused, playing the big points well with careful shot-making and variety, using the one-two punch where I could, serving big and then either following up with a huge forehand or changing it up and coming to the net and volleying on the really important break-point questions. Before I knew it, the interview was over. Game, set, Jason Arday – but not yet the match. As I acknowledged everyone and thanked them for this opportunity, I felt calm. The result was immaterial; just to have arrived at this moment was monumental enough.

Interview over, I changed out of my clothes and walked to Cambridge station to get the train to London. I almost fell asleep on the journey home, I was so exhausted; getting off at King's Cross, and taking the Tube to Clapham Common, eventually arriving home at 5 p.m. Thankfully, I didn't have to wait long after that to find out the result. When the call came in from Cambridge in the late afternoon, I ran upstairs to my parents' room to take it. I didn't want Giff to see my disappointment if the answer was 'Thank you, but we have decided to go with another candidate.'

Sure enough, it was Professor Ramchandani.

After a polite preamble, he offered me the job. I was speechless, struggling to hold back the emotion. I thanked him, thanked the whole panel and all the decision-makers.

'You really deserve it,' he told me. 'Huge congratulations.'

As soon as the call was over, I went downstairs and told Giff.

We hugged and she cried, then she held my hands, and we prayed, thanking God for his favour and his mercy, and praying for the candidates who were not successful today. For Giff, it had been a very long journey with many, many milestones, not just this latest one. The first time I managed to understand how to follow instructions to halve and eat an apple at age seven. The first time I spoke at nearly twelve. Sandro accepting me onto the course at Merton. My first day at university. My first graduation. My first job in academia. Any one of these would have been enough for her.

We prayed and gave thanks for all of it. And then we did what we always did during celebratory moments: we put on some music. We didn't play records anymore, so I got my phone out. The first song that came on was The La's 'There She Goes', and it was perfect. We danced in the living room, just the two of us – Giff mumbling through the words she didn't know until we got to the euphoric, unforgettable hook, about feelings so powerful they can't be contained. Hand in hand, out of tune, we sang along together.

Epilogue

It was Thursday, 23 February 2023, and after the usual blast of 'Even Flow' by Pearl Jam – my morning alarm – the first song to come on shuffle was the Oasis classic 'Morning Glory'. Listening to Manchester's finest while still in my bed, I was experiencing the intense inertia of a chronic insomniac who had fallen into a fitful doze sometime around daybreak, just in time to get up.

Hauling myself out of bed, I grabbed my phone from the side table – and that's when I saw the text messages. Normally, I might have a couple of messages pop up, but this time, there were hundreds of alerts, all saying the same thing: 'Congratulations, mate!' 'Amazing news!!' Some of the messages were from people I knew; others were from unknown numbers. Confused and still half-asleep, I followed my normal routine, flipping to my BBC Sounds app to listen to Radio 4. The newsreader was finishing up a segment about protests against the war in Ukraine when I heard something else: 'Coming up later in the hour, a thirty-seven-year-old man from south London, Jason Arday, makes history as the youngest Black professor to be appointed to Oxbridge in a thousand years.' I went downstairs and switched on the television. There it was on *Good Morning Britain*, the same story but this time with a picture of my silly, shiny face, grinning ear to ear, wearing my graduation cap.

It's a strange thing to go to bed a complete unknown, only to wake up to your name on the radio and television. It's even stranger when you're waking up in the same house where not so long ago, you used to sit with your mum in front of the TV, trying to make out the words, without any idea of what anyone was saying. Giff and my dad weren't up yet, and I didn't want to wake them, so I got myself ready as I had a *very important* appointment and I didn't want to be late: I was going to a second suit fitting at Huntsman on Savile Row. Despite what was happening with my name in the news, obviously, tailoring always takes precedence, and this was unashamedly my priority for the day.

Outside, it was chilly, somewhat damp and drizzly, as I left the house to walk to the Tube. I hadn't gone very far before I met a man coming towards me, who nodded, smiled and said: 'Congratulations, brother, we are all so proud of you. This means a lot to our community.' Unused to this kind of attention, I replied with a bumbling thank you. In fact, he was the first of many strangers who stopped me that morning to say, 'Well done!' or give me the thumbs up. On the platform, I opened up the free *Metro* newspaper, only to see an article with the headline: 'Man Who Couldn't Read until 18 Becomes Cambridge's Youngest-Ever Black Professor' alongside a full-colour photo again with my silly shiny face, which explained why so many people seemed to be doing double-takes in my direction. It was all quite surreal.

After getting off at Oxford Circus, I walked down Regent

Street towards Savile Row, excited to see the new Fox Brothers double-breasted, navy flannel chalk-stripe suit that I knew was waiting for me. Stepping in through the door at Huntsman, I was met by the usual suspects – Dario, Michael and David amongst them – who burst into a spontaneous round of applause. All the other customers were looking over their shoulders, trying to figure out *Why the clapping? What's the occasion?* After all, you don't get that many Black people walking into a Savile Row tailor – especially not ones wearing beaten-up Adidas Gazelles, a patchwork, multicoloured hippie coat from Camden Town, and thigh-length locs – who are met with cheers from the staff. Clearly, my dear friends at Huntsman had heard the news, because they all hugged me, offering their congratulations. I'd only ever told them that I worked in education, so they'd had no idea about the rest of my story until now. To say they were pleased for me would be an understatement. After I thanked them, we quickly got down to the business of trying on my suit, making any final adjustments.

As I stood in front of the mirror at Huntsman, admiring my friends' immaculate handiwork, I had no way of knowing that the news of my Cambridge appointment was already spreading, not just throughout the UK, but around the world. Having your story go viral is quite a bizarre experience. Before 23 February 2023, no one really knew anything about me; I was just quietly getting on with my life and work. But after that day, I was thrust into the public eye in a way that someone can't really prepare for or predict. If I'm being honest, it's something I'm still getting used to.

~

Life changed in a lot of ways. I began commuting to and from Cambridge, settling into my new office in the Faculty of Education Donald McIntyre Building, the same place where I'd had my interview for the job only a few months before. Many times I would find myself sitting in my office, looking out of the window at the perfectly mown lawn and red-brick turret of next-door Homerton College, thinking to myself, *How did I end up here? This is absolutely insane!* I still can't easily explain it all, but I hope this book goes some way to describing the long and winding distance travelled.

There have been many times when I have thought about the midwife who helped deliver me, the one who warned my mother to take care of me because my long fingers meant I was destined for something special. In many ways, I suppose her prediction has come true. But it's the woman I met on the volunteer trip to Brazil – the one who said that the great would be accompanied by the unfortunate in my life, who turned out to have the most accurate prophecy. Sadly, almost every good thing that has happened to me has come with some kind of cost, and my appointment to Cambridge has been no exception. I cannot sugarcoat the fact that there have been those who have been outraged and offended by the idea of a Black professor at such an elite institution. I have continued to face harassment and persecution as the subject of targeted campaigns driven by racial animus. There have been days when I can only describe the experience as traumatising. It's hard for people to begin to even comprehend or imagine the toll this can take on a person.

What keeps me going are the *other* messages, the positive letters, texts and emails from people all over the world that come in daily; I've received hundreds of thousands of them now, so many that I've lost count. People write to me because they've read an article or seen a video clip, and they want to tell me about their own challenges regarding either them or their children; others are just writing to express their joy at a victory for the underdog. Many tell me that hearing my story has inspired them, that what had seemed impossible to them may seem less impossible, regardless of what any one person or expert says.

If I could, I would respond to everyone who has written to me, but even if I lived another century, I'd never have enough time to write to every single person. So, I hope this epilogue will serve as a heartfelt reply.

To those who are struggling: This is not a story about me; it's a story about us. I know I'm not unique in my difficulties. Many people have exhausted every sinew and fibre trying to scale their own mountaintops, personal or professional. And I know not everyone is as lucky as I have been to find people who have stuck by me, breathing belief and life into my aspirations. What I will say is that whenever I felt ready to give up, when my head was submerged and I was barely able to breathe, Giff has always reminded me that I'm anchored by a greater purpose, one that goes beyond my own need and serves a greater good. I hope this way of thinking will help you, as it has helped me.

To the parents of neurodivergent children who write to me: I know you are cradling equal amounts of hope and fear in what can be a very unforgiving world. I know that the current system isn't built to help you or your child, and my promise to you is that I will continue to do everything I can to advocate for the greater support that you and they deserve. Giff's creed has always been that success looks different for everyone, that sometimes the biggest milestone can be the smallest step, and that every child develops in their own way and on their own timeframe. This approach helped me long before I had the words to explain it. I truly believe in harnessing *everyone's* potential and that recognising each person's difference as an eternal gift will help your children to flourish and develop a sense of worth and belonging in a society that can often marginalise our community. Many parents write to me in genuine and understandable desperation, asking if there was a magic pill or potion that I took that helped me. The truth is, there was no elixir, just a lot of love. Love isn't a tonic that will guarantee a perfect outcome; it's more like a well to draw on in ever-more trying times. When you put love first, you help us to feel valued and acknowledge that we have something to contribute, despite what rigid medical models say and the observational tests that seek to limit our often complex and spiky range of abilities.

To those who are neurodivergent: If I could have any wish for us, it would be that the world would be a kinder place, one where our differences were accepted, and we could be our entire, unapologetic selves without the constant fear of dehumanisation. In this version of the world, we wouldn't have to mask, suppress, or assimilate; we could just exist without having to always adapt; in fact, the world would adapt to us. But until this wish comes true, I hope you can find places where you can take shelter from the storm, like I always did, lying on my back as a kid on the Common, the sun on my face, or dancing in the living room with Giff, music on full blast.

To my fellow siblings of colour: This is not an easy time for us. As Jean-Baptiste Alphonse Karr once said, 'The more things change, the more they stay the same.' When the stressors of invalidation are pressing down on you and feel unbearable, remember that you are part of a long legacy of survival. Like the Sankofa bird, I hope you can look behind you and draw strength. And at the same time, never forget you are deserving of well-being and joy in your life, that our existence is not based purely on survival and nor should it be. It's my sincerest hope that, wherever possible, you attempt to harness all the happiness and balance to your life you can find, and that you thoroughly deserve.

To everyone else: I hope you'll take the time to wonder how your own life might change if you listened and connected with someone who might seem, on the surface, very different from you. We're all different. We're all human. Every human life has a purpose. Imagine what might happen if we were all united in the just cause of valuing human beings equally? Then maybe, just maybe, all kinds of great things might become possible.

As Giff always said to me, 'Everything has a beginning and everything has an end.'

This is life. Hello, goodbye, everybody. Thank you for existing, hold each other tightly, and no matter what, always keep the faith . . .

All my love, Jason x

Sources

Extract from *A Burst of Light: And Other Essays* by Audre Lorde (1988). Copyright © 1988 Audre Lorde.

Extract from *The Cancer Journals* by Audre Lorde (1980). Copyright © 1980 Audre Lorde.

Extract from *Killing Rage: Ending Racism* by bell hooks. Copyright © 1995 bell hooks.

Extract from writings by Angela Davis. Copyright © Angela Davis.

'Invictus' by William Ernest Henley (1875).

Quotes from *Rocky*, *Rocky III* and *Rocky IV* by Sylvester Stallone. Copyright © MGM.

Extract from 'Footprints in the Sand', Anonymous. Copyright © Anonymous.

Scripture quotations taken from The Holy Bible, New International Version® NIV®. Copyright © 1973, 1978, 1984, 2011 by Biblica, Inc. Used with permission. All rights reserved worldwide.

Acknowledgements

First and foremost, I want to thank my family and friends who appear in this book for entrusting me with their story and those who have gone above and beyond to help me: LA, Sandro, MCC, SW, Giff, Dad, Joseph, Simon, Debs, T. and N., Mr Trace and Angela. Your interventions at different stages throughout my life are the reason I ever amounted to anything. I will be forever indebted to you all for what you have done for me. You are my life.

Thank you to my agent and beautiful Sister, Jennifer Gates. Your email in the middle of the night over three years ago turned out to be one of the most important messages I have ever received. I consider it to be one of the greatest blessings of my life to know you and to be able to call you my kin. This book would not exist without you. I will be eternally grateful for all you've done for my family and me, and I love you beyond words.

Thank you to Ben Clark, my agent in the UK, for your initial insights and support. I am immensely grateful for everything that you have done and your belief in me from the outset.

Thank you to Dawn Davis, my editor at Simon & Schuster in the US, for being the best champion an author could wish for.

You took a chance on a complete unknown, had a vision for this book and brought a passion to this project that was unwavering. Your belief in me is still something I struggle to fathom. I have been immensely fortunate to have been under the guidance and editorship of 'The Best Editor in the World'.

Thank you to Kris Doyle, my editor at Simon & Schuster in the UK. You are one of the most genuine, warm and caring people I have ever met. Your kindness, compassion and understanding have brought immense comfort in what have been very challenging times during the writing of this book. Your insights, sensitivity and editing have sharpened this telling of my story. You are quite simply one of the most exceptional human beings I have ever met.

At Simon & Schuster, I'd like to also thank President and CEO Jonathan Karp and Associate Publisher Irene Kehradi for all their belief and support of this project.

Thank you to everyone involved in the production of the book: Maudisa King, Gail Hallett and Jo Edgecombe in the UK; and Amanda Mullholland, Amy Medeiros and Beth Maglione in the US. Thank you to copy editors Janice Weaver in Canada and Kerri Sharp in the UK; as well as angliciser Amanda Rutter in the UK. I'm so grateful for your attention to detail.

Thank you to everyone in the Simon & Schuster Sales, International Sales, Marketing and Publicity departments in both the US and the UK who believed in this book from the first meeting and have done so much to help me share my story with booksellers and readers, especially Cat Boyd, Julia Prosser and Ingrid Carabulea in the US; and Hayley McMullan, Kate Kaur, Sabah Khan and Victoria Purcell in the UK.

On the design side, thank you to Matthew Monahan and

Wendy Blum in the US, and Matt Johnson in the UK, for the elegance of their vision.

Thank you to assistants Maria Mendez in the US and Oli Hunt in the UK, who brilliantly supported this project.

Thank you to Iman M'Fah Traoré, who fact-checked this book and lent a hand in other important ways too.

Thank you to the audio team in London for producing the audiobook, led by Alice Twomey.

Thank you to my colleagues at the University of Cambridge for their continued support.

Thank you to my friends at Huntsman, Savile Row. As Okwui Enwezor said, 'Style is the resistance to confine oneself to where circumstances say that you belong ... to live with a sense of constant affirmation of the beauty of one's own life, of one's own possibility ...' You have helped me to achieve that sense of affirmation, and I'll always be grateful.

Eve, it is hard to know what to say. We have been through quite the journey together, having spent hundreds of hours across differing time zones writing this book together. You are one of the most important people I have ever met in my life. Your diligence, kindness, understanding, commitment and passion for this project have elevated it beyond what any of us could ever have imagined. I will never forget this experience and the incredibly difficult times we have faced during it. You helped me transition from my academic voice to one that was more personal, something that is hard for such a private person who finds it very uncomfortable to talk about himself. You are my beautiful Sister, and we have been bonded by the most unique of experiences. I love you more than words can express, and I cannot wait for us to dance again.

Thank you to everyone who has ever extended a kind word, message or prayer; it has meant everything and carried me through what has always seemed to be the choppy, turbulent waters of my life. There are too many people to mention, but you know who you are, and you know how grateful I am to you for your existence and everything you have done for me, and I hope you know the depth of my gratitude and love for you.

God in heaven, thank you for delivering me, my family and friends to this point. With God, all things are possible.

The Great and Unfortunate Things Playlist

Tangled Up in Blue – Bob Dylan
Sonnet – Richard Ashcroft
Slide Away – Oasis
Stand by Me – Oasis
Hope You're Feeling Better – Santana
New Kid in Town – Eagles
Take It to the Limit – Eagles
Young, Fresh 'n' New – Kelis
Set Adrift on Memory Bliss – PM Dawn
No Easy Way Out – Robert Tepper
Underdog – Kasabian
In My Life – The Beatles
End of Days – Enya
Why? – Tracy Chapman
Tomorrow (Sadio) – Salif Keita
The Boxer – Simon & Garfunkel
Graceland – Paul Simon
Pali Gap – Jimi Hendrix
If Not Now – Tracy Chapman

Johnny Was – Bob Marley & The Wailers
Iron Lion Zion – Bob Marley & The Wailers
Believe – Lenny Kravitz
Late in the Day – Supergrass
Nessun Dorma – Andrea Bocelli
The Great Beyond – R.E.M.
Kings of Kings – Ladysmith Black Mambazo
If You're Ready (Come Go With Me) – The Staple Singers
Everything Is Everything – Lauryn Hill
Try Again – Aaliyah
The Rain (Supa Dupa Fly) – Missy Elliott
Rock Star – N.E.R.D.
Ocean Drive – Lighthouse Family
Finally – CeCe Peniston
Small Axe – Bob Marley & The Wailers
Qongqothwane (The Click Song) – Miriam Makeba
Shiver – Coldplay
Made of Stone – The Stone Roses
No Questions Asked – Fleetwood Mac
Back to Life (However Do You Want Me) – Soul II Soul
Crashed – Daughtry
What A Day – Greg Laswell
People Everyday – Arrested Development
Lucky You – The Lightning Seeds